Engines for Education

ENGINES FOR EDUCATION

Roger C. Schank
Chip Cleary
The Institute for the Learning Sciences
Northwestern University

Lawrence Erlbaum Associates, Publishers
1995   Hillsdale, New Jersey   Hove, UK

Lawrence Erlbaum Associates, Inc., Publishers
365 Broadway
Hillsdale, New Jersey 07642

Library of Congress Cataloging-in-Publication Data

Schank, Roger C., 1946–
    Engines for education / Roger C. Schank, Chip Cleary
        p.   cm.
    Includes bibliographical references and index.
    ISBN 0-8058-1944-4 (cloth : alk. paper),   — ISBN 0-8058-1945-2
(pbk. : alk. paper)
      1. Education—Unites States—Data processing. 2. Computer
-assisted instruction—United States. 3. Educational change—United
States. 4. Progressive education—United States. I. Cleary, Chip.
    II. Title.
LB1028.43.S32   1995
371.3'34—dc20   95-13897
                                                                      CIP

Books published by Lawrence Erlbaum Associates are printed
on acid-free paper, and their bindings are chosen for strength
and durability.
Printed in the United States of America
10 9 8 7 6 5 4 3 2 1

Contents

Colophon

Usually when you see a colophon in a book, it's tucked away at the back and dedicated to telling you about typefaces. We think that it's worth telling you up front about how we constructed this book, although we are not concerned with fonts.

The book you are looking at is the paper version of a text which we are releasing simultaneously as a computer-readable hypermedia "text" on CD-ROM. For now, the paper version does have the edge of being convenient when you're relaxing at the beach, but over time the advantages of traditional texts over computerized ones will fade. What will *grow* over time is the ability of computerized texts to give you functionality that paper books cannot.

For instance, the CD-ROM version provides 3 features that the paper version does not:

- *Guided Tours:* The CD-ROM version offers tours of a selection of the educational software that we have built at the Institute for the Learning Sciences. Although the paper version describes these programs, taking the tours gives you a better sense of them and is simply more fun than reading about them.
- *Multiple Paths:* The paper book, like any traditional book, lays down a single path for you to follow. The CD-ROM version, however, offers customized paths for four different audiences: educators, business people, those interested in new forms of media, and those who are just curious. It also provides customized overviews for each audience, allowing readers to efficiently zoom in on the high spots of text.

- *Mixed Initiative:* In the paper book, it's not easy for you to carve out a path through the material other than the one we provide for you. The CD-ROM version allows you more control over your "conversation" with the text. you do not have to accept the suggestions that the CD-ROM makes about which page to go to next. The program also offers a series of questions for each page relevant to what the page says. By choosing one of these questions, you may jump to the parts of the book which directly address your interests. The program will then take into account your decisions when suggesting a new next page, and you may again take the suggestion or not as you please.

If the CD-ROM version has all these advantages, you might ask why we are publishing a traditional paper version at all. One answer is that readers have asked us to. A number of people who saw an early version of the computerized text asked for a paper copy to use as a reference or to share with others.

The more basic reason is that although hypermedia texts like this one are exciting and full of fancy features, they are also still in their infancy. Most people do not own the hardware required to run the CD-ROM version; almost none are equipped to browse it while relaxing on the living room couch with a cup of coffee. Some day computerized texts will all but eliminate the niche for paper texts. That day, however, is not quite here.

Preface

Most six-year-olds can't wait to go to school on that first day in September. It's a sign of coming of age. They get to go to school like the big kids. For an alarmingly large number of these children, however, boredom, anxiety, and fear of learning quickly set in.

This happens because societies build schools that achieve much less than they promise, are frustrating for students, and generally fail to help children become adults who can think for themselves. Education has always been considered to be a process whereby some essential body of knowledge is transmitted to students; schools have simply been places where that transmission officially takes place. The development of flexible, inquiring minds has rarely been the primary consideration in the design of educational systems. Making students into proper members of society has usually been of much greater concern than developing students who are creative thinkers.

Today, the level of dissatisfaction and even outright anger at the educational system is tremendously high. We hear a great deal about the failure of our schools, about falling test scores, and about inequalities in education. A variety of solutions have been put on the table, solutions that run the gamut from applying corporate methods to gain efficiency to simply spending a lot more money. Some of the proposals to fix the situation are even more frightening than the situation they are trying to fix.

Clearly, the schools are a mess. Today's schools are organized around yesterday's ideas, yesterday's needs, and yesterday's resources (and they were not even doing very well yesterday). Consider the most common classroom approach: One teacher standing in front of 30 children trying to get each one to be at the same place at the same time. This approach has the advantage of being relatively inexpensive, but it flies in the face of everything scientists have discovered about children's natural learning mechanisms, which are primarily experimentation and reflection—in other words, learning by doing. Consider also the concept of curriculum: that there is a particular body of knowledge everyone should know. This idea may comfort those who are concerned that our children know the "right stuff." Children, however, learn facts about the world because they feel the need to know them, often because these facts will help them do something they want to do. What is the right stuff for one may be the wrong or irrelevant stuff for another.

The purpose of this book is to raise consciousness about the changes needed in our educational system. Certainly some changes are going to occur soon on the American educational scene. People are justifiably upset about education, but the proposals that most school reformers are advancing will not work. Though well-intentioned, the reformers are confused.

This book is about what is wrong with the educational system and how to improve it. Our ideas are largely aligned with what the historians of educational reform call the Progressive Reform Movement, which has a history tracing back almost two centuries. The radicals of this movement have tried out such ideas and found them to work, most notably in alternative schools. Fragments of these ideas, though often distorted, have even made their way into mainstream schools. But, by and large, the Progressives' reforms have not been implemented on a widespread basis. Why? One reason is that they have been hamstrung by economics—progressive programs require that children get individual attention, and individual attention is at odds with student–teacher ratios of 30-to-1.

This book, however, does not give an idealistic view of what education could be if only we had unlimited resources. Rather, it is pragmatic. Early reformers did not have computers; we do. We are now building computer technology that allows us to pursue seriously the radical notion that we must allow children to guide their own education because interested learners learn more. Children can and will become voracious learners if they are in charge of their own education. This does not mean allowing them to play video games all day. But it does mean allowing them to pursue the intellectual goals that interest them, rather than being force-fed knowledge according to someone else's schedule. It also means that the school system should be creating excitement in children about learning and enticing them to want to learn more.

As a cognitive scientist, I have been studying how people think and learn for 25 years. Specifically, I have been working in the field of artificial intelligence, which involves trying to understand people by modeling human processes on machines. Earlier in my career, my research centered on the question of how we learn. Over the last decade, my research has shifted to the question of how we can teach. I currently direct one of the handful of research institutions in the world that is dedicated to understanding how learning takes place in people, and then uses those findings to develop new educational technologies. The Institute for the Learning Sciences at Northwestern University consists of a team of educators, psychologists, and artificial intelligence researchers who have banded together to produce the educational technology of the future.

Why do I care about reforming the schools? I was a terrible student. In grade school, I got bad grades in "conduct." I did not find school to be particularly interesting. My lack of interest in what was being taught and the way it was being taught generally led me into endless confrontations with authority. I began to doubt my own intelligence as others who were more willing to play by the rules got better grades than I did. Later, as I began to study the mind, and learned more about the way it works, and met many people who had troubles in school similar to mine, I began to realize the problems I had in school were hardly unique to me.

When my own children went to school, I watched the same thing happen all over again to them. I had, by this time, become a professor at Yale University. Even so, I realized I would still have trouble getting A's in school if I were taking classes rather than teaching them. I watched what happened to my children, who entered school eager to learn, but who later became anxious, troubled, and generally discouraged by the educational system. Watching them, I became convinced that the system simply does not work.

By building the right computer systems, we can deliver expert resources as students need them and that can react to students' decisions. Through such systems, we can show students the implications of their individual decisions.

What we will be able to do with tomorrow's computer systems is a vast step forward from what we were able to do in the past. At the Institute for the Learning Sciences, we are now producing computer systems that interact with people in more engaging ways than before. The systems allow children to try out things in simulated worlds of our own making, and sometimes of their own making; they allow children to fly their own ship to the moon, design their own animal, or direct their own newscast. This technology will allow us to support what is one of the most important parts of a good educational system—the cultivation of individual initiative in students.

This book is about what can be done to change education now. This is not a work of fantasy about what might exist one day. Nor is it an academic tome that presents irrelevant theory. Rather it is a work that applies what we know about how people learn to the design of computer software that can revolutionize the schools. A large portion of it is dedicated to discussing specific examples of such software. This book is about what we can do today to make learning fun, to make learning less stressful, and to build a world of thinking citizens. This book is about harnessing the power of the world's experts so that they all will be available as needed by students who want to learn from them. This is quite possible to do using today's technology.

Computers are already in the classroom. Unfortunately, for the most part what is there is awful. To date, these computers have been used to play games and to teach children to run spreadsheet programs. Until now no one has cared enough about education to begin to build what is needed. But enough is already known about natural human learning to start the process of change via the computer. Computer software can change the way we learn in school. This book discusses what needs to be done and how to do it.

Roger C. Schank

Acknowledgments

The ideas about education that ground this book are not new. Whenever parents encourage their children to "have a go at it," they are showing that, deep down, they understand how vital learning-by-doing is. Whenever businesses employ "on the job training," they too are relying on learning by doing. These ideas have long been found in books as well, having been written about by such educational pioneers as John Dewey and Francis Parker, among others. The problem with learning-by-doing is that we have not yet found a way to make it the core of our educational system. The primary reason is that it has been too expensive to implement on a massive scale.

Ever since computers were first developed, computer scientists have wanted to apply their machines to education, but they have been hampered by not having machines powerful enough as well as by not knowing quite what to do with them. Today, we are at a juncture. The machines are powerful enough and continue to rapidly become more powerful. The question that challenges us now is how to take that power and use it to make learning-by-doing the foundation of our educational system.

Engines for Education is not just another manifesto about the need for educational reform. The software it describes—software that we are now building at The Institute for the Learning Sciences (ILS), shows how to use computers to let students learn things by doing them, and, most important, demonstrates our progress towards making reform real. As such, this book is really a product of the whole of ILS. Literally every person at ILS has contributed to the software discussed in this book; without their contributions the book would not have been possible.

Projects at ILS influence each other in many ways. Though only so many program descriptions can fit into a single book, thanks go to all of the ILS members who worked on projects that are not directly described here. The following project teams require special mention because of the prominence their software takes in *Engines for Education*:

- *Broadcast News:* Alex Kass, Noreen Burke, Christy Conroy, Scott Dooley, and Frank Luksa;
- *Creanimate:* Danny Edelson, Riad Mohammed, Bob Kaeding, John Cleave, Will Fitzgerald, Diane Schwartz, Ken Greenlee, Ian Underwood, Ben Bell, David Newton, and Charles Earl;
- *Dustin:* Enio Ohmaye, Vitas Daulys, Beth Beyer, Mark Chung, and Faina Mostovoy;
- *GuSS:* Alex Kass, Eli Blevis, Chris Riesbeck, Mark Ashba, Robin Burke, Samir Desai, Debra Jenkins, Smadar Kedar, Jarrett Knyal, Ann Kolb, Brad Kolar, Charles Lewis, Doug MacFarlane, Joyce Montigny, Tom Murray, Miquel Rodriguez, Mark Schaeffer, Jeff Sherwood, Karen Smith, Mary Williamson, Ellen Winnick, Yihua Wu, and Thomas Zielonka;
- *Movie Reader:* Ric Feifer, Richard Beckwith, Christy Conroy, Scott Dooley, Ann Holum, Yat-Keun Keung, Mike Korcuska, June Loeffler, Frank Luksa, Frank Luksa, Wayne Schneider, and Jenneken VanKeppel;
- *Road Trip:* Alex Kass, Scott Dooley, Dave Faloon, and Steven McGee;
- *Sickle Cell:* Ben Bell, Ray Bareiss, Richard Beckwith, Ann Kolb, Tamar Offer-Yehoshua, and BarbaraThorne;
- *The Sounding Board:* Alex Kass, Beth Beyer, Rob Campbell, Scott Dooley, Mike Engber, Kerim Fidel, Jon Regalis, and Pete Welter;
- *The Story Archive:* Ray Bareiss, Andy Fano, William Ferguson, Eric Goldstein, Richard Osgood, and Eric Shafto;
- *TransASK:* Ray Bareiss, Don Frega, Bob Hooker, Ann Kolb, Carolyn Majkowski, Jim McNaught, and John Welch.

Writing *Engines for Education* has been a group effort almost as much as building the software it describes. Each project leader (the person mentioned first in the lists above) contributed a section to their program, with the exception of the section on Movie Reader, which was drafted by Ann Holum and the section on the Story Archive, which was drafted by the first author. Richard Beckwith lent us his vast knowledge of the education literature on several occasions. Kemi Jona provided a section describing Goal Based Scenarios. Liz Gearen, William Graham, Heidi Levin, and Lisa Stolley helped whip the text into consistent, readable form.

Special thanks as well to the team that has taken the text version of *Engines* and converted it into something better—a hypermedia version that lets you sample the programs the text describes. Chris Riesbeck gave this team direction in its early days and always made sure that it received the resources it needed. Laura Zielinski and Bob Kaeding put the right content in the right places. Carolyn Caballero and Diane Schwartz produced the graphics that make the software visually effective. Pamay Bassey and Jon Revelos developed the program's guided tours. Jeff Lind did much of the programming. Mark Schaefer and Ralph De Stefano helped produce the video.

The work we describe here also would not have been possible without the assistance of our sponsors and Institute Partners. In particular, the projects we describe were supported in part by the Defense Advanced Research Projects Agency, monitored by the Office of Naval Research under contracts N00014–91–J–4092 and N00014–90–J–4117. The Institute for the Learning Sciences was established in 1989 with the support of Andersen Consulting, part of The Arthur Andersen Worldwide Organization. ILS receives additional support from Ameritech and North West Water Group plc, Institute Partners, and from IBM.

Although the reform we advocate will take much more effort than any one organization can produce, the work being done at ILS offers a path for forging ahead. We are proud of and grateful for the efforts of the members of the ILS community.

Roger C. Schank
Chip Cleary

1

Time for A Change

CLASSROOM LEARNING

Picture a freshman introductory psychology class, about 350 students, who are still trying to find their seats when the professor starts talking. "Today," she says, "we will continue our discussion of (blah, blah, blah)." She might as well be addressing a crowd at the airport. Like commuters marking time until their next departure, students alternately read the newspaper, chat with friends, or prop their feet on the chair ahead of them, staring into space. Only when the professor defines a term that she says "might appear on the exam" do they look up and start writing notes.

Machelle Robinson

Machelle Robinson was an undergraduate in a course I taught. I asked students to comment on their college education and this passage was part of her response. Her response is not atypical. Increasingly, school at all levels is seen as a chore, a rite of passage to be endured, rather than an exciting place to grow and learn. Students are turned off to learning in school. They worry about how well they are doing, about passing the next test, about pleasing the teacher, about getting along with the other kids. Rather than be excited by the classroom, they have learned to fear it. They realize that what they are learning in school is unlikely to apply to their adult lives. They are often discouraged from following their own interests. School fails to excite them. And the rest of us, as observers of this scene, have virtually forgotten that learning is supposed to be exciting.

Learning Prior to School

Small children love to learn, at least before they get to school. No 2-year-old has ever taken a walking class, yet any physically healthy 2-year-old can walk. No 3-year-old has ever taken a talking class, yet every physically healthy 3-year-old can talk. No 4-year-old has ever taken a course in geography or planning, yet every physically healthy 4-year-old can find a room in his home, knows his neighborhood, and can navigate around in his own environment.

Children are little learning machines. Before they ever reach school, they manage to progress from newborns with innate abilities and minimal knowledge to children with an enormous amount of knowledge about the physical, social, and mental worlds in which they live. They accomplish this feat without classrooms, lessons, curricula, examinations, or grades. They are set up for learning before they enter this world. It is the job of parents to help them learn by protecting them from danger and exposing them to new situations. This should be the job of teachers in school as well, but we have long since lost the model of education that would allow it to happen.

In their natural state, that is, prior to school, children do not have motivation problems. Excited by learning, they are eager to try new things and are in no way self-conscious about failure. We never see a 2-year-old who is depressed about how his talking is progressing and so has decided to quit trying to improve. We never see a 2-year-old who has decided that learning to walk is too difficult and thus has decided to not try to get beyond crawling. For almost every child, the love of exploration, the excitement of learning something new, the eagerness for new experiences continues until he or she is about 6 years old.

The natural learning mechanisms children employ are not much more sophisticated than experimentation, and reflection, with a small amount of instruction thrown in when they are in the mood to listen. They try new things and, when they fail to get what they want, they either try an alternative or are helped by an adult whom they then attempt to copy. Children learn by trying to do something, by failing, and by being told about or by copying some new behavior that has better results. This perspective is founded on the simple but central insight that children are trying to do something rather than to know something. In other words, they are learning by doing. Doing, and attempting to do, is at the heart of children's natural acquisition of knowledge. They see things they want to play with and learn to grasp. They see places they want to go and learn to walk. They feel the need to communicate and they learn to talk. Learning is driven by the natural need to do. Knowing is driven by doing. Children learn facts about the world because they feel the need to know them, often because these facts will help them do something they want to do. It isn't until school that knowing becomes uncoupled from doing.

Failure and Education

Because we cannot do what we want perfectly the first time we attempt something new, failure is critical in the learning process. If you don't fail when you try to do something, it is probably because you have already learned to do it. Doing something for the first time and failing at it are intimately intertwined. When children fail, they discover they need to expand their capabilities. Although they may be frustrated by initial failures, they are rarely so frustrated that they don't try and try again. Also, children are not embarrassed by failure until they get to school. It is there that their failures result in the ridicule of their peers and the approbation of their teachers. In school they learn to view failure as something to fear. The willingness of young children to fail is a critical prerequisite to their ability to learn. Without failure there is no second try, no thinking about what needs to be changed, what needs to be learned. The loss of this willingness to fail is highly detrimental to the very curiosity that drives education.

Formal Education Versus Childhood Learning

Small children rarely receive formal instruction. Instead, parents answer questions when they are asked, expose their children to new phenomena that lead them to ask more questions, and are there to help when a child is frustrated by his failed attempts. Often, however, small children reject the help offered by others, preferring to "do it myself" until they get it. Children don't learn because they are ordered to by some authority. They control their own learning using the individual attention of an adult to support and guide them through new areas of investigation. One-on-one assistance, on an as-needed basis, is the basis of a child's education until the age of 6.

At 6 all this changes. Children begin to learn that failure is problematic, and, consequently, that learning is less exciting. They are learning what someone else wants them to learn anyway. No longer do they learn because they want to and because they have a need to know. They learn because someone tells them to. In addition, quite often no one tells them what they might be able to do with what they are about to learn. The motivation they themselves had previously supplied has been taken away and has not been replaced. Further, what previously had been a private experience is now done among a peer group all too happy to ridicule their errors. What has happened? The 6-year-old has started school.

In public schools from first through twelfth grade, much of the classroom routine is shaped by an emphasis on rote learning, a strict adherence to standardized textbooks and workbooks, and a curriculum that is often enforced with drill and practice. The methods and the curriculum are molded by the questions that appear on the standardized achievement tests administered to every child from the fourth grade on. Success no longer means being able to do. Success comes to mean "academic success," a matter of learning to function within the system, of learning the "correct" answer, and of doing well at multiple-choice exams. Success also means, sadly, learning not to ask difficult questions. When we ask how our children are doing in school, we usually mean "are they measuring up to the prevailing standards?" rather than "are they having a good time and feeling excited about learning?"

Example of Natural Versus Formal Learning

In his essay, "The Loss of the Creature," the novelist Walker Percy (1982) contrasted how learning arises spontaneously to how learning is structured in the classroom. Here's his description of spontaneous learning: "A young Falkland Islander walking along a beach and spying a dead dogfish and going to work on it with his jackknife has, in a fashion wholly unprovided for in modern educational theory, a great advantage over the Scarsdale high school pupil who finds the dogfish on his laboratory desk" (p. 56).

Compare that description to how Percy described learning canned for the classroom, as it is for the typical high school biology lab. There, the student is handed an assignment that includes a list of every item he will need and all the steps involved. He finds his tools laid out on the table. Every contingency has been provided for in advance except his curiosity about dogfish.

The problem is, of course, that without curiosity the dissection is, at best, busywork. If the student's own motivation is disregarded, even the most careful preparation will backfire because he will be relegated to an entirely passive role. In the worst case, this passive, compulsory experience squeezes the life out of his interest in biology altogether.

Were you ever required to dissect a frog, compare what you saw to pictures in your textbook, then memorize the scientific names for the organs and structures you "discovered?" If so, then you recognize Percy's classroom exercise. You probably also recognize how far it is, how much less it is, than the experience of the Falkland Islander.

Boring Science Assignments

Of course, ideally, every learning experience would arise as naturally as it does for a curious child roaming the beach and poking into what he finds around him, but in the context of formal education that is very difficult. For one thing, the ratio of students to teachers makes individual discovery very difficult. Novelist Percy, however, described a plausible scenario in which students are captivated in the classroom while in the middle of the standard, boring biology dissection lab exercise:

> One day a great biologist walks into the laboratory; he stops in front of our student's desk; he leans over, picks up the dogfish, and, ignoring instruments

and procedure, probes with a broken fingernail into the little carcass. 'Now here is a curious business,' he says, ignoring also the proper jargon of the specialty. 'Look here how this little duct reverses its direction and drops into the pelvis. Now if you would look into a coelacanth, you would see that it . . .' And all at once the student can see. (pp. 60–61)

Percy's expert treats the students as though they were the first people on earth to think of looking inside a dogfish. He captures the students' attention by pointing out its unusual features. Together, they formulate questions that come from their observations. He fills the gaps of the students' knowledge spontaneously, as the students become curious, rather than in a textbook-like sequence. By involving the students in the act of discovery, he covers the principles of the lesson in unforgettable detail. Most important, long after the students can list the organs and skeletal structure of the dogfish, they retain the impression of what an actual scientific probe feels like.

Learning Process Reversed

What is curious about the dissection exercise as it is usually conducted in the schools is that the natural learning process is reversed. The answers are provided before the student has asked the questions. At every level of school, students face this reversed process. They learn to write before they have the genuine desire to communicate in writing. They learn to read before they want to find out the information contained in books. They learn history before they try to analyze current political decisions. They learn economics before they ever try to run a business.

This reversed process delivers education through a prerequisite-driven scheme in which curriculum planners demand that students initially learn basic things they feel those students will likely need to know later to do more advanced things. But two problems arise from this scheme. First, predicting which basic things different students will need to pursue their different interests is almost impossible. Second, it is almost impossibly boring for a student to learn basics when these basics are divorced from the context of something the student really wants to do.

Imagine that you are an undergraduate considering majoring in history, which means that you may eventually need to do some quantitative research. Consider the plight of the math department trying to decide what to teach you. Can the department deliver in advance the math you really will need for your eventual research? To answer this, you need to first consider the fact that they probably do not know that you are a history major and certainly cannot be sure that you will remain one. Second, the math department faculty are mathematicians, not historians. Even if they knew where you were headed, they are not likely to know what kind of math that direction requires, much less how to teach it in an appropriate context.

The likely outcome is that you will be taught some standard form of statistics by the math department that you will forget in a year or two. If and when you actually do conduct your quantitative research, you will probably have to relearn those parts of the math lessons you've forgotten, but that you now need. You will learn them because you have developed your own need to know them.

The children who learn to read earliest are those who find things they actually want to read. A teacher's or parent's first job is to cause the child to want to read something, to motivate him to care, so that the natural order of learning can kick into action. The educator's job is to provide the one item that today's education system leaves out: motivation.

Problems with Traditional Classroom Biology

There is a big problem, from the perspective of assessment, with the biologist's visit to Percy's Scarsdale classroom: it isn't clear ahead of time what particulars will be covered. An authentic learning experience simply does not lend itself to objective assessment. A biologist can lead the curiosity of the class in whatever direction it is wont to go only as long as there is no standardized test or Biology II class waiting to be cued up.

Tapping A Child's Interests

We must be prepared to be flexible in the way we try to tap into our children's innate interests. For instance, if children do not like the notion of doing dissection, they might instead find it fun to playact the role of a white blood cell in a drama built around biology. Or, perhaps they will find using the analogy of biology practical when they are trying to design some mechanical structure. If one approach doesn't work, we should drop it and try another.

Why Biology Lab is No Fun

The dissection assignment doesn't hold the student's attention because both the method and the content of the lesson are static—the procedure's beginning, middle, and end were predetermined. The implication that there is exactly one appropriate method for dissecting a dogfish crushes the authentic spirit of discovery that might compel someone to look for some other way to get at it. Even worse is the implication that the goal of experiments should be to uncover in the lab what is already laid out in the textbook. The untold connections between the dogfish and other subjects are not accounted for.

The typical classroom dissection is not really an experiment at all. The idea of authentic scientific inquiry is replaced by the dictum to follow the rules and learn the required material. The small child in us cries out because we wanted to do more or less or something different. We were interested in the dogfish, but not in naming its organs. At home, we could explore what interested us, but here we are on an intellectual chain gang, following the leader and the pace set and doing the work required. This method of instruction discounts any connections the student might make between the dogfish and what he already knows about other subjects, except those that are precoded in a text. It does not allow for students to see what science is all about. No real hypotheses are formed because no student-initiated hypotheses are allowed. And it's just not fun.

Schools Fail to Use Students' Natural Questions

As individual students are exposed to new information, they ask themselves questions, corresponding to their specific internal needs for answers. Schools often fail to answer their questions during the course of instruction. Thus, the material they teach often fails to stick in their students' heads for very long. And, for this reason, the phenomenon of the finals cram is born. Students labor to cram material into their heads, but because they haven't generated the questions the material might answer, there are not receptive places for the material to be indexed. Nevertheless, they fight against the natural learning process to try to get the material to stick, if only for a little while. Students then take their tests and forget the material a few weeks or months later. A few students do manage to succeed in this system by finding a way to become curious about the material. Most who "succeed," however, simply force themselves to temporarily retain the material that so readily slides off their memories.

For those who succeed through sheer discipline, even the fraction of the material that does stick tends to not be very useful. The reason for this has to do with the types of internal memory labels students use when indexing what they learn. When students are studying, they typically have the goal of "covering the material" or "getting ready for the test." The way they label the information they memorize is under mental headings such as "stuff I need to know for the chemistry midterm." Such labels are satisfactory if the goal is to recall the material for the test. But if the goal is to be able to apply this knowledge in the real world, then mental indices need to be generated that relate to real-world concerns, that is, that help one achieve real goals or create real plans to achieve those goals. When information enters memory that in no way relates to goals that the possessor of the information may want to accomplish, it is quickly forgotten because there is no meaningful place for it to reside.

Studying Versus Practicing

Competency tests like those found in today's schools force students to cram, to study. Natural learning does not involve studying. It involves practice, but that is a performance concept. Studying (as opposed to reading about something you are interested in) is a concept that has nothing to do with natural learning. No child studies until he is forced to either by a parent, or by the fear of doing badly on an exam.

Practicing, on the other hand, is a natural concept. Animals practice their skills while growing up. Children practice all the time prior to school. However, children practice naturally only what interests them. Children naturally practice sports because they are interested in improving their performance for next time. Performance tests are real tests, ones that natural learners work towards if the task itself interests them.

Faulty Indexing

Many students learn when studying chemistry that acetone, the chemical in fingernail polish, dissolves glue. But when faced with a glue spill in their basement at home, few students can access this knowledge to help them with their problem. The way students mentally index what they learn in school often does not pertain to the issues they face in life. If a student spilled glue in the chemistry lab and his teacher suggested that he use acetone to clean it up and explained why, the student would likely exclaim, "Yes, I already knew that!" And, in some academic sense, that is true. But in a real-world sense, not having knowledge properly indexed is about as valuable as not having it at all.

Such knowledge is called *inert*. Inert knowledge is simply knowledge that is improperly indexed. Unfortunately, the only way to create more flexible indexing is to ask questions and pursue the answers. The kind of memorization that comprises most studying (and most schoolwork) rarely involves such question asking. Hence, most of this work leads to inert knowledge.

Succeeding in School Today

Those who succeed in today's school often do so by learning what the rules are and slavishly following them. Occasionally, in the last few years, I taught an undergraduate course that attempted to get students to think for themselves. (I taught this course twice at Yale and twice at Northwestern. It was disguised as a computer science course at Yale and listed as a psychology course at Northwestern.) In this course, I attempt to get students to do some original thinking. The class focuses on discussing unanswered questions about human thought processes. The students may say what they want, they just have to do so in a rigorous manner. I say very little. Many students are uncomfortable with this situation. They want to know what I think and I refuse to tell them. They are reluctant to think for themselves and are eager to tell me what they think I want to hear. My failure to encourage this kind of behavior leaves many of them confused about what it means to succeed at this game. Academic success is what drives them, and I take away the usual means.

Grade System Limits

Given the opportunity, students at places like Yale and Northwestern will, on average, spend time using their intelligence to figure out how to get an A without doing the real work of the course and without thinking, rather than spending the same time thinking and exploring, regardless of what grade this may bring them. It isn't that these students are not motivated. It's just that they're not as motivated to learn as much as they're motivated to get good grades. Once you are grade oriented in your thinking, it is difficult to stop thinking that way.

Anybody who gets into these schools is, in some sense, a winner of the system. But these seeming winners are, far too often, losers of a more important game. To win the grade competition in high school, most of these "winners" learned to ask what was expected of them and then do just that. They had to make sure they got high SAT scores by memorizing endless vocabulary words and by practicing a thousand-and-one uses of the Pythagorean theorem. They wanted to know from their high school teachers if the material being covered on a given day was going to be on the test, because they realized early on that the test is all that matters.

When these "successes" of the system arrive in college, they, of course, have not changed their attitudes. They fear open-ended assignments. They are impatient with discussions that are not going in any particular direction except where the interests of the discussants dictate, because they know that such discussions waste time that could have been better spent studying for a test. What these students have learned from school is the underlying message that the world is run by authorities who have definite points of view. The system has taught them that the way to get along in the world is to understand and to cater to those points of view espoused by the educational "authorities." Cleverness pays, but disagreement does not. Such students are in the process of becoming "yes men." They are confused and frustrated by professors like me, professors who refuse to don the mantle of authority so that their real education can begin.

On the other hand, students who do poorly in high school are often rebelling against curricula they see as irrelevant to their lives. This type of student judges what goes on in school according to how well it relates to his own day-to-day concerns. If algebra does not seem relevant to the problems such students face, then they see little need to pay attention to it. The school might have been able to embed algebra instruction inside a task they cared about, causing them to want to know algebra because it would help them do something they wanted to do. But schools generally don't think like this, so the conclusion drawn by many students is that, because so much is irrelevant, they might as well tune it out. These students learn to get by as well as they can, separating themselves from others who are willing to play the game.

Fear and Students

Most students perform passably, being neither stellar performers nor problem students. But they are governed by fear. Their greatest hope in the classroom is to escape without being called on. In his book, *How Children Fail*, Holt (1964) captured their essence when he described how his class approaches playing Twenty Questions:

> Many of them are very anxious when their turn comes to ask a question. We ask them to play Twenty Questions in the hope that, wanting to find the hidden thought, they will learn to ask more informative and useful questions. They see the game quite differently: 'When my turn comes, I have to ask a question.' They are not the least interested in the object of the game, or whether their question gains useful information. The problem is simply to think of a question, any old question. (p. 32)

Holt described the impact of this stifling fear:

> For many years, I have been asking myself why intelligent children act unintelligently at school. The simple answer is 'Because they're scared.' . . . What I see now for the first time is the mechanism by which fear destroys intelligence, the way it affects a child's whole way of looking at, thinking about, and dealing with life. (p. 49)

With 30-to-1 student–teacher ratios, these students usually get what they are after. By keeping their heads down, they manage to escape attention. They get left alone. So they learn that life is fraught with risks, but if one plays it safe, one may get through without too much trouble. Of course, they don't learn much, but that is not what they are after. After a few years of school, it is the lucky student who manages to retain the eager curiosity most kids bring with them into kindergarten.

The Failure of Schools

Schools make students learn in ways quite different from how they learn in the real world. Because schools were designed around economic considerations, and because curricula are inevitably controlled by the list makers who want to tell us what everyone should know, school learning has traditionally been something quite different from "real-world" learning. Schools have not attempted to provide an environment within which natural learning can operate.

In their eagerness to fill students with knowledge, schools typically try to short-circuit the natural learning process. When we learn naturally, we start by developing an interest in what we are learning about. We try things out and get hands-on experience. We suffer expectation failures and we ask questions. Schools are not built around steps such as these. Instead, they try to cut to the chase. They rush to present answers to questions students have not asked and generalizations about experiences students have not had.

Schools are forever in the position of the parents of a teenager who asks why their child cannot learn from their bad experiences, wondering why the teenager has to repeat all their mistakes. The teenager replies that he has to live his own life and make his own mistakes, without realizing how accurate a picture of learning he really has. Schools cannot simply tell the answers, they have to motivate the questions first. Schools that fail to do this will simply not work.

The Goals of the Schools

One reason why the schools are troubled is that they don't have the right goals. You can ask why the education system does not fulfill its charter and complain about shortages of money or the number of hours kids spend in school or teacher burnout. These may even be reasonable things to complain about. Still, the place to start when considering why the education system is broken is to start with the charter itself. What are the goals of the schools?

Goals Underlying Education.   The educational system is full of goals. Teachers, for example, have teaching goals, goals of a particular lesson, goals they wish to achieve with individual students. Students, too, already have goals. They wish to get into good colleges, get good jobs, get approval from their peers, parents, and teachers, and get good grades as one means of doing this. They have the goal of studying for tests, and taking good notes to study from, and understanding the lesson, and so on. Further, state boards of education have goals. They have goals for minimal achievement of graduating students on standardized tests, for example. Administrators want to keep order in the system and high test scores and coverage of the curriculum. Indeed, the school system seems rather full of goals.

But are these relevant goals? One thing to notice is that most of these goals are held by those who run the system (i.e., administrators and teachers), not by those the system is to educate (i.e., students). To make the system effective, we must concentrate on the goals of the students.

Students Learning Naturally.   From an educator's point of view, the goals that the current system leads students to adopt are curiously content free. The system does not lead students to want to investigate some scientific question. Nor does it encourage them to get involved in activities that will, for example, lead them to want to write a persuasive essay. It does not put them in situations in which they care about what happened in early American history so that they might, for instance, be able to provide an informed opinion on some current policy issue they are facing in a class project.

Through natural learning, students will become experts in those areas in which they have strong interest. Giving the goals students usually hold, this means they will become experts at trying to get approval, getting good grades, and studying for tests. Yes, some students will gain more expertise than others, but natural learning assures us that all students will become adept at pursuing such goals (except those who intentionally buck the system—they will then become adept at system bucking). Are these the areas in which we want our children to become proficient?

Goals can be characterized in terms of their relevance to the content we would like students to learn. The goals that we (mostly inadvertently) encourage students to adopt are not particularly relevant to the material we would like them to learn nor the way in which we would like them to learn it.

The Goals of the Current Educational System.   The current educational system is constructed around the goals of educators first and students second. Educators want students to know the Pythagorean theorem. So they create a math class and expose students to it. Educators want students to be familiar with Shakespeare. So they create an English class and expose students to him. This method of teaching is the basis of the entire subject-matter organization of schools. Students go to one room for an hour to hear about math. Then they go to another room to hear about English. However, they rarely go to a room organized around some task they care about and then get help with math or English as they need such help to progress with the task. Instead of starting with the things students care about, today's subject-centered system is oriented around the things educators care about, the things the system wants students to learn.

Given that starting point, it is difficult to get students to care in a productive way about the content the system intends to convey. Yes, we can hold the threat of grades and tests over students' heads. These threats will cause many students to want to "master" the material for the test. But such mastery will not last long. During the period before students forget the material, it will be inert. Because students have not thought about it in terms of how it helps them solve some problem they face in the real world, it will be difficult for them to access it when they do face such a problem.

Students Should Learn to Question

Schools today are based on the underlying assumption that students should learn answers. This commonsensical assumption is wrong. Students should instead learn how to ask questions and pursue their own answers.

Much of the current system is oriented around giving students answers. If we only care that students know some fact, then it's fine for us to simply give it to them at some point when they are ready to hear it. But a rational educational plan wouldn't care so much that students know some fact X as that they know how to reason using X. In other words, we should care that they know how to use X in an argument, or how X might be disputed, or how to find facts similar to X, or how far X can be pushed. For this to happen, students must have goals that lead them to care about reasoning with X. They must be given situations in which they come to care about how X might be disputed or how it might be used to bolster some point they wish to make. An education system that offers such environments cannot be oriented around facts. It must be oriented around questions.

In this view, there is hardly any reason to concern ourselves with whether students learn the underlying facts. In a fact-obsessed culture, this idea is anathema to what education seems to stand for. But in chemistry, for example, do we really care if students know the details of the periodic table? In physics, do we really care if they can apply the formula for calculating torque? In history, do we really worry if a student cannot name all the Presidents or Kings? In English, do we really worry if a student fails to memorize lines from Beowulf? In these situations, we are primarily interested in helping students become curious enough about these subjects to genuinely want to know more. This means that we want to help students build the memory structures that encode knowledge in such a way that the encoding itself starts to demand more knowledge. Or, to put this another way, we want students to know what they don't know so that they will be motivated to find out more.

Questions in Class.   Any parent will tell you that one of the most annoying habits young children have is their penchant for the "Why Game." In this game, the child observes something and demands that the parent explain it. "Why is the sky blue?" is the classic example. But more bizarre questions often pop up, such as "Why doesn't the week start with the weekend?" or "How does my brain know what my name is?"

These questions are irritating not only because they are time-consuming, but also because they often show us the limits of what we ourselves know. We don't like being reduced to the answer "Just because." Nonetheless, we encourage our children to ask such questions because we realize that they help to develop intelligence and curiosity.

How much time do you remember taking in school to ponder such questions? If you are like most people, your answer will be "Not much." Why? Student–teacher ratios of 30-to-1 make it impossible to consider everybody's questions, but they don't make it impossible to consider anybody's. Why don't teachers take more time to sit and wonder with their students about the questions the students have about their world? If adults in their role as parents consider the Why Game worthy of time because it helps their own children to develop, why don't adults adopt the same approach in their role as teachers?

The answer is not that teachers consider students' questions to be unimportant. It is that teachers consider such questions to be less important than all the other stuff curriculum development boards have crowded into the classroom agenda, such as the names of all 50 states, or the structure of the periodic table, or the Pythagorean theorem.

A teacher of third-grade geography, fifth-grade math, or seventh-grade social studies just does not have time to sit and wonder with the class why weekends don't start the week. Teachers have a long, predetermined path from which they cannot stray if they are to reach the required destination. Further, such open-ended questioning admits the possibility that the teacher might not know the answer. Not knowing the answer is both possible and perfectly acceptable from an educational perspective, but it is not at all acceptable in a world where the teacher is the ultimate authority.

Asking the Right Questions.   Imagine that you go to a meeting at work every Monday morning. You never quite understand the pertinence of the topics that are discussed. Every week you ask, "Why are we worrying about this?" or "Wouldn't our time be better spent talking about some other aspect of our business?" You are playing the Why Game, the same game that children play with their parents, except that years of experience have taught you not to let your questions go too far afield.

Now, imagine that every week the chair of the meeting says, "That would be a good question to ponder if we didn't have so much ground to cover." How long will you continue to ask questions? If you want to keep your job, you will stop asking why and instead figure out how to play whatever game is being played in these meetings. In short, you will learn to cater to the desires of the authorities in the environment. This may be appropriate in business where the ultimate purpose is certainly not the enlightenment of all concerned, but in a classroom it sets a tone that is antithetical to the learning process.

This is exactly what happens to children in today's classrooms, particularly those who are most eager to please the grown-ups. Their job is to sit in classes that are, for the most part, assigned to them. Often, they cannot figure out how the content discussed in these classes relates to their lives.

Although they are assured that it matters that they learn about cosines, the Entente Cordial, and iambic pentameter, they really have no choice anyway. When they ask questions that go in the "wrong" direction, that is, questions that diverge from the curriculum, the teacher is forced to respond, as did the meeting chair, "Good question, but we have no time for it." And, if the child is eager to please, as most are, he will learn to drop the Why Game and learn to participate in "classroom discussion."

Classroom Discussion.   Classroom discussion is not to be confused with real discussion. The purpose of classroom discussion is to enable the teacher to pull the content dictated by the curriculum out of the class by imposing a limited discussion-like format. Most everyone who has been in the American school system has experienced hour upon hour of these pseudodiscussions. In classroom discussion, the questions the "successful" student asks are the questions he knows follow the direction the teacher wants to take.

Other questions generally get gently put aside. Asking why, though (when it's not clear that the teacher wants the question), causes trouble. Thus, we breed students who learn that there is a right next question, and if they're not sure what that question is, they are better off not asking anything. We breed students who therefore really become quite skilled at asking and answering only one question: What is it that the authority figures want me to do next?

Fixed Curricula

Fixed curricula centralize control. They remove control from the hands of teachers. Therefore, teachers cannot pass on control to students. Teachers often would like to reward children for asking the big-picture questions that don't fit the lesson plan, but they cannot afford to. Curriculum development boards fill up the time allotted to classes with content that teachers then need to cover. By doing so, they automatically determine that nothing else can be covered.

The Why Game, conducive to curiosity and creativity, falls into the category of "anything else." Classroom discussion squelches children's curiosity as they learn that their own questions don't matter. Their creativity destroyed, these children look to others for guidance rather than trusting themselves. Self-confidence, a commodity most successful people have in abundance, ought to be what schools try to instill in students. What is actually instilled, however, is the fear of doing something wrong.

To get real inquiry into the classroom, we must give teachers the possibility of allowing it. Without real inquiry, an inquiry that comes from a student-directed need to know, real learning cannot take place.

Motivation in the Classroom.   Children locked into classroom discussion are no different than adults locked into boring, irrelevant meetings. If you do not understand how something relates to your goals, you will not care about that thing. If an adult cannot see the relevance of the material covered in a meeting and has no desire to score political points, he will tune out or drop out. If a child does not understand how knowing the elements of the periodic table will help to address the concerns of his life, and he is not particularly interested in pleasing the teacher, he will do the same.

Because we do not want our children to be motivated solely by a desire to please the teacher, what we need to address is how to make the content of the curriculum fit into the concerns of the child. Sometimes, this is easy. The child who wants to design a roof for the family doghouse will gladly sit through a lesson on the Pythagorean theorem if he understands that the lesson will teach him how to calculate the dimensions of the roof he needs. If a piece of content addresses a particular concern of a student, or even a general area of interest, that student will not tune it out.

Most children as they work through their years of school do, in fact, find areas of study they genuinely enjoy. But these areas are different for different people. The general problem of matching individual interests to fixed curricula is one that is impossible to solve. People obviously have different backgrounds, beliefs, and goals. What is relevant for one will not be relevant to another. Of course, we can force something to be relevant to students— we can put it on the test. But this only makes it have the appearance of significance; it does not make it interesting.

Some children decide not to play the game this system offers. Instead, they continue to search for ways in which what is taught makes sense in their day-to-day lives, becoming frustrated as they realize that much of what is covered is irrelevant to them. If children are unwilling to believe that their own questions do not matter, then they can easily conclude that it is the material covered in class that does not matter.

What is left, then, if the content has no intrinsic value to a student? Any teacher knows the answer to this question. Tests. Grades. When students don't care about what they are learning, tests and grades force them to learn what they don't care about knowing. Of course, students can win this game in the long run by instantly forgetting the material they crammed into their heads the night before the test. Unfortunately, this happens nearly every time. What is the point of a system that teaches students to temporarily memorize facts? The only facts that stay are the ones we were forced to memorize again and again, and those we were not forced to memorize at all but that we learned because we truly needed to know them, because we were motivated to know them. Motivation can be induced artificially, but its effects then are temporary. There is no substitute for the real thing.

Curiosity Versus Curriculum.   In a classroom when 30 students each have good questions, 29 of them will be frustrated. In fact, they may all be frustrated, because teachers are bound by the curriculum to march endlessly onward in a very particular direction. But students' curiosity tends to go in directions for which teachers have not planned. In today's schools, teachers' plans are preordained, dictated by the curriculum. The plan, not the individual ideas or questions of the student, dictates how the lesson proceeds. Curiosity and curriculum are antithetical concepts.

The Cause of Conformity.   Because motivation is such a critical issue in learning, and because failure is such an idiosyncratic affair, school reformers often miss the forest for the trees. Although reformers worry about standards, test scores, and cultural literacy, the real issue is the curriculum. Students who are held to rigid curricula with tests at the end cannot help but begin to believe that learning means getting a good grade. When a student knows what is expected of him, he will usually conform, and therein lies the problem.

Teaching Children in the Classroom

Teachers need to play a variety of roles for their students, but schools usually limit them to the roles dictated by the transfer model of education. In this model, the teacher performs three jobs: selecting the material children are to absorb, presenting that material, and then administering tests that seek to determine exactly how much has been absorbed. The problems of today's schools come to the fore when you think about the challenges teachers face in each of these jobs. How can the teacher know what each student needs to learn? How can the teacher effectively "present" the material? Are the children ready to hear it? How can the tests that are commonly used determine whether children have made the appropriate generalizations or are able to use the material in real life?

The transfer model limits the teacher to the three roles of selector, presenter, and evaluator. What about the roles of motivator, challenger, and critic? What about the roles of brainstormer, manager, and leader? Each of these roles leads to a different style of teaching, and each plays an important part in helping students learn a class of knowledge worth knowing. You might claim that, even if it isn't supported by their school, a teacher can serve as a motivator and leader. That may well be true, but only the exceptional teacher will summon up the energy and effort required to go beyond what the system naturally supports. How long until that teacher burns out?

Motivator Versus Expert.   It's particularly important to separate the role of the motivator from the role of the expert. Teachers are too often forced into the role of being the expert and too seldom given the chance to motivate their students.

The motivator is concerned with helping the student develop the right questions. Parents easily adopt this role, taking children to the zoo and pointing out the animals, for example. Once a child has a question, then it is the role of the expert to get the child to an answer. Before the expert can start, though, the child must already have had a question. The expert must follow the motivator.

The expert role is one that both teachers and parents get trapped into playing, often to their own potential embarrassment. Children can easily ask questions about animals they see in the zoo that the parent cannot answer. But parents usually do not refrain from taking their child to the zoo because they worry this might happen. Teachers, on the other hand, do fear being asked questions they cannot answer. They have become, not always willingly, the expert in the classroom. This need not be the case, however. Computers offer the possibility of separating the roles of motivator and expert, with the latter going to the computer and the former going to the friendly human who no longer needs to take the role of the answer man.

Role of Feedback.   Students need to get feedback as they work. Studies by a number of cognitive psychologists (Anderson, Reiser, and others) have shown that the right feedback at the right time helps students understand and correct their own misconceptions, helping them learn to do things better.

What specific feedback they need depends, of course, on exactly what they are doing and how they are doing it. Take two students who are learning biology by playing the part of a manager of a wildlife park. One might need guidance on how to balance short-term and long-term goals. Another might need details about what habitat herons prefer.

Schools are not very good at giving students the feedback they need. Sometimes, the only feedback a student gets is a grade. When students do get feedback that has some content to it, it's typically because they get it during class discussion when all the students are getting the same feedback at the same time.

Testing

Fixed curricula are developed with a noble goal in mind: to help our children learn The Right Stuff. This goal provides the cornerstone of any educational system; it is beyond challenge. The way this goal is pursued, however, is not. In our system we pursue the goal of knowing The Right Stuff about history by translating it into the goal of knowing a series of dates. We implement the goal of knowing The Right Stuff about math by converting it into the goal of knowing a set of formulas or the steps of some proof. How has this happened?

The answer lies in the term, "teaching to the test." This term has gathered negative connotations, but it refers to a quite innocent practice. Tests play the central role in the incentive system underlying today's schools. Students are admitted to colleges based on how well they do on tests. Teachers receive raises based on the tests their students take. The measurements go all the way up the ladder. Even our sense of national pride partially hinges on how well this year's students do on the Scholastic Aptitude Test, or whether we have beaten the Koreans at math.

Teaching to the test means tailoring the work of the classroom to the goal of improving scores on tests. Because the benefits of the education system are doled out on the basis of test results, teaching to the test seems to be a sensible thing to do.

The problem is not only in the practice of teaching to the test but in the tests themselves. The really important tests in the school system are mass produced and mass graded, and thus they are populated with questions that have simple, objective answers. As a result, our national definition of what it means to be educated translates into how readily one can recognize the right word among five options listed after a multiple-choice question, or how quickly one can apply the right formula to a one-paragraph word problem.

Because most schools teach to these types of tests, they emphasize the memorization of facts and formulas. Then, we begin to believe the material that was taught primarily because it was easily testable was in fact what should have been taught in the first place. You might think that tests should be built around our conception of what it means to be educated. But today's tests are just the opposite. In today's system, tests do not so much derive from our notion of education, they drive it.

Inflexible System.   The rigidity of the nation's curricula stems from the fact that if something is difficult to test, we don't include it, but if it is easily testable, we dwell on it. In determining the mathematics curriculum, for example, one might think we would first ask whether mathematics should be taught at all, second, what aspects should be taught for which purposes, and third, how we can assess competence in those aspects. Instead, the answer to the last question has come to dominate how we answer the two logically prior questions. The most important aspects of mathematics, in the reality of today's schools, are those necessary for a student to do well on California Tests, Iowa Tests, and SAT tests.

We have come to accept multiple-choice tests in places where we know they make no sense at all. At least in mathematics one can formulate reasonable problems that have objective answers. But we also test (and therefore teach) liberal arts in a multiple-choice format. We go so far as to use this ubiquitous format when judging skills instead of knowledge. We find ourselves in the odd situation of asking people to objectify knowledge they simply use and never need to explicitly state, because the tests demand it.

Piaget and Intelligence Tests.   Early in his career, Piaget, one of history's most significant psychologists, went to work with Simon, the co-author of the Binet–Simon IQ test. Piaget realized that the Simon team, who were focusing on the total number of correct answers in their intelligence tests, were overlooking what was perhaps the most interesting data—the kinds of answers students were giving. Piaget believed that by looking at the answers themselves (rather than their correctness) he could see how the children were thinking. He noted that, although many children were giving the same incorrect answers, this important pedagogical fact was not even noticed by the Simon team because they looked only at the numbers of correct answers. He studied these wrong answers and learned that, although children were giving incorrect answers, they were reasoning in ways similar to each other. Piaget recognized that teaching needed to focus on how children were reasoning rather than focusing on how well they might recall facts for a test. Nevertheless, although his work is lauded by most researchers, it has had little effect on the school system.

Test of Everyday Knowledge.   Let's consider what one has to do to get a driver's license. The driver's license exam consists of two sections: a driving test and a written test. The driving test is usually pretty simple. It typically requires the applicant to negotiate a car through an obstacle course at speeds somewhat under what the typical driver achieves before getting out of the driveway. The harder section is the written exam. The written exam tests how well the driver can call to mind details about the rules of the road. One of the questions I was asked when I last applied to renew my motorcycle license was whether a horn must be able to be heard from (a) 100 feet, (b) 200 feet, (c) 50 feet, or (d) 150 feet. (The answer, incidentally, is 200 feet.) Another question asked whether it is necessary to push on the inside of the handlegrip in order to turn quickly. Other questions were similar. How relevant are such questions to the skill of driving?

The written driver's test is just an exercise in meaningless memorization, as are most such tests. The odd point here is that even when a skill can be tested in the normal way, by seeing if the student can actually do it, we still rely on good old multiple-choice tests, simply out of habit. An experienced driver does not have to brush up on the driving part of the test when he changes residence and needs to get a new license, because he knows that he knows how to drive. But he has to memorize the booklet the state gives out, as if he were reading the material for the first time, because the objective knowledge contained within it is so irrelevant to what he knows about driving.

The sad part is that the schools have outdone the motor vehicle bureaus. They have eliminated any testing of doing at all. All they have left are the multiple-choice tests of stuff no one ever needs to know.

Multiple Choice Tests.   The multiple-choice test is the standard model today for assessing education in this country. In various fields, and at various times, we use other forms of assessment, but when the stakes are high, we almost always come back to the multiple-choice test. And at the moment, standardized testing is the only "objective" method we have to determine whether "the standards" have been reached. Testing has come to mean multiple choice or fill-in-the-blank and therein lies the problem. Multiple-choice or fill-in-the-blank tests cannot be used unless the answers sought are well known, explicit, and precise. Because the content of the tests must be clear and agreed upon, what is taught has to share the same characteristics; no teaching of debatable points or open questions or curiosities to be mused upon. The premise is that facts must be taught and then tested. To get children to be intellectually committed to fact memorization is difficult.

The convenience of the multiple-choice test (and other tests that have simple right answers) is incontrovertible. But these tests perpetuate the myth that is the crux of what is wrong with today's education system: The Myth of the Right Answer. In a multiple-choice test, there is a right answer. This is rarely true in real life, however. In real life, there are nearly right answers, answers that were missing a step, and most important, situations in which there is no right answer at all. Should the United States have invaded Iraq? There is no right answer to this question, but there are many interesting answers. But tests being tests, those are not the answers that will be called for in any standardized exam, where it is always better to test a date instead.

The Right Answer System.   The Right Answer System insists that there is a single correct answer to every question. Students do not have any control over what the Right Answer is. Answers are doled out by the teacher. But the teacher really has no control either. He is simply a delivery mechanism. In today's system, control is centralized. The Right Answer is found in the standardized test and is delivered to the classroom by way of the fixed curricula. Answers are selected not so much because they are important to teach as because they are easy to assess.

What schools are really teaching students through this system is that the formula is the key to success in school. They come to believe that reasoning without the formula is futile, even though this could not be farther from the case in real life. And because they quite often do not know the formula, they react by believing themselves to be stupid and incapable. They develop strategies to avoid getting called on, to avoid taking the risks that are so central to learning. After all, when you have a deficiency, the last thing you want to do is display it in front of 30 of your peers. The stress that comes from this is a real inhibitor to learning. No one can learn if they are afraid to be wrong.

Those who do know the answers are in even worse shape. They wind up believing they know all the answers to life's important questions. Unfortunately for them, life isn't a multiple-choice test.

Testing and the Love of Learning.   In *How Children Fail,* Holt captures the devastating effect that testing has on children:

> Our "Tell'em-and-test'em" way of teaching leaves most students increasingly confused, aware that their academic success rests on shaky foundations, and convinced that school is mainly a place where you follow meaningless procedures to get meaningless answers to meaningless questions. (p. 151)

> We destroy the disinterested (I do not mean uninterested) love of learning in children, which is so strong when they are small, by encouraging and compelling them to work for petty and contemptible rewards—gold stars, or papers marked 100 and tacked to the wall, or A's on report cards . . . in short, for the ignoble satisfaction of feeling that they are better than someone else. . . . We kill, not only their curiosity, but their feeling that it is a good and admirable thing to be curious, so that by the age of ten most of them will not ask questions, and will show a good deal of scorn for the few who do. (p. 168)

Problems with Standardized Tests.   On the surface, the objective measures of today's standardized tests sound sensible. In theory, they give every student a solid picture of achievement and an equal opportunity for advancement. But after years of rote memorization and drills, what were once intellectually excited and motivated 5-year-olds have become bored or grade-obsessed teenagers. Their thrill over accomplishing real tasks and exhibiting real skills is replaced with anxiety over upcoming tests and a concern for high grades.

The problem with standardized tests and the fixed curricula they engender is their tendency to kill off the kind of education that matters most. But who can blame a teacher or school for orienting the lesson toward helping students pass those tests with high marks? The temptation to teach students to do well on standardized tests is almost unavoidable when performance on such tests is how entire school systems are evaluated.

It is difficult to avoid being evaluated in our society. We have arrived at the point where we are so used to being graded all the time that we expect it in every aspect of life. What is interesting to note is the way in which we evaluate ourselves. We are forever striving for "hard" numeric ranks that allow us to pit ourselves against "the competition." We rarely ask how we are doing in life, or if we are happy, because these things are so difficult to quantify. The curious thing is that how much someone has learned is difficult to quantify as well, but we still try.

Solving the Testing Problem.   The root of the solution of the education problem in America has to do with the need to eliminate competitive test scores, not with the need to improve students' performance on them. It is critical to recognize that the schools cannot be changed in any important sense until fixed curricula are eliminated. But fixed curricula will not be eliminated until we change the way we assess progress.

Bear in mind that when adults take courses in subjects for which they pay money—courses in photography, weight loss, yoga, home repair—there is no test at the end. There isn't a need for a test because the students are their own masters. They set their own standards and, rather than having themselves be judged, they judge the teacher. Lack of motivation is not a problem when the student deliberately sets out to learn a new skill.

We shouldn't be distracted by trying to win the unofficial world test score competition. Instead, we should measure the success of our educational system by whether or not we are producing graduates who have internalized the ability and desire to learn. The best sign of a successful education system would be that students want to go to school, that they remain excited about learning once they get there, and that in the end they are prepared to creatively respond to the kinds of open-ended problems they will actually face in the world.

TOP TEN MISTAKES IN EDUCATION

Obviously, I believe that the school system is making a great many mistakes. Here are 10 of the most important; important because eradicating them would go far toward helping kids learn:

Mistake #1: Schools act as if learning can be disassociated from doing.

There really is no learning without doing. There is the appearance of learning without doing when we ask children to memorize stuff. But adults know that they learn best on the job, from experience, by trying things out. Children learn best that way, too. If there is nothing to actually do in a subject area we want to teach children, it may be the case that there really is nothing that children ought to learn in that subject area.

Mistake #2: Schools believe they have the job of assessment as part of their natural role.

Assessment is not the job of the schools. Products ought to be assessed by the buyer of those products, not the producer of those products. Let the schools do the best job they can and then let the buyer beware. Schools must concentrate on learning and teaching, not testing and comparing.

Mistake #3: Schools believe they have an obligation to create standard curricula.

Why should everyone know the same stuff? What a dull world it would be if everyone knew only the same material. Let children choose where they want to go, and with proper guidance they will choose well and create an alive and diverse society.

Mistake #4: Teachers believe they ought to tell students what they think it is important to know.

There isn't all that much that it is important to know. There is a lot that it is important to know how to do, however. Teachers should help students figure out how to do stuff the students actually want to do.

Mistake #5: Schools believe instruction can be independent of motivation for actual use.

We really have to get over the idea that some stuff is just worth knowing even if you never do anything with it. Human memories happily erase stuff that has no purpose, so why try to fill up children's heads with such stuff? Concentrate on figuring out why someone would ever want to know something before you teach it, and teach the reason, in a way that can be believed, at the same time.

Mistake #6: Schools believe studying is an important part of learning.

Practice is an important part of learning, not studying. Studying is a complete waste of time. No one ever remembers the stuff they cram into their heads the night before the exam, so why do it? Practice, on the other hand, makes perfect. But you have to be practicing a skill that you actually want to know how to perform.

Mistake #7: Schools believe that grading according to age group is an intrinsic part of the organization of a school.

This is just an historical accident and it's a terrible idea. Age-grouped grades are one of the principal sources of terror for children in school, because they are always feeling they are not as good as someone else or better than someone else, and so on. Such comparisons and other social problems caused by age-similar grades cause many a child to have terrible confidence problems. Allowing students to help those who are younger, on the other hand, works well for both parties.

Mistake #8: Schools believe children will accomplish things only by having grades to strive for.

Grades serve as motivation for some children, but not for all. Some children get very frustrated by the arbitrary use of power represented by grades and simply give up.

Mistake #9: Schools believe discipline is an inherent part of learning.

Old people especially believe this, probably because schools were seriously rigid and uptight in their day. The threat of a ruler across the head makes children anxious and quiet. It does not make them learn. It makes them afraid to fail, which is a different thing altogether.

Mistake #10: Schools believe students have a basic interest in learning whatever it is schools decide to teach them.

What kid would choose learning mathematics over learning about animals, trucks, sports, or whatever? Is there one? Good. Then teach him mathematics. Leave the other children alone.

This list does not detail all that is wrong with school. Moreover, the teaching architectures we propose will not fix all that is wrong with education. Nevertheless, they give an idea of where to begin. And I believe that high-quality software could help make these changes possible.

2

What Makes People Smart

Everybody has opinions on politics and religion. These days, everybody also has an opinion on the school system. In particular, everybody seems to have his or her own pet solution for how to fix the system, solutions that run the gamut from reinstituting corporal punishment to eliminating the schools altogether. How are we to figure out which ideas make sense?

The first question to ask about a proposal for reform is whether it meshes with what we know about the process of learning. It may be important later to ask questions like "What's the cost?" and "Is it practical?" but if a reform plan violates basic learning theory, there is no real need to pursue it further.

Cognitive science is in many ways a fledgling field. Few of its theories, taken at a very detailed level, are widely agreed upon. But our concern here is with the general lessons that cognitive science has uncovered rather than the details. There is a general consensus on these lessons.

THE MECHANICS OF INTELLIGENCE

If we want to build a better school system around what we know about how people think and learn, the place to start is with what makes people smart in the first place. Thirty years of research has shown that many of the ideas that people intuitively have about intelligence just do not hold.

Human Reasoning

Perhaps the most harmful misconception people have about intelligence is that being smart comes from knowing a lot of rules. Behind this notion is the sense that reading a lot of textbooks and absorbing what they say will lead one to become an expert. It's funny, though, that this is largely what students do for the first two years of their graduate education, and nobody would want to be operated on by a second-year med student, no matter how well he did on his test. It makes sense to say that intelligence comes from knowledge, but most of that knowledge looks quite a bit different from what you find in a textbook.

Much of human reasoning is case based rather than rule based. When people solve problems, they frequently are reminded of previous problems they have faced. Everyone has vast experience in facing the problems brought up in daily life. How often are you reminded? When you wait in line for a long time at the post office, are you reminded of other times you have waited in line? When you face a problem at the dry cleaners, are you reminded of other problems you have had with the dry cleaners?

People constantly experience such remindings, comparing one experience to another so as to learn from both. Often we believe that our mind is wandering as it seems to flit from thought to thought, leading us in directions that often seem irrelevant to our needs at the time. But the reminding process is reflective of our mind's constant search for old information to help in processing new information. We are, in essence, creating theories about the minute details in the world around us, trying to create a theory of dry cleaners that will help us to select the right one, or a theory of state government, or the behavior of our friends that will allow us to better function in the world. We are constantly accumulating cases and comparing those cases to the cases we have already accumulated in an effort to understand the next case that will appear.

The world is too complex a place to be adequately characterized by the theories we develop, and for the most part we know this. Our rules may be useful for the most common situations we encounter, but we cannot help but encounter many situations that violate or are outside the bounds of the generalizations we make. Having a broad, well-indexed set of cases is what differentiates the expert from the textbook-trained novice. Or, to put this another way, being educated means, in its deepest sense, having access to a wealth of cases from which to generalize.

Cases

Cases contain and relate individual bits of knowledge about instances of things you have experienced. So the car your parents owned that always broke down on long trips is a case. A relationship like the one you had with your first boyfriend or girlfriend is a case. So is an event like the last time you went to get ice cream.

Cases of Sending Troops

We often see people reasoning from a single case. In examining examples of man-on-the-street interviews that focused on what the United States should do about Central America, we found that all the respondents replied that the situation in Central America reminded them of Vietnam, and that we should not send troops. Most Americans had one case in their memories about the effects of sending troops overseas and reasoned from that one case. When the Gulf War broke out, however, most Americans were in favor of American occupation. What happened to the Vietnam case?

The reason why respondents didn't get reminded of Vietnam when thinking about the Gulf War has to do with how they label the Vietnam case. In Vietnam , we intervened in an internal conflict. Thus, the case Americans remembered might have had this label: "Sending American troops overseas to intervene in internal conflicts leads to failure." The Central America case also fits this label, so it tends to bring Vietnam to mind. The Gulf War, however, was precipitated by an invasion of a small country. In this case, Americans may have used this label: "Sending troops to help out country invaded by dictator." Now this case looks a lot more like World War II to most Americans, and most Americans feel World War II was a success. The fact that Saddam Hussein, after the invasion of Kuwait, was often compared to Adolph Hitler no doubt helped people make this connection.

Reminding

The central process in case-based reasoning is the process of getting reminded. The key idea in reminding (Schank, 1982) is that when we hear a story we attempt to understand that story by labeling it in our memories. That label will often correspond to one we have used before and will thus evoke a reminding.

Because our experience is so varied, many of our labels are quite detailed. Suppose you hear a story that has all the details stripped out of it: "The Smiths mistreated their son and it really affected him." You might get reminded by such a story, but even if you do the remindings are often vague and uncompelling. If you get some details, however, things change. Suppose you hear this story: "When he was a child, Chris Smith's parents took away his allowance for a month every semester because he didn't get enough A's. Nothing he ever did was good enough for them. Now he works 80-hour weeks and is obsessed about being perfect in everything he does." Even though this story is still abbreviated, it has enough detail in it to give you strong, concrete remindings.

Bull sessions that last late into the night consist of chains of such remindings. Someone tells you a story and you get reminded. You tell your story and they get reminded. Such story swapping is valuable because it augments the conversants' libraries of cases. If you hear a good one, you can use it the next time you are in a similar situation. Likewise, by telling a good story, you can give others a piece of your experience in a form they can use.

An Example of Case-Based Reasoning

To understand case-based reasoning in more detail, let's consider someone who wants to become a member of the sushi cognoscenti, one who is really an expert in sushi. This domain is a good one to discuss because everyone is familiar with learning about new foods. Also, as with most "real-world" domains, this is one for which there is no fixed curriculum. What exactly is it that an expert on sushi knows? What memory structures get built and changed as the person learns?

To start, let's assume that our subject has never tasted sushi before. Having never had sushi, what happens when you eat it for the first time? The answer is that you create a case for that experience. This case contains the story of your sushi-eating experience. It packages information about where you were, what you ordered, how you liked it, and other related details.

Where is this case located in memory? Well, when eating the sushi (or doing any other task), you are comparing it with other things you have eaten before. Because each person has different experiences, each person will have a distinct set of memory structures to use to understand the sushi experience. Typical ways of understanding the experience might be "an example of uncooked food" or "an example of Japanese food" or "an example of seafood." Each of these general categories would then be used to "index" the case in memory. "Indexing" is the process that people use to attach labels like these to the cases they experience. They can then use those labels at a later time to recall relevant cases. So, if you were later asked "When was the first time you ate raw fish?", you would then be able to answer "I had sushi once in such-and-such a place."

What happens if you are asked at this point, "Do you like sushi?" Having eaten sushi only once, you have no generalizations about it. The way you would answer this question is to use case-based reasoning. You would be reminded of your one sushi-eating experience and build an answer around how much you enjoyed it.

One case does not a gourmet make, however. If you wish to become an expert on sushi, then you must get more experience—you must eat more sushi. You need to experiment with the different variables that affect sushi. If you want to know the extent to which freshness matters, you have to eat some sushi that isn't fresh and some that is especially fresh. To understand how sushi compares to other forms of raw fish, you must try them as well. This means eating sashimi, for example, or eating rare tuna in a restaurant that grills tuna steaks.

What happens as you gain these experiences? One result is that you build additional cases. But you will find, as you gain cases, you begin to build organizational structures in memory that capture what you learn from those cases. You begin to build a theory-of-sushi around your experience, capturing that theory in your organizational memory structures. After becoming experienced with sushi, when asked the question "Do you enjoy sushi?", you no longer get reminded of your initial sushi-eating experience. In fact, you will probably not be reminded of any particular case at all. Instead, you will be able to tap into your organizational memory structures and use rule-based reasoning to give a reply such as, "Normally I don't much care for sushi, but when it's fresh, it's wonderful." The additional cases allow you to distinguish nuances in sushi, and the organizational structures represent the rules you have learned from those cases.

People are constantly building theories such as the theory-of-sushi we have been discussing. How do we create such theories? Three processes are critical: expectation building, expectation failure, and explanation.

Building Expectations.   The first time you eat sushi, you take that experience as your prototypical sushi-eating experience. The next time, you expect the experience to be roughly the same as the first. You use your past experience to provide expectations (i.e., predictions) for what your future will be like. As you gain experience, those expectations that turn out to be always true get embedded into generalized memory structures that capture the commonalties.

Expectation building then is simply the generation of generalized memory structures based on similarities among the events we experience. In the sushi example, these structures give you predictions that you can use when thinking about sushi. Unless you sit back and ponder about your sushi-eating experience, these structures will contain little more than knowledge about the typical sequence of events in a sushi-eating case and the typical outcomes from such cases.

Expectation Failure.   The discussion about expectation building is based on a critical assumption. It assumes that new experiences are like old experiences (or in other words, that the expectations we build turn out to be true). But what happens when our expectations turn out to be wrong? As the saying goes, there is an exception to every rule. What happens when the type of sushi you always enjoy tastes bad to you one night?

When your expectations fail, you know that your theory-of-sushi needs to be adapted. If your theory was perfect, after all, you would never have generated an incorrect expectation. When faced with expectation failures, we, logically enough, attempt to repair the structure that generated the expectation. But this is not simple to do. Because many different memory structures provide expectations at any one time, how do you know which of those structures needs work? When your sushi tastes bad, do you fix the structure that organizes what you know about eating or the one that organizes what you know about ordering? Perhaps neither needs to be changed. Perhaps you need to add a mental addendum that tells you not to go out for food when you have a bad cold.

Explanation lies at the root of how you know which knowledge structures need to be repaired. You need to explain the failure to yourself. You might determine, for example, that the cause of the bad sushi was the fact that the fish was old. Such an explanation tells you which structures to update. Here, you might index this case under the sushi memory structure. You might also index this case under your ordering memory structure with the admonition to check how old food is before ordering it. Whenever you reach a tentative explanation, you use the explanation to index the case under the appropriate knowledge structures.

When we experience a number of failures that have the same explanation and point to the same knowledge structure, we then know to refine that knowledge structure. Imagine you have bad sushi again, and again the explanation is that the fish was old. When indexing this case, you will come across (i.e., be reminded of) your previous experience. On the basis of these matching explanations, you can build a generalized knowledge structure that indicates that when sushi is old it is bad.

The Right Time to Generalize

Schools, though, tend to present generalizations before specifics. But a generalization is really only valuable if you make it yourself. The reason for this is simple enough. Generalizations come from cases, lots of cases. If someone teaches you a generalization (a formula for example is a type of generalization that is typically taught), then it better be useful nearly every day or you will most likely forget it. The generalizations we remember we make ourselves, drawing on the rich case base we have acquired that has, in a sense, forced us to make that generalization as a way of tying together what we know in a useful form. When we make such a generalization ourselves, we can be sure to remember it because we obviously needed it. We needed it because the same kind of cases kept coming up and we needed to understand them. Generalization and understanding are intimately connected. Generalizations that we are told have no place to sit in memory and no cases to tie together are quickly forgotten from lack of use. They are "lean" generalizations, isolated from the knowledge that would answer questions like "Why is it so?", "Why do I want to know it?", "What are the exceptions?", and "How does this impact on other things that I know?"

Cases and the Process of Fixing a Broken Generalization

It makes sense that the process of building new generalizations is grounded in individual cases. What is not so obvious is that the process of repairing them is similarly grounded. To repair generalizations, we need to construct explanations. And those explanations require data to support them. We cannot wonder if old fish makes for bad sushi unless we keep around those cases in which we have experienced sushi made from old fish. Likewise, if we later find out that one of our explanations is incorrect, we need access to the source cases for that explanation to try to construct an alternative. To construct a new explanation, we need to be able to access the details of our past cases and "see them in a new light."

The Problem with Expert Systems

The dependence on cases poses a problem to those who treat human cognition as being primarily rule based. Much work in artificial intelligence, for example, is done in "expert systems." These systems are based on the notion that expert knowledge consists of a collection of rules. By determining the rules an expert in a domain uses, the idea goes, we may then simulate expert behavior in that domain. Not surprisingly, expert systems have run into a significant problem: They are brittle. When faced with a problem that bends the rules, they are unable to cope. They fail because they are not grounded in cases. They are unable to fall back on the details of their experience, find a similar case, and apply it. Likewise, they are unable to use similarities between tough problems and previous experiences to update their rules. Their failure to retain cases cripples their ability to learn from their experiences.

The Value of a Misguided Generalization

In an expert system, if a rule is wrong, it is worthless (or worse). People, however, can repair faulty generalizations. Therefore, for people, even if a generalization is wrong, it isn't necessarily useless. The organizational structures we build in memory serve three purposes:

- Providing us with expectations;
- Storing our theories-under-construction; and
- Organizing the cases of our experience so they can be recalled when relevant.

When an organizational structure provides incorrect expectations, it has only failed in the first purpose. The incorrect expectation serves to actually further the other two purposes. It allows us to upgrade our theory and it gives us a place to index the new case, along with its explanation. Without such structures, we would not be able to recall appropriate cases when faced with new ones.

Learning and Memory

To understand enough about learning to be able to understand more about teaching and what should go on in education, we must look more deeply at human memory. If memory is a place where active processing and learning takes place, then what we learn about memory should tell us a great deal about what schooling should look like. We need to understand what kinds of structures are contained in memory and how those structures operate.

The Importance of Memory

To understand how we learn, it is first necessary to understand something about how we think. Intelligence is fundamentally a memory-based process. Learning means the dynamic modification of memory. It means change— change that causes a system to act differently on the basis of what is contained within it. Human memories are in a constant state of dynamic modification.

Learning depends on inputs. Each word you read and each sight you see changes your memory in some way. It follows, therefore, that one of the key media of learning are the senses. The role of memory is the interpretation and the placement of those inputs. Memory must decide what's worth keeping by determining what the meaning of an input is and where it fits in relation to previous knowledge it has already stored.

One commonsense but incorrect view of memory is that it is simply a warehouse where we keep our knowledge when we are not using it. This warehouse notion implies that learning is the stocking of memory with uninterpreted knowledge. The corresponding notion of remembering is that when we need a piece of knowledge, we go into memory and pull it off the shelves. This notion is appealing but misguided. There are no alphabetically listed bins in memory. When I ask you to tell me an incident where your mother was mean to you when you were young, you don't look under M for mother or M for mean and run into information about moths located nearby. Memory organization depends on meaning and thus is organized in a way that might have you run into something about your father or something about punishment while you were looking for the incident I asked for. This meaning-based organization has great importance for theories of learning.

The Warehouse Model

In the warehouse model view, thinking is accomplished by some mysterious outside processes in which knowledge structures are pulled off the shelf when knowledge from memory is needed. In such a simplistic model, being intelligent has a lot to do with these mysterious other processes and not so much to do with the knowledge structures stored in memory. But knowledge is what organizes memory in the first place. This matters because new knowledge must perturb the system to find its place in memory in relation to what is already there. Does it amplify old knowledge, or contradict it? The mind needs to resolve these questions as new knowledge appears, getting reminded of what it already knows or believes each time some new experience occurs. This process of reminding and comparison is a critical part of learning. Thinking depends on our ability to generalize and merge new knowledge with older memories. Teaching must make use of this natural process or fail miserably in getting anyone to ever remember anything at all that has been taught.

The Error of the Warehouse Model

People use many different types and levels of knowledge structures when they do even simple tasks like understanding what someone tells them. When you read a book, for example, you have built up expectations about what will come in the next sentence from structures that contain what you know about (among other things) the ways paragraphs are typically organized, the way an intellectual argument is structured, and your views about what has been said so far. Under the warehouse model, some mysterious process requisitions the appropriate model when needed. The knowledge itself is static and passive.

However, when you read, you can always learn something about each of the varied types of knowledge you are applying. You can learn a new word or a new fact or a new opinion or a new way of presenting an argument. It does not make much sense to consider your memory a site of passive knowledge when this knowledge behaves so actively, each piece always trying to align your experiences with itself and modifying itself when needed.

Computers Should Get Bored Too

At Yale during the late 1970s, students in my laboratory built a number of simulations that operated by retrieving a variety of static knowledge structures from a memory, then applying it to the current problem. Typically, we would build a program to read a story about an earthquake, and it would take what it knew about earthquakes in general and use that information to interpret what had happened in the story it was reading. It would use its prior knowledge to help it verify its expectations of possible loss of human life and extensive property damage. In other words, such a program operated on the warehouse model, by finding knowledge it needed and using it and then returning it untouched. At the time, we were happy with this model because we were interested in investigating the kinds of knowledge structures people must use to understand stories. And our programs did quite well in translating, summarizing, and answering questions about stories they had read. The key insight at that time, attributable to these programs, was that knowledge played a key role in understanding, or, to put this another way, that one could not understand a story about earthquakes unless fairly extensive knowledge about earthquakes was already present in memory.

But, unfortunately, there was a serious flaw in our work. The knowledge structures our programs used did not change during the process of reading. Our programs would happily read the same earthquake story a hundred times and never complain about being bored. Why was this the case? Clearly, the reason was that human beings update what they know from what they read. We never accounted for this in our programs because we didn't see the use of it, and the idea behind it created havoc in our view of memory as a static warehouse of information.

An Experiment in Memory and Knowledge

The simulations built at Yale in the 1970s laid out some of the processes and knowledge structures people use in understanding the world. One of the central insights we reached through these experiments was that the warehouse view of memory is wrong. Instead of being a place where knowledge structures are stored when they are not in use, we found that the structures that memory contains must be processing structures as well-acknowledged structures; that is, the very knowledge that was stored away in memory helped to process new situations. Or, to put this another way, the intelligence that helps us understand the world is the very same stuff we have been remembering about the world all our lives. Memory mechanisms and information-processing mechanisms have to be exactly the same stuff to work the way they do.

The Dynamic Memory View

Memory is changed with each use. When you read about Bosnia it helps you learn enough so that you can read tomorrow's Bosnia story, too. In the work we did in Artificial Intelligence (AI) at Yale in the 1970s, we had been trying to avoid working on learning because, as we didn't even know what people knew, it seemed premature to attempt to understand how they changed what they knew. What we discovered was that it was unrealistic to work on static memory structures because such structures really didn't exist in people.

Instead of viewing memory as a warehouse then, we instead began to see it as a workhouse. The notion of a "dynamic memory" implies that memory structures are not shipped off for use by some outside process but instead employ internal processes. Each of the structures actively proposes expectations and then tracks what comes next to see whether the expectations are fulfilled or not. The structures not only provide knowledge; they update that knowledge. They are the nexus of learning. Memory certainly is a place where we store knowledge, but it is much more. It is a place where we process knowledge, dynamically changing what we know by the processing we do.

An Example of Dynamic Memory

When a person reads a story, the knowledge structures they used to understand the story change during the reading process in an attempt to absorb what has been read. It isn't that memory is trying to learn the story; memory really isn't an intentional entity. Rather, during the process of attempted understanding, memory must self-adjust to accommodate the information it is trying to process. As memory is engaged in understanding a story, learning, in some sense, has to take place. However, the learning that takes place is not simply the adding of information to memory. Consider, for example, the following story from the *New York Times* (June 2, 1993):

King of Saudi Arabia Urges A Formal Peace With Israel

Mecca, Saudi Arabia, June 1 (AP)—King Fahd pledged today to support all efforts to end the state of war formally between the Arabs and Israel and to promote peaceful coexistence in the region.

In a statement marking the Feast of Sacrifice, Islam's holiest feast, he also criticized Muslim militants for projecting the Islamic faith "as if it were the force that would destroy human civilization and take the world back to the Middle Ages."

The statement was read over state radio and television on the second day of the feast, which marks the end of the pilgrimage season to Mecca, Islam's holiest city. (p. 3)

To understand such a story, an understander must relate the information in it to what is already in the understander's memory. In this instance, this means taking previous beliefs that may have been in memory and attempting to use them to help comprehension. Each person understands such a story differently, because each person has different beliefs about the Middle East. So, if our reader's memory contains beliefs like "Arabs never want to make peace with Israel" and "Arabs promote terrorism in the name of

Islam," then this reader would need to confront the fact that this new story violates both of those beliefs. There are many ways to deal with such memory conflicts. One is to ignore the new input. In this case, this story will not be remembered at all; the reader will have "forgotten" it because he or she failed to integrate it into memory. Another strategy is to say that prior beliefs were wrong and that the new story supersedes them. The problem here is that someone with this attitude would be purging prior memories in a way that is uncharacteristic of most readers. This isn't learning exactly, as the elimination of the old makes the new material a kind of orphan in memory.

A much more realistic situation is that of an understander trying to reconcile the conflicts by explaining the differences to him or herself. He or she might think the Saudis are different from other Arabs, for example, and seek to explain this difference by recalling that they were allies of the United States in the Gulf War. Further, he or she might recall that the Saudi government is, in general, more religious and more right wing than the terrorists they are condemning. However the understander resolves these conflicts, the resolution itself results in new beliefs. The learning that has taken place was actually a modification of old beliefs and generalizations that cause failed expectations and the creation of new beliefs that are anchored by the example, also added to memory, of the new news article. Memory has thus changed by adding both new information and a new place to put that information and a new way to link that new information with older, and now modified, information. Learning is, we can see, a memory process—the result of the attempt to understand new information.

Looking at the Structures in Memory

To understand the variety of structures we have in our memories, let's consider an example. How good an answer can you give to this question:

When was Bill Clinton born?

Now think about how you answered the question. Different people answer this question in different ways. Most people use one of these three strategies:

Strategy 1.   They know the answer immediately.

Strategy 2.   They know how old Clinton was at some important point (such as when he was inaugurated President) and do some simple math to figure out how old he is now.

Strategy 3.   They don't know how old he is but try to figure it out by comparing him to another individual whose age they know. So, a high schooler might guess that Clinton is the age of the high schooler's parents. Senior citizens might compare Clinton to one of their children.

Each of these strategies uses different memory structures. The first strategy is simple: Locate the fact in memory that gives the answer. The second strategy is more complex: Locate some episode in memory that gives an age for Clinton and then use that episode to calculate the desired value. The third strategy is also more complex: Locate some "reference" individual and use that individual's age, perhaps adjusting it a bit one way or the other.

All three strategies use some bottom-level knowledge structure as input data. The first strategy requires a single fact: Clinton's age. The second strategy requires a bit more knowledge: Clinton's age at some point in time and when that point was. The last strategy is more complex: It requires locating a person who seems similar in age to Clinton, figuring out how old that person is, and then perhaps adjusting the answer a bit. To use this strategy, one must know a lot more than a single decontextualized fact. One must know enough about the reference person to be able to bring him or her to mind in the first place as well as to be able to adjust his or her age before responding. We call the structure that holds this latter kind of knowledge a "case."

The Purpose of Memory Structures

Memory strategies depend, in part, on the mental structures that organize our memories so that we can locate knowledge when we need it. It is implausible to believe that we activate every structure in memory every time we try to answer a question. Instead, our memories use organizational structures that help them figure out which knowledge is relevant when. Although we could not keep track of the enormous number of things we know without such structures, they are not always perfect. Have you ever had the experience of knowing that you know something but not being able to bring it to mind?; Or the experience of having to use a circuitous route to remember some piece of information? The classic example of this is when you mislay your keys. How do you find them? One good strategy is to mentally retrace your steps. The reason this strategy works is that in the process of retracing your steps, you activate additional memory structures. You may not be able to retrieve "on top of the kitchen counter" when you first want to locate your keys. But when you retrace your steps, you activate your memory structure for being in the kitchen, and that structure allows you access to the memory for your act of putting the keys down on the counter.

The Role of Organizational Memory Structures

Our memories contain a number of different types of organizational structures that categorize and interrelate other memory structures. So, for example, we have structures that group together "times we have been in a doctor's waiting room." We also have structures that group together "people we find annoying because they talk too much and listen too little." And we have structures that group together memories under abstract categories such as "times that we labored hard against the odds and managed to win out in the end." These organizational structures segment the full complement of our memories so that we can locate the right ones when we need them.

Our lab has studied a variety of these organizational structures. It is not important for the current purpose to go into the details of these structures and how they operate. But it is important to understand the roles these structures serve. Organizational structures help us classify and locate lower level structures like facts and cases. Organizational structures also capture the generalizations we make about those bottom-level knowledge structures. They capture knowledge such as the order events happen in a restaurant or the way bosses react when their employees are tardy. These structures then allow us to make predictions about the world. We know when we walk into a restaurant that a waitress will bring us a menu after we sit down. And we know that if we don't want to irritate our boss we should not be caught coming in late to work very often.

It is organizational structures like these that tell us how to go about trying to figure out President Clinton's age. Most people have had enough experience trying to figure out other peoples' ages that they have built up a library of generally useful techniques for doing it. They can use the generalizations they have constructed as rules to guide their behavior. In this case, these rules contain knowledge that looks like: If I want to figure out someone's age, then I can try strategy X.

Scriptlets and MOPs

Dynamic Memory (Schank, 1982), proposed two different types of memory structures that we use to capture knowledge. The first were called "scripts" in that book and are now called "scriptlets" to emphasize their limited scope. Scriptlets are memory structures that capture what we know about how things happen in typical situations we find ourselves in. Scriptlets are confined to small portions of our experience located within one physical scene. Examples of scriptlets include looking at a menu, putting ketchup on a hamburger, brushing one's teeth, or parking the car.

Scriptlets are extremely important in human cognition. The secret to being skilled is bound up in them. When we say we know how to do something, we are often referring to some set of scriptlets we have built up over the years. Such scriptlets often operate subconsciously. We can use them quite fluidly, but we may have difficulty describing just what it is they contain to someone who wishes to develop the same ability.

Because scriptlets cover such small portions of our expertise, we need to have other structures that tie them into larger sequences. A second type of structure serves this function. I call these MOPs (for Memory Organization Packets). MOPs contain knowledge about typical sequences of events; they break down events into individual scenes. A restaurant MOP, for example, contains scenes such as "being seated," "ordering," or "paying." Those scenes then point to scriptlets that contain our knowledge about how to understand and handle ourselves in those situations.

The splitting up of memory into the two levels of scriptlets and MOPs gives us a critical ability. It allows us to take what we learn in doing one task and apply it to another task (to the extent that those tasks share common scriptlets). Thus, for example, one might pay for a meal in a restaurant, an airplane ticket, and a hospital visit in much the same way—by going to a person seated behind a counter and presenting a credit card, taking a form that the person fills out, signing it, and keeping one copy. Of course, there are differences between paying in each situation, which means that what we know about the scene must be "colored" by different MOPs. Nevertheless, we can transfer what we learned in a scene while using one MOP and apply it while using another. For example, if you find out that you sign credit card forms incorrectly when at a restaurant and are corrected, you will probably sign the next one you get correctly even if you are at the travel agent. We use scriptlets to capture commonalties and transfer learning between the MOPs that organize our experiences on a larger scale.

Questions Driving Knowledge

The process of building up and correcting knowledge structures is driven by the questions we ask ourselves. Expectation failures are a primary source of questions. Such failures force us to ask ourselves questions like "What caused the failure?" and "How can I prevent the failure from occurring again?" But expectation failures are not the only times when we sit back and ask ourselves questions. Sometimes, we are faced with a new problem and need to develop a new plan. In such cases, we might proceed by asking ourselves "What old problems is this new problem like?" or "How can I break down this problem into simpler problems?" Other times, we puzzle over our experiences, asking questions such as "What would have happened if I had behaved differently?" and "Why did X act as he did?" Still other times, we ask more mundane questions like "How do I get to 1243 Rose Avenue?" or "How much does a cup of coffee cost here?"

Although these questions are of different types and are generated in different ways, they share a common characteristic. Like all questions, they play a central role in learning. They point to holes in our memory structures that we wish to fill. They provide the starting point for the processes through which we integrate new information into memory, tie old information together in new ways, and correct our faulty generalizations. It is probably not too strong to say that until we ask a question we are unable to integrate an answer into our memories. Further, the more questions we ask about an item, the more ways we index that item in our memories. Better indexing allows our memories to be more flexible. So the more questions we ask, the more easily we can recall the items that we think about.

Asking Questions to Build Knowledge.   Here's a story from the *New York Times* (June 2, 1993):

Libyans Strangely Cut Short Their Strange Visit to Israel

Jerusalem, June 1—Muslim pilgrims from Libya suddenly cut short their visit here today after calling for the overthrow of the "Zionist leadership," the "liberation" of Jerusalem and the establishment of a "democratic" Palestinian state of Arabs and Jews.

Israeli officials, some of whom had hailed the visit as a portent of peace, were surprised and outraged by the remarks, made at a news conference. The strange collapse of an already strange pilgrimage quickly dampened speculation that the trip might promote ties with Libya after years of unbending hostility.

The pilgrims announced that they would depart on Wednesday, a day ahead of schedule, canceling planned visits to several Israeli cities.

The motives behind their abrupt departure remained unclear. They said they were leaving because they had completed their prayers, but their Israeli travel agent said they had decided to leave after Palestinians obstructed and harassed them today as they tried to visit Al Aksa Mosque (p. 7).

Here are some questions I had after reading this article: (a) Did Libya really want to improve relations with Israel?; (b) Was it Libya's intention all along to do what they did?; (c) Is the PLO really annoyed at Libya?; (d) What does this all have to do with the new Saudi Arabian viewpoint about wanting to make peace with Israel that I read about earlier?

If you were a teacher who wanted to teach me about the Middle East, you would now find a willing student, because I have been made curious. I am curious about the issues I have noticed, so I won't respond well to a lecture on whatever it is you wanted to say before I asked those questions. I asked those questions because my memory got confused when it tried to integrate the new story with my old beliefs. The answers to these questions are needed by my memory for me to remember the preceding article. I will not remember much more of this article besides the answers to these questions because the questions indicate what I had to think about and what I wanted to think about to absorb the article into my memory. Learning depends on following one's own internal mental path in an idiosyncratic fashion.

Because questions kick off the processes of integration and generalization and therefore ultimately have an impact on the issue of long-term retention of information, it is important to understand what conditions lead us to ask questions. It is important to recognize that it is internally generated questions that drive memory and hence drive learning. Once a question has been generated by memory, memory is set to learn because it knows where to place any answer it finds. But memory is obsessive enough to fail to pay attention to information provided that is not an answer to any question it may have, thus making learning of information it is not seeking fairly difficult.

Ignoring Questioning Skills.   Most of school has to do with understanding answers. But generating questions is often more difficult than generating answers. When questions ask for facts, we can rapidly tell whether we know the fact or not. If we don't know it, we usually know how to rapidly find it out (at least for the facts that tend to get covered in school). When questions ask for explanations, people are remarkably capable of rapidly generating hypotheses. This is because, besides pointing out the need for an answer, questions also point out which type of answer is required.

Questions have buried within them the seeds of the kinds of answers they will permit. These answers then allow us to build generalizations that tie together our experiences. Imagine you get old sushi at a restaurant and want to figure out a way to avoid having that happen again. If you ask yourself the right questions, you can tap into your previous experiences to help you figure out what to do. Perhaps you ask yourself what getting bad sushi has in common with getting bad seats at the baseball park like you did the week before. You know that arriving earlier at the ballpark helps you get better seats. So you think about trying to arrive at the restaurant "earlier," which in this case might mean just after a fresh shipment of sushi comes in. Or you might ask yourself what getting old sushi has in common with getting old milk at the grocery. This question leads you to try to adapt your plan for getting fresh milk, grabbing containers from the back of the shelf. You might then decide to go to a sushi place late at night to see if the food seems fresher because by then they have had a chance to run through their older stock.

The Importance of Good Indices.   Asking questions leads us to think more deeply about our experiences. The more deeply we think about the cases we experience, the more detailed the indices we build between them get. And the more detailed these indices are, the better we are able to use knowledge gained in one context in some other context. For example, if I eat sashimi for the first time, I might label it as "sushi without the rice." Or I might label it as "sushi without the rice, leading to a blander taste experience due to the lack of contrast in textures." The second label is not only more detailed; it is more useful. It allows us to apply experiences we have had with other examples of "lack of contrast" to what we know about raw fish. The better our indexing, the more prepared we are to plan for and react to the world we operate in.

THE FUNDAMENTAL LESSONS OF LEARNING THEORY

Cognitive scientists and educational researchers may be frustrated by the limits of what they know. Still, few schools are bumping up against the limits of this knowledge. There is much to be learned about what kinds of things people know, how they use what they know, how they come to learn it, and how we can "teach" it to them (by which I mean only how we can help them learn it). Most of today's schools flagrantly violate even the little we do know. The system needs to change, and it is not enough to say what it should not change to. A positive and clear guide for reform is possible by focusing on two mottoes:

An interest is a terrible thing to waste

- and -

Students must be in control of their own learning

3

Cultural Unliteracy

LISTS AND DESIGNING CURRICULA

It's been a favorite hobby of educators over the years to churn out extensive lists that supposedly provide the definitive answer to the question, "What should an educated person know?" If you know everything on the list, the idea goes, you are well educated. School-age children have good reason to fear such lists.

During the 20th century, the methods for producing such "literacy lists" have become increasingly "scientific." One of the most famous of such lists was produced between 1915 and 1919 by the Committee on Economy of Time in Education, a committee of the National Education Association (NEA). This group performed an extensive study of the activities people engage in on an everyday basis and tried to isolate what knowledge they need to effectively perform those activities. The list that resulted filled a staggering eight volumes of things one should know.

This NEA effort was based on a seemingly right-headed idea: Look at the things adults do, then teach children what they need to know to do the same things. At the heart of this effort was the idea that teaching children the things that tie into their everyday experiences and interests will help with what they will want to do. But the committee made a basic mistake. Instead of producing a guide that could help different children pursue different interests, the committee instead produced a uniform list dictating what was necessary for all children to know.

Literacy lists inevitably harm educational efforts. They take control away from teachers and students and cede it to distant authorities. The more detailed such lists are, the more harm they do. The longer these lists grow, the more teachers need to rush through the items and teach to the test, and the likelihood decreases that teachers or children will be allowed to think for themselves in the classroom. This problem is endemic to the notion of literacy lists. Although the NEA effort set a standard for rigorous analysis, it also legitimized the idea of bulky literacy lists, an idea that, unfortunately, is gaining currency today.

The Cultural Literacy Movement

The historic tendency of educators to promote literacy lists goes today under the moniker of Cultural Literacy. This current incarnation promises to be even more dangerous than usual. The Cultural Literacy movement has replaced the NEA committee's emphasis on living experience with an emphasis on static academic knowledge. This movement in its various guises has filled the bookstores with books that claim to explain exactly what it is that a person must know to be "literate" in fields as diverse as science, culture, religion, and art history. The philosophy of the literacy list is even being advocated for each grade level. E.D. Hirsch, Jr., the major proponent of Cultural Literacy, edited a set of books called *The Core Knowledge Series*, which includes titles like *What Your First Grader Needs to Know*. In this work, Hirsch (1991) explains that his goal is to define "a specific core of knowledge for each grade that motivates everyone through definite attainable standards."

E.D. Hirsch Jr. and What Your First Grader Should Know

Among other things, according to Hirsch (1991), your first grader needs to know the following Indian myth about why owls have big eyes:

Why the Owl Has Big Eyes
(An Iroquois Tale)

Raweno, the spirit who makes everything, was busy creating animals. This afternoon, he was working on Rabbit. "May I have nice long legs and long ears like a deer?" Rabbit asked. "And sharp fangs and claws like a panther?"

"Certainly," Raweno said. But he had gotten no farther than shaping Rabbit's hind legs when he was interrupted by Owl.

"Whoo, whoo. I would like a nice long neck like Swan's," Owl demanded. "And beautiful red feathers like Cardinal's, and a long beak like Egret's, and a royal crown of plumes like Heron's. I want you to make me into the swiftest and the most beautiful of all birds."

"Be quiet," Raweno said. "You know that no one is supposed to watch me at work. Turn around, and close your eyes!"

Raweno shaped Rabbit's ears, long and alert, just like Deer's.

"Whoo, whoo," Owl said. "Nobody can forbid me to watch. I won't turn around and I certainly won't close my eyes. I like watching, and watch I will."

Then Raweno became angry. Forgetting Rabbit's front legs, he grabbed Owl from his branch and shook him with all his might. Owl's eyes grew big and round with fright. Raweno pushed down on Owl's head and pulled up on his ears until they stood up on both sides of his head.

"There!" Raweno said. "Now you have ears that are big enough to listen when someone tells you what to do, and a short neck that won't let you crane your head to watch things you shouldn't watch. And your eyes are big, but you can use them only at night—not during the day when I am working. And finally, as punishment for your disobedience, your feathers won't be red like Cardinal's, but ugly and gray, like this." And he rubbed Owl all over with mud.

Then he turned back to finish Rabbit. But where was he? Poor Rabbit had been so frightened by Raweno's anger that he had fled, unfinished. To this day, Rabbit must hop about on his uneven legs, and he has remained frightened, for he never received the fangs and claws he had requested. As for Owl, he remained as Raweno shaped him in his anger—with big eyes, a short neck, big ears, and the ability to see only at night, when Raweno isn't working. (pp. 56–57)

Now this is certainly an interesting story, and it can be used to draw out a number of useful lessons. But the advocates of the Cultural Literacy movement do not propose it as an example that might be used to illustrate some potentially useful points. They do not claim that it might be useful for a child to learn such lessons in some way. Rather, they claim that to be "culturally literate" every American child should know this specific story. They are not concerned with making sure the child understands why this is a potentially useful story. They are not concerned with making sure that the child can do something with the story. They only want the child to be exposed to the story, to absorb its "facts."

In addition to "Why the Owl Has Big Eyes," there is "Puss-in-Boots" and "The Princess and the Pea" among the other 20 stories Hirsch presents as necessary reading. Or you have a choice of one of the 42 rhymes, 13 sayings, or 13 myths and fables also advocated by Hirsch. This is only the beginning of the 5,000 things he proposes as core knowledge for every American adult.

Cultural Literacy Gaining Ground

The Cultural Literacy movement is gaining ground today as the public demands some assurance that schools are really teaching the "right stuff" and that children are learning it. What better way is there to achieve these goals than to write down exactly what the right stuff is, tell it to students, then test them to make sure that they got it? Such a system seems to be rational.

The problem is that such a notion of the right stuff flies in the face of what we know about how the mind works. The Cultural Literacy movement, which purports to be founded on scientific findings concerning how people use knowledge, is actually based on a flawed notion of what people are and how they operate. Not only does the Cultural Literacy movement suffer from the generic problems inherent in other fixed curricular systems, it also faces a set of problems that stems from its rigid and faulty theories of what knowledge is, how people learn, and how teaching should be conducted.

Goals of Cultural Literacy

Perhaps the best way to describe the goals that motivate the Cultural Literacy movement is to quote Hirsch as he described them himself. This series of quotes, drawn from Hirsch's (1987) book, *Cultural Literacy*, lays out the major purposes of the effort:

- In an anthropological perspective [the name which Hirsch chooses for the Cultural Literacy point of view], the basic goal of education is acculturation, the transmission to our children of the specific information shared by the adults of the group or polis. (p. xvi)
- literate culture has become the common currency for social and economic exchange in our democracy, and is the only available ticket to full citizenship. . . . Membership is automatic if one learns the background information and the linguistic conventions that are needed to read, write, and speak effectively. (p. 22)
- Cultural literacy constitutes the only sure avenue of opportunity for disadvantaged children. (p. xiii)
- Mature literacy alone enables the tower to be built, the business to be well managed, and the airplane to fly without crashing. (p. 2)

Most of the goals underlying these statements are laudable. But can Hirsch's tool achieve them? Hirsch believes that by dint of pursuing Cultural Literacy, which, as we see later, is nothing more than the accumulation of a large set of specific, fixed facts, we can satisfy the basic goal of education, create better citizens, help the disadvantaged, further all other "fundamental" improvements to the education system, and, as the last quote indicates, do just about anything else that modern society might require of us as well.

Flaws in Hirsch's Program

Hirsch's (1987) Cultural Literacy program has a number of flaws:

- It promises more than it could ever hope to accomplish. If everyone should know facts about airplanes, for example, we can make them memorize lists. But if they ever want to do anything with a plane (fly one, repair one, design one, even be a passenger in one), more is needed. Literacy does not ensure that an airplane will fly without crashing.

- It is distinctly conservative—the facts Hirsch believes to constitute cultural literacy tend to be the ones known to those in power. Hirsch vigorously believes that the best way to even society's playing field is to make the underprivileged familiar with these facts. Because "Puss-in-Boots" is part of a European heritage, let's make everyone know about this heritage and everyone will be equal. What Hirsch fails to comprehend is that in a multicultural society neither of the obvious fixes works. You can't make everyone the same by forcing them into one mold. Neither can we teach everyone something about everyone else. When he throws in an Iroquois folk tale, presumably for breadth, he leaves out Apache folk tales, Egyptian folk tales, and Thai folk tales. Trying to cover everyone leaves many people out. Trying to make everyone the same means making them like those in power. Neither approach will work.

- It advocates methods that are contrary to its goal. In his attempt to build a more democratic society, Hirsch is willing to destroy democracy in education. Literacy lists deprive students of the very choices they will exercise as soon as they are freed from school. Hirsch wants to make everyone the same, as if this somehow were the real mission of education. The concept of "acculturation" fails to account for the hallmark of a democracy, individual difference. Not everyone has the same interests. To presume so, or to assume that the task of educators is to make students the same is simply not democratic.

The irony of all this is that Hirsch justifies his cultural literacy program by cloaking it in the mantle of science, specifically in what cognitive scientists have learned about the important role that background knowledge plays in communication. Cognitive psychologists have learned quite a lot in this area, but Hirsch, an English professor, has profoundly misunderstood our results.

Hirsch's Theory of Knowledge

Hirsch's central concern is that we all have the ability to communicate with each other. Due to the increasing complexity and specialization in today's society, Hirsch says, citizens need to have some common basis, some common vocabulary, through which they can communicate. He then focuses on the background knowledge that is required to form such a common basis. For Hirsch, such background knowledge is important because it facilitates communication. To select an example at random from Hirsch's list, two people cannot successfully use a reference to Little Big Horn in a conversation unless both of them are familiar with it.

Taken at this level, and assuming that communication about all subjects is equally important, it is understandable why Hirsch would attempt to create such lists. Still, even if we grant him these premises, Hirsch's reasoning is faulty. He has misunderstood the role that background knowledge plays in communication. And he has failed to account for how people learn background knowledge in the first place.

Hirsch and His Theory

Hirsch roots his claims in what cognitive scientists call "schema theory." Schema theory lays out a picture of how people organize the truly astounding amount of background knowledge they accumulate about the world. This theory asserts that such knowledge is organized into mental units called "schemas." When people learn, when they build knowledge, they are either creating new schemas, or linking together preexisting schemas in new ways. Many of the schemas that people develop are idiosyncratic. Everybody has different experiences, so everyone develops a somewhat different view of the world. However, we also share many common experiences. Most Americans have seen a baseball game, know who the President is, and have eaten at McDonald's. So, many of the schemas that people develop are shared schemas, ones that others have developed as well. Shared schemas constitute an important part of our shared cultural knowledge.

When people communicate, they depend on these shared schemas. Jay Leno can't make a joke about McDonald's unless he can reasonably assume that most of his audience has eaten there. The more background knowledge two people share, the less they have to make explicit in their conversations. This is the central observation on which Hirsch bases his program. His reasoning seems straightforward enough: To enable each American to communicate with any other American, we must make sure that every American shares a common set of schemas that may be taken for granted as shared background knowledge.

The Goal of Teaching Communication

What background knowledge do two people need to share to be capable of communicating with each other? Let's take an example.

I play intramural football every year. Imagine I am telling a team member about a game he missed. In telling the story of the game to a fellow team member, I can count on him having an enormous amount of concrete knowledge about the team. So I can give him a terse description of the game, something that might look like this:

> They tried to do what they always do. But we used the new option a couple of times and we used the quick pitch and they fell for it. By the end, they didn't know which way to turn. We pretty much steamrolled over them.

This story will make little, if any, sense to you, because you are missing the concrete information needed to tie it together. Who are "they"? What is the "new option"? What do I mean by "which way to turn"? Without knowing some facts about the game, you will not be able to make heads or tails of such a communication. Here's the same story as I would tell it to a typical adult under the assumption that he or she knows the things that most American adults do, but may not be particularly familiar with football, or my team:

> I am probably one of the world's oldest intramural athletes. Every year, there is one team that gives my intramural football team trouble because on defense they always fanatically rush whoever has the ball. This style upsets my team's rhythm and we always have a hard time scoring against them. When we played them this year, however, we plotted out a few special plays to take advantage of the risks the team left themselves open to and we really shredded them up. By the end of the game, they had stopped taking such risks because they knew we could take advantage of them. But they did not know how to play defense without taking such risks, so they more or less just fell to pieces.

Most adults will be able to understand this story. One reason for this is that this version fills in the concrete facts that were missing in the first version. Another equally important reason is that most adults understand the abstract knowledge about life that underlies the story. Every adult knows what it means to take a "risk." Every adult knows what it means to plot a strategy. Every adult knows what it means to have a plan of action that usually works go wrong, and not know how to react. Adults can understand this story because they know stories that, in the abstract, are just like it. They understand the abstract schemas on which the story is based.

Children and Schemas

Children, who have not yet had experiences with building strategies, changing plans, and taking risks, are not able to understand, for example, a story about adults playing football. If one were to try to convey what such a story is about to a young child, one might focus on one particular play and describe how it worked, thereby adding more concrete information to adjust for the child's lack of abstract information. Or one might playact one of the football plays with the child, thereby giving the child a sense of what the experience is like. But until the child generates the abstract schemas that underlie the story, he will not have a very complete understanding of the story. Learning is inextricably linked with the ability to abstract and generalize. If all we ever knew were isolated and unrelated facts, then, we might do very well at a game like Trivial Pursuit, but we wouldn't be able to reason coherently. When we try to teach facts to our children, we must realize that the facts themselves are meaningless unless they are linked to generalizations.

Hirsch and Schemas

Hirsch (1987) seems to recognize the need for abstract schemata and generalizations, saying: "In modern life we need general knowledge that enables us to deal with new ideas, events, and challenges. In today's world, general cultural literacy is more useful than what Professor Patterson terms 'literacy to a specific task,' because general literate information is the basis of many changing tasks" (p. 11) and "To understand how isolated facts fit together in some coherent way, we must always acquire mental models of how they cohere, and these schemata can come only from detailed, intensive study and experience" (p. 129).

Still, Hirsch (1987) insists that we teach the specific bits and pieces he collects in his literacy lists. He informs us: "To know what educated people know about tigers but don't know about elm trees is the sort of cultural knowledge, limited in extent but possessed by all literate people, that must be brought into the open and taught to our children" (p. 16) and "What distinguishes good readers from poor ones is simply the possession of a lot of diverse, task-specific information" (p. 61).

Hirsch and Today's Curricula

Hirsch goes so far as to propose that schools should have a split curriculum. He calls the half aimed at imparting Cultural Literacy, a specific set of concrete schemata, the "extensive curriculum," and the half aimed at imparting skills and abstract schemata the "intensive curriculum."

Of course, when one gives two goals to an already overloaded system, it may well turn out that only one of them will be attended to. Hirsch makes it clear that the halves of the curriculum are not meant to be equal for him. The so-called "extensive curriculum" is really what is important to him.

Hirsch is correct to point out that facts are quite important in how people think. But he only half understands their role in how we think and communicate. He says that they are to give us knowledge that we could never figure out on our own (Hirsch, 1987):

Critical thinking and basic skills, two areas of current focus in education, do not enable children to create out of their own imaginations the essential names and concepts that have arisen by historical accident. The Rio Grande, the Mason-Dixon line, "The Night Before Christmas," and "Star Wars" are not products of basic skills or critical thought. Many items of literate culture are arbitrary, but that does not make them dispensable. Facts are essential components of the basic skills that a child entering our culture must have. (p. 28)

What do these catch phrases and code words mean in the absence of the generalizations they serve to illustrate? To his credit, Hirsch recognizes the inherent emptiness of such bits and pieces. "The crucial knowledge held by literate people is, as I have pointed out, telegraphic, vague, and limited in extent." Nevertheless, Hirsch believes such empty knowledge is worth forcing on our children. This desire shows that Hirsch fails to understand how students must be able to relate facts to abstract schemata if they are to be able to use them in everyday life.

Hirsch and Knowledge Building

Let's consider in detail the specific bits of concrete knowledge that Hirsch believes all Americans should have. First, take a minute to build your own idea of what a Cultural Literacy list should look like. Imagine situations in which you might find yourself talking with somebody from a very different background than yours. In what situations might this happen? What topic areas will you be talking about? These are the questions that one would expect Hirsch would ask himself. One would expect that on the basis of answers to these questions, Hirsch would build his literacy list.

I, for example, frequently talk with people from different backgrounds during job interviews, baseball games, or public lectures. If I consider written communication instead of oral, I also have such interactions when I write a book, when I read the newspaper, or when I wade through my junk mail. What concrete content does one need to master to communicate successfully in such situations?

Hirsch himself provides one answer to this question. He points out that people tend to interpret their experiences using what psychologist Eleanor Rosch calls "basic-level categories." Such basic-level schemata include things like dogs, trees, and flowers. From an educator's point of view, these basic-level categories have one very convenient characteristic and children pick them up along the way as they grow up. Such schemata do not need to be taught; children learn them automatically. So even though these pieces of knowledge do provide important background knowledge that we must share to communicate, they cannot be what Hirsch decided to build his lists around. There is no need to build a curriculum around things we all learn automatically.

Knowledge and Lists

Hirsch (1987) proposes that becoming literate is a matter of covering the territory on his Cultural Literacy lists. He assures us that this territory is, in fact, quite small. He states: "It should energize people to learn that only a few hundred pages of information stand between the literate and the illiterate, between dependence and autonomy" (p. 143). This is actually quite a phenomenal concept. Those of us who put knowledge into computers in order to make them intelligent can tell you that it would take a few hundred pages just to describe the simplest of ideas, such as eating in a restaurant. The amount of detail people know about such situations is phenomenally large. (What kind of fork is likely to be found at a three-star restaurant? What is the relationship between the coffee shop waitress and the short-order cook likely to be?)

It's not surprising that as Hirsch has pursued building literacy lists, he has had trouble keeping them down to "a few hundred pages." His books for first graders through sixth graders total over 2,000 pages! Who knows what will happen once he gets to junior high and high school?

Determining what literate people know is a rather daunting undertaking. We know so many details about the world around us that any list of them can at best be superficial. The issue after all is not really knowledge in the first place. The issue is that Hirsch and others are appalled when they hear that students in America don't know who Lincoln was or where Seattle is. However, telling them the answer to these questions fails to tell them a few million other facts they don't know that might help make sense of the first facts and in no way assures that they will remember all this stuff anyway. If they now know Lincoln was the sixteenth president, so what? Hirsch's concern is that children don't understand American history, which may well be an important concern, but it will be in no way remedied by trivia about Lincoln. Knowing a random fact is simply that and no more.

The Cultural Literacy List

Here are the first 20 terms from the Cultural Literacy list. Imagine yourself in a conversation with a stranger. How many of them would you expect to surface? Are they even the kind of terms you would expect? If these terms did indeed arise, would the conversation come to a grinding halt if either party were not familiar with them?

Aaron, Hank
absolute zero
Abandon hope, all ye who enter here
abstract art
abbreviation

abstract expressionism
Aberdeen
academic freedom
abolitionism
a Cappella
abominable snowman
accelerator, particle
abortion
accounting
Absence makes the heart grow fonder
acculturation
absenteeism
AC/DC
absolute monarch
Achilles

These bits and pieces might be important to some particular conversations under some particular circumstances, but they are not essential to one's knowledge. In any case, and this is the key point, if you mention the rock group AC/DC to me, I can always ask you who they are or decide to talk to someone else with whom I might have more in common.

Is the lack of familiarity with such terms the stuff from which social decay is made? To say the least, it's questionable whether these are the pieces of knowledge on which national unity and full citizenship are based. Even if they are important for some conversations in some circumstances, the major impact of a list like this is only to build the myth of the Right Answer. Children faced with random pieces of information cannot understand why the knowledge is important (in fact much of it probably is not at all important) but can only come to believe that there is so much that they don't know that all is lost.

Hirsch's Reading Method

What is the problem with Hirsch's method? Well, for one thing, it doesn't work very well. A child wants to read about things to which he can relate. He expands his horizons by building on what he already knows. He should not be instructed about the Incas in order to read about the Incas. He should learn about the Incas because he was reading about something he already cared about that caused him to become curious about the Incas.

Because he does not understand that how you learn determines what you learn (the Acquisition Hypothesis), Hirsch is able to hold the task of rote memorization dear. If you are interested in teaching reading, the problem is to use materials that build upon the child's own experiences, that relate to the knowledge the child has already acquired in a natural way. What is being read should tie into and extend the background that the child has developed. At least that was the message until Hirsch came along and perverted it by claiming that first children should be explicitly taught the knowledge that forms the background of what they are then to read.

Reading Process and Background Knowledge

What types of knowledge do people need when they communicate? Let's consider the process of reading. Here are eight key processes that people do when they read (Schank, 1982b):

- Make simple inferences
- Establish causal connections
- Recognize stereotyped situations
- Predict and generate plans
- Track people's goals
- Recognize thematic relationships between individuals and society
- Employ beliefs about the world in understanding
- Access and utilize raw facts

The proponents of Cultural Literacy assert that simply by teaching children facts they will become literate. But facts are useful only so far as they help with the processes that underlie communication.

Some of these processes do indeed involve facts, although not all of them do. Even when facts are involved, they are ancillary to other types of knowledge, like knowledge about the types of goals people hold and the plans they use to achieve their goals. If you read a story about Lincoln running for President, for example, and you didn't know who Lincoln was, you could infer who he might have been and still comprehend the story. If, on the other hand, you knew who Lincoln was but had no idea what the process of running for President might involve or the results that it might have, then you would not understand very much. Reading does indeed depend on background knowledge, but it depends on a lot more than that, with most of the latter stuff being fairly difficult to get into a list of what one should know.

Hirsch and Schema Theory

When describing his views on schema theory, Hirsch cites as authorities Spiro, Collins, and Bransford. Experiments done by these psychologists have indeed shown the significance of background knowledge in reading. The curious thing is that Hirsch cites their research as his evidence. These three authorities each find the concept of Cultural Literacy just as appalling as I do. And, as it happens, each has done research that Hirsch apparently never really understood.

It is worthwhile to look at the reading process for just a bit to see what the real issues are. The following is a typical article that I have taken from a recent *Wall Street Journal* (May 24, 1994):

> **Heart Surgery Battle in Michigan Is Struggle Over Cost, Care, Profit Firms, Unions Join to Block Expansion That Hospital Needs for Its Own Health, Safety Is Part of Fight, Too**
>
> There are 28 open-heart surgery programs at hospitals in Michigan. Joseph Damore wants to have number 29.
>
> The chief executive of Sparrow Hospital here is building the kind of full-service health-care organization he believes will be needed to compete in the era of managed competition. Open-heart surgery is the capstone of his strategy.
>
> But his dream has collided head-on with an extraordinary campaign waged by Michigan's most powerful economic interests—including both the auto makers and their unions. When it comes to open-heart centers, these opponents insist, more is not better, just costlier and riskier.
>
> So determined is the opposition that John F. Smith, Jr., General Motor's Corp.'s chief executive, told a surprised Gov. John Engler in their very first meeting last fall that one of GM's top priorities was blocking new heart-surgery units. Other top corporate officials and union leaders flooded hospital executives across the state with letters, phone calls and visits to protest plans for new programs. (p. 1)

Let's consider what readers need to know to understand this story, asking ourselves how relevant a literacy list might be in helping us attain that knowledge. Recall the eight key reading processes. To read a story like this, what does one need to know to perform each process? Let's take a look at some examples:

- Make simple inferences
  1. People pursue dreams because they think they will accomplish things that they hold to be valuable.
  2. Executives of big companies are interested in keeping health costs down.
- Establish causal connections
  1. GM wants to block new health care units because health care is too expensive.
  2. Sparrow Hospital wants new units because it wants to make money.

- Recognize stereotyped situations
  1. More medical care requires taxpayers to pay more taxes.
  2. The governor of a state wants better health care for his citizens so he can get more votes.
- Predict and generate plans
  1. Sparrow Hospital will sue GM.
  2. The governor will be afraid to go against GM.
- Track people's goals
  1. The head of Sparrow wants his hospital to be more important and will find another way to do so if this one doesn't work.
  2. GM wants to run things in the state of Michigan and will soon become active in other social issues.
- Recognize thematic relationships between individuals and society
  1. The governor wants to appear to have done the right thing and make everyone happy.
  2. The hospital wants to make people believe it is interested in people.
- Employ beliefs about the world in understanding
  1. Hospitals usually care more about profits than patients.
  2. GM cares more about profits than about patients.
- Access and utilize raw facts
  1. GM is in Michigan and is very important to the governor of the state.
  2. "What's good for General Bullmoose is good for the USA."

A reader who does not make these inferences, establish these connections, and so on did not fully understand the story. Readers get much more from the story than what we've listed here, but the facts, beliefs, and general ideas we have listed show the kinds of knowledge that are critical for understanding a story like the preceding one.

None of this knowledge would be found on any literacy list. Furthermore, this example is no different than any typical newspaper article. Hirsch has misunderstood the processes people use to communicate and the kind of knowledge they need to communicate successfully.

How Schools Teach Literacy Lists

To really understand the impact that literacy lists have, it's necessary to take a look at how lists are taught. Inevitably, lists get taught by forcing students to memorize. If you are dead set on having children learn a specific set of things, there is no other way that seems as straightforward than simply having them sit and stare at them, trying to commit them to memory.

Hirsch's Method for Cultural Literacy

To be fair, Hirsch appears not to be explicitly convinced that memorization is a good method for learning. He (Hirsch, 1987) wishes that children be led to learn the facts of Cultural Literacy in an interesting way, telling us, "Indeed, if traditional facts were to be presented unimaginatively or taught ignorantly or regarded as ends in themselves, we would have much to deplore" (p. 125).

However, it is clear that if it comes down to a choice between forcing children to memorize facts or allowing them to pursue their own interests with the risk that some facts will be missed, Hirsch will choose forced memorization. When it comes down to it, Hirsch (1987) just does not find forcing children to memorize lists to be distasteful:

> Our current distaste for memorization is more pious than realistic. At an early age when their memories are most retentive, children have an almost instinctive urge to learn specific tribal traditions. At that age they . . . are eager to master the materials that authenticate their membership in adult society. Observe for example how they memorize the rather complex materials of football, baseball, and basketball, even without benefit of formal avenues by which that information is inculcated. (p. 30)

Pragmatically, Hirsch's opinion on the virtues of memorization is a moot point. Hirsch does not propose an alternative. And in the absence of an alternative, those educators who are forced to use Hirsch's list in the context of overcrowded fixed curriculum will inevitably turn to memorization.

Hirsch and Memorization

The idea that memorization is useful comes from the warehouse model of memory that assumes facts can be inventoried in memory to be pulled out whenever needed. Memory does not work this way, however. Consider these three phenomena:

- Everyone has experienced the difficulty of trying to memorize disconnected facts.
- Everyone has experienced trouble in trying to recall things they had once memorized.
- Everyone has experienced trouble remembering something they actually do know when they need to remember it in a context different than the one in which it was learned.

If you grew up in the United States, you probably spent a lot of time as a child memorizing the names of the presidents. Can you now write down all the Presidents' names? Can you now remember who was President during the War of 1812? Unless you are a history buff, the answers are probably "No." Learning the list of Presidents is a project on which schools are traditionally willing to spend a great deal of effort. But does that effort really pay off? Such knowledge, even in this high-visibility example, tends not to stick very well, nor to make itself available when it would be useful. Sure, people can memorize disconnected facts, but they are notoriously bad at it, and, as the manufacturers of Rolodexes and calendars will tell you, they typically avoid doing so whenever possible.

What the Experts Say About Memorization

Numerous studies (by Ross (1987), Holyoak (1985), Gentner (1989), and others) show that what students learn needs to be grounded in a way that is meaningful to them. Yet, schools still insist on rote memorization of principles and facts taught independently of their potential use. We have learned from these studies that when students learn in meaningful contexts, they can transfer knowledge they have learned in one domain to another. When learning tasks are grounded in things students care about, students can establish mental indices from old situations to new ones, thus allowing natural case-based reasoning to function. However, when students are just given principles and facts, out of the context of their use, they simply do not have the concrete experience they need as raw material to be able to properly apply what they have learned.

Where Is That Fact When You Need It?

Memorization does not work very well. As Gardener (1991) discussed in his book, *The Unschooled Mind*, we frequently ignore the knowledge we memorize in classes, relying instead on the knowledge we picked up in passing. It's not that the knowledge we picked up in passing is necessarily better (in fact, it's often wrong); it's just that such knowledge comes to mind more readily. When faced with problems that deviate only slightly from the standard form of school problems, we are often unable to access our memorized schoolbook knowledge and instead use what we have picked up in passing from the real world.

Imagine what this says about the value of what we learned in school! How many times in a day are you faced with problems neatly framed in the terms your old physics textbook used? The world does not often present itself in terms like "You have a rope attached to a pulley which itself is attached to a 50 lb. weight. . . ."

The reason why schoolbook knowledge fails to come to mind when it's needed is that it is not well indexed in memory. When students learn, they are often not encouraged to try out the new knowledge on problems they face or relate that knowledge to what they already know. So the schoolbook learning forms isolated islands of structures in their memories. They know how to apply these islands to the schoolbook problems they face because that is the context in which they learned it. But the knowledge does not come to mind when they are faced with a problem in a different context.

Memorization has another problem. It's just not fun. Why should we force our children to memorize if it does not work and only ends up making them dislike learning?

Transfer Model.   A great deal of the most educationally significant work psychologists have done in the past 20 years has been all but ignored by the educational establishment. When teachers stand before students and lecture, they are assuming a model of education that has been shown to be far too simplistic. This model has often been called the "transfer model" of learning. The idea behind this model is that a student is a kind of sponge: Give him facts and he will absorb them. A popular version of the transfer model sees the student as a TV viewer. This version is quite in vogue these days, for obvious reasons. The premise behind it is that there is lots of interesting stuff available on television; whether it is appropriate in level or content for a particular child is irrelevant; he ought to watch it anyway when it becomes available.

The transfer model proposes that one learns effectively by being told. No doubt learning occurs in this way sometimes. We can learn by being told. However, we can only learn in this way when we care about, and are ready to hear, whatever it is we are being asked to learn. The trick to learning, in fact, is to be at the point where one is ready to hear something. The transfer model, teachers talking at students, is not particularly effective at getting students to that point. As an alternative, educational psychologists have shown the value of having children participate in "authentic tasks"; tasks they care about, understand the relevance of, and actively engage in. This view is consonant with the work of Piaget, Bruner, Resnick, and others, who discussed intelligence as actively constructed by a learner, building upon previous knowledge in pursuit of real goals. The learning that occurs outside school always involves "authentic tasks," with real goals and real challenges that children are interested in meeting.

The Acquisition Hypothesis

This is the Acquisition Hypothesis:

When considering what someone should know, it is vital to simultaneously consider how they will come to know it. How we learn determines what we learn.

Often when someone acquires some information in one context, they are unable to access it in another. This effect means that if you have learned some fact by memorizing it for a test, you may not be able to access it when it applies to some other problem you face in your life. This effect also underlies the common capability that people have to hold one belief in one context but a conflicting belief in a different context. Knowing a fact is quite different from being able to use that fact. Information needs to be grounded in some reality to be really useful but cannot be so grounded if it hasn't been acquired in terms of that reality. To understand new information well, students must link the information with what else they know. Students must generalize the information, but they will not make generalizations unless they have a need to do so. But memorization does not create such a need. Only when they are trying to do something with a new fact will students build generalizations from it.

The Function of the Acquisition Hypothesis

Why is it that, as Hirsch points out, children can "memorize the rather complex materials of football, baseball, and basketball" without the benefit of "formal avenues" (i.e., teachers and tests)? The answer lies in the link between learning and knowing. Children will be able to retain material when they can see how the material relates to some goal they want to pursue and the material builds upon something they already understand. Every schoolchild has the background to learn about team sports because every schoolchild has played games and has built generalizations that capture some of their abstract nature. They want to learn more because they understand the potential use for that knowledge in a conversation with a friend, in a trade for baseball cards, in a fantasy team. Those children who have elders or friends who are involved in sports, and want to be like those elders or friends, will strive to find situations where they can get sports experiences. In trying to become better athletes or pretend sports commentators, children will see where they fail and they will be ready to learn from the corrections and suggestions their elders and friends give them after such failures. They will already have the proper schemas active that tell them where new sports knowledge should go. This is how natural learning works.

Children who do not particularly care about sports, who do not play them, and who do not talk about them, will not learn the complex facts that they involve. If you believe sports should be a part of Cultural Literacy, you might believe children should be forced to sit down with a list of the rules of football and memorize them. But such a strategy would fail because it would not tap into what children already know and what they want to do. Those children would end up not knowing most of the rules and, even those they could reproduce for a test, they would find themselves constantly violating in practice. Not until they were able to tie those rules into their experiences would they really come to know them.

Knowledge and the Natural Learning Process

For a person to be able to use a fact, he must first be able to remember it. Natural learning ensures that facts are richly linked with the rest of one's knowledge. It is through such rich links, for example, that a doctor can, upon learning a few vague and partial facts about a patient's condition, confidently declare which condition can be inferred from those facts. Such links allow people to confront a situation that presents itself as a confused set of data, link the facts of the situation to abstract schemata, and infer the pattern that underlies the situation. The facts themselves are only half of what the student requires. The half that goes missing when facts are taught isolated from their use is the links to schemata. Facts that are taught in isolation can be recalled only in isolation, good for Trivial Pursuit and little else.

Indexing Facts

The important issue in learning a new fact is having someplace relevant to put it in memory. New facts are absorbed only in terms of old facts that are already present in memory. If we are told about pirates and can understand them only as an instance of muggers in the street, we will have missed something important. To understand them in a more complex way, we must have understood something more complex in the first place. The kind of understanding necessary to comprehend complex issues does not come from memorizing terminology or sets of facts from lists. It comes from discussing, playing, imagining, and, in general, thinking.

Before we can absorb new background knowledge we must understand to what that knowledge relates. It is easy enough to say, as Hirsch has said, that to be culturally literate one must understand "L'etat c'est moi." But to do this one must know about kings and France, and Louis, and why what he said is worth caring about. As it stands now, teachers and parents who listen to Hirsch will settle for a recitation without understanding so that students can pass the inevitable state administered standardized test.

MIKE ROYKO AND CULTURAL AWARENESS

Mike Royko, a columnist for the *Chicago Tribune,* recently wrote about what it means to be culturally aware in a society saturated with too many things to be aware of. Royko tells a story of being at a cocktail party where "everybody in the parlor had taken a firm position of one of the great issues of the day." The issue in this case was who the better talk show host was: Jay Leno or David Letterman. Royko was forced into confessing that he hadn't watched "The Tonight Show" in 15 years and had only seen "The Late Show" with David Letterman once. The other guests were appalled. As

Royko tells it, one serious-looking guest told him, "I would think that as an observer of popular culture and social trends, you would feel it is your professional obligation to watch shows that are so much a part of the American fabric."

Royko's response to this is a heartfelt refusal to bow to some rule that demands one know certain things. He said (*Chicago Tribune*, Jan. 3, 1993)

> The fact is there was a time when everybody would have had to have had an opinion on David Letterman and Jay Leno. But that was before TV viewers could say, as Martin Luther King Jr. once did, "Free at last!" Yes, there was once a time when the choice was ABC, CBS, NBC, and one or two local stations and the visual trash they tossed my way. But now, thanks to the miracle of cable TV, satellites, and the VCR, I have been freed from network tyranny and have my choice of every conceivable form of visual trash.

When today's world is so full of options, why should Royko be held responsible for something he has no desire to know about? Hirsch's idea that to be intelligent we should strive to know everything that makes up the "core" of our culture is an impossible and useless goal. When culture was younger and more tightly defined, it might not have been unreasonable to ask that an educated person be able to recognize all the cultural icons. But the depth and breadth of today's culture makes that a ridiculous requirement.

THE UNLITERACY POLICY

The schools should reject Hirsch's ideas about literacy in favor of an opposing policy that we can dub the "Unliteracy Policy." The Unliteracy Policy states that there is no one fact or set of facts that everyone should know. If we discovered a fact that did seem worth knowing, the interesting issues would be the reason it was worth knowing, how other facts were related to it, and what a person had learned when they compared that fact to similar or contradictory "facts." It doesn't matter which historical facts one has learned; it matters that one has learned to think about history in a reasoned way. It doesn't matter what mathematical formulas one has memorized; it matters that one has learned to solve problems in a logical way. It doesn't matter if one can recite every conjugation in French; it matters that one can communicate in French.

The subject matter we use to motivate students is not as important as the need to motivate them. It makes little difference what children learn; it matters that they learn and that they want to continue to learn. Regardless of what they learn, certain things that we want them to know will come along for the ride anyway. You can hardly learn about some specialty area of interest without also learning how to reason, how to learn more, and how to communicate what you know.

DANGERS OF LITERACY LISTS

We, as parents, educators, and students, need to understand the real danger in assuming that we can build a literacy list the contents of which each student should know. To the extent that we believe there are facts everyone must know, we will create exams to test that people know them. Such exams will inevitably disrupt natural learning, replacing it with techniques that are detrimental to learning.

We, as a country, must take the competition and stress out of education and put the joy back in. To do this, we must stop thinking about national standards for achievement, about grades, and about the role of schools as places to channel students into their rightful role in the workplace. We must think about how to get students involved in thinking, learning, and being engaged in the process.

4

Natural Learning

NATURAL LEARNING

People have powerful natural mechanisms for learning that allow them to master an enormous volume and variety of material during their lifetimes. Some people learn enough baseball statistics to fill a book. Others learn such a variety of conversational tactics that they can literally talk to anybody. Others learn which political strategies great leaders employed and when those strategies worked. And almost everybody learns where the milk is in their neighborhood grocery store, as well as how to navigate the streets of their home town. This kind of natural learning occurs outside of school.

Rather than fighting against these natural learning mechanisms, schooling should make use of them. The very nature of school must be changed so that it reflects rather than opposes natural learning. The way mainstream schools are structured now goes against much of what we have learned about learning. Schools fail to educate because they don't leverage the natural learning process. Natural learning is not compatible with lockstep classrooms nor with rigid curricula, nor is learning measurable by multiple-choice tests.

History of Progressivism

Many of the basic ideas about natural learning talked about in this book have been around for a long time. Various members of the Progressive Movement, in particular, proposed that education should respect natural learning, not fight against it. They may not have used those words, but they had the same ideas about the importance of starting with students' interests and letting students learn to do instead of making them listen.

The Progressive Movement was diverse; its members held varied and sometimes even contradictory beliefs. The thread that held it together was a unifying concern for the problems caused by the growth of industrialization and the expansion of the cities in America. The movement affected the way Americans viewed the nature of society, the role of government, and the goals of the education system.

As education historian Lawrence A. Cremin (1961) pointed out, the education branch of this movement was tied together by a simple message: "Progressivism implied the radical faith that culture could be democratized without being vulgarized."

Progressive Versus Traditional Education

How successful was Progressivism in changing the traditional educational system in America? Progressivism's most dramatic impact has been limited to so-called "alternative schools." The nation contains a range of alternative schools like the University of Chicago Laboratory School, the Montessori schools, and others that are built on the foundation of Progressive ideas. These schools are notable for the quality of students they produce. They are also notable for how much they cost to run.

Although some mainstream elementary schools today embrace aspects of Progressive ideas in their earlier grades, elementary schools in their later years, secondary schools, and universities have been affected more by the form than by the substance of the movement. School features such as gym classes, so-called "industrial arts" classes, school projects in the community, and the broad range of available extracurricular activities come from the work of Progressive reformers. However, these features seem like adornments on the system—students typically do not view them as what school is really about. The core of the educational system remains largely untouched despite 100 years of attempts at Progressive reform. Classes aimed at teaching reading still often have all students reading the same book as if it were the book and not the reading that mattered. Classes aimed at teaching math still often present math as something that will be useful only at some vague point later in life, rather than as something that applies to students' immediate concerns. Classes aimed at teaching history rarely show how the lessons of the past can inform choices students face today.

Progressivism in America

The primary problems that have prevented Progressive reformers from changing the core of the educational system are the schools' dependence on fixed curricula, the stranglehold of standardized testing, and the impossibility of giving individual attention with student–teacher ratios of 30 to 1. For Progressive reforms to succeed on a widespread basis, we need to break the lockstep of the classroom. We must give students individual attention and customized support. Since we cannot afford to have a full-time teacher dedicated to each student, the solution rests with technology that allows students to learn naturally aided by one-on-one instruction.

The goal here is an attempt to build an educational system that can take the natural interests of any given student and use them as a vehicle for teaching just about anything. If a student likes trucks, why not teach him to read about trucks, do the math that is needed to understand fuel economies, and know the economics and politics needed to run a trucking company?

One primary reason Progressive reformers could not carry out their program earlier in the 20th century is that they did not have the means to deliver such individualized instruction. Although the Progressive movement acknowledged the importance of students controlling their own learning, it had no way to create an environment that would allow such self-management to occur. The computer has the power to change all this.

LEARNING BY EXPERIENCE

In a graduate class of mine, in which there were a few undergraduates, we were discussing learning. The students were making a variety of assertions about learning that caused me to wonder whether we were all talking about the same phenomenon. People learn every day, but these students had managed to make learning into an entirely academic affair. They were failing to see themselves as the best examples of learners and learning that they could possibly know.

To get them to see this point, I asked various members of the class what they had learned recently. One told me he had learned that a wok will rust if left overnight with the cooking residue in it. Another told me she had learned that cheap paint doesn't work as well as expensive paint. Another told me she had learned that she could buy cough medicine across the street and didn't have to walk a long way for it as she had thought. Another told me he had learned that I liked to sit in a certain place in the classroom. Another said he had learned how to handle himself better in certain social situations. These learners were all graduate students.

The undergraduates, on the other hand, noted that they had learned various facts such as certain events in history or certain methods of calculation in mathematics.

Why the difference? The graduate students were much older than the undergraduates. Their environment was not as sheltered as the undergraduates. In addition, the undergraduates were engaged in the process of getting

"A's" by learning what they were told. The graduate students were trying to find out about their new environment, living in new houses, cooking for themselves, trying to understand what was expected of them in graduate school. The graduate students were being forced, both in school and in life, to think for themselves.

What method were the undergraduates using for learning? Basically, they were copying what they were told. They learned by studying. The graduate students were experimenting, hoping to find out what was true by trying things out and attempting to make generalizations about what might hold true in the future. And although the undergraduate who learned how to perform symbolic integration will likely soon forget it, the graduate who rusted his wok will never make that mistake again.

THE LEARNING WATERFALL AND NATURAL LEARNING

From a bird's-eye view, the natural learning process consists of three steps. These steps must follow in sequence, like stages in a waterfall. The first lesson we can draw from the preceding learning theory is that schools must be configured to support, not short-circuit, this learning waterfall.

Figure 4.1 stresses the importance of setting the stage for learning. Getting answers is only the last part of the process. Without the earlier parts, people cannot learn from answers that are given to them.

The secret to why people are able to learn so much in their daily lives is really no secret at all. They learn about things that pertain to their goals—they learn about things in which they are interested. Because they are

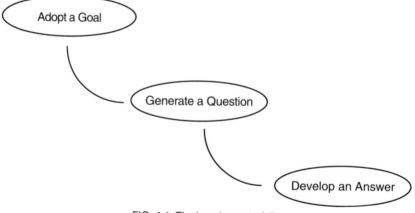

FIG. 4.1. The learning waterfall.

interested, they try things out and sometimes fail. These failures, as well as their interests, cause them to ask questions. Sometimes these questions are directed to outside sources like friends or books. But, often, these questions are internally oriented, as when we ask ourselves, "Why did I do it that way?" or "How could I avoid looking so foolish again?" Once we have developed a question about some topic in which we are interested, then we are ready to learn the answer. After we have developed an answer (or are given one), we then have little trouble remembering it.

Moreover, in natural learning a person has some experiences, wonders about them, and draws some conclusions. The specifics come first, the generalizations come later. The process of wondering serves to create indices in the person's memory. Those indices then tie the cases to each other, and to the generalizations the person forms. As the person has subsequent experiences that do not fit the generalization, they become indexed under it as exceptions. This process results in a "rich" generalization, to which is attached the following: a collection of cases that support the generalization, a collection of cases that are exceptions to it, and the goal that the person was attempting to satisfy through the wondering.

This rich indexing helps the student get reminded of the relevant generalization, and to go beyond it when it fails.

In summary, to take advantage of students' natural learning abilities, we must provide an environment that supports the learning waterfall. This means students must be allowed to pursue goals that interest them. And it means students must be allowed to try things out and fail. It also means students must be given answers only after they have generated questions. To leverage the processes of natural learning, we must offer answers on an as-needed basis. Instead of making the student conform to a schedule of instruction, we must make the schedule of instruction conform to the student.

The education system should take first things first. The system must first be concerned with goals, because before they can proceed to later stages of the waterfall students must first acquire goals that interest them. Goals must underlie education.

THE TEACHING ARCHITECTURES IN THE LEARNING WATERFALL

We have investigated a number of types of teaching that we feel are particularly amenable to computer implementation, developing what we call "teaching architectures." Figure 4.2 shows which part of the natural learning process is targeted by each architecture:

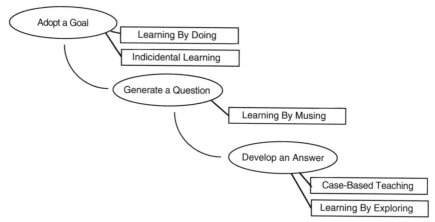

FIG. 4.2. Teaching architectures and the natural learning process.

The Five Teaching Architectures

Next is a brief description of each of the five different teaching architectures we have developed.

Simulation-Based Learning by Doing.   This architecture aims to have students learn every possible skill through learning by doing. Because the doing of the task is what prepares the student for real life, it is important that the student be able to actively engage in such tasks. Simulations of all kinds can be built. But the designer must understand the situation well enough that the simulations will be accurate portrayals. This can mean, in the case of simulations of people-to-people interactions, having to create complex models of human institutions and human planning and emotional behavior. The Simulation-Based Learning-by-Doing Architecture is critical when the subject matter to be learned is experiential at heart. Much of natural learning is the accumulation of experience.

Incidental Learning.   Obviously, not everything is fun to learn. In fact, some things are terribly boring to learn. But people do habitually learn a variety of information that is quite dull, without being completely bored by it. Often, they do this by picking up the information "in passing," without intending to learn the information at all. The Incidental Learning Architecture is based on the creation of tasks whose end results are inherently interesting, and which can be used to impart dull information. We have built programs that impart incidental information while engaging the user in a fun and interesting task.

Learning by Reflection.   Sometimes a student doesn't need to be told something but rather needs to know how to ask about it. It could be that the student has a vague plan he wishes to mull over. Or perhaps the student has a problem and needs to figure out a way to approach it. Or maybe the student has finished a project and wishes to think back on how he could have done it better. In such cases, a teacher's job is to open the student's eyes to new ways of thinking about his situation, to help the student articulate the situation and generate ways of moving forward. The teacher's job is to muse with the student.

Case-Based Teaching.   This architecture depends on these two ideas: Experts are repositories of cases, and good teachers are good storytellers. The task of this architecture is to tell students exactly what they need to know when they need to know it. When students are learning by doing, they experience knowledge failures, times when they realize that they need new information to progress. Such are the times when Case-Based Teaching can provide the knowledge that students need. Because isolated facts are difficult for students to integrate into their memories, useful knowledge is typically best presented in the form of stories.

Learning by Exploring.   The previous architectures deal with the difficult problems of getting students involved in their own learning and letting them learn through performing tasks that they care about. As we've pointed out, when students get involved, they naturally generate questions. And they are ready to learn from those questions. An important method of teaching is to answer a student's questions at the time he generates them and carry on a conversation with him, answering whatever follow-up questions he generates. The Learning-by-Exploring Architecture is intended to provide such answers in a conversational format.

Implementing the Teaching Architectures

Each architecture is an attempt to isolate a type of knowledge or activity that occurs during some part of the natural learning process and to build a machine that helps learners gain that type of knowledge or engage in that type of activity. In order to build such machines, we have had to study the kinds of knowledge that expert teachers have and impart that knowledge to our machines. These architectures use the ideas and methods of artificial intelligence to provide capable components that can be used in the construction of teaching systems.

All five architectures are based on methods that are found, in one form or another, in daily life. It is precisely because these teaching methods are quite natural that they should be exploited in schools. Although the teaching architectures themselves are targeted for implementation on a computer, each is based on an underlying teaching method that is not dependent on computers. The teaching methods capture the general point about teaching on which the architecture is based—they may be furthered through computers, but by no means do they depend on them. Because descriptions of computer programs are not necessary in order to illustrate these underlying principles in action, why frame this discussion in terms of computers at all?

For massive educational change to take place in this country, the computer will have to be the medium of change. We cannot make entire states, entire school systems, entire training organizations, or all teachers and textbook publishers change their ways overnight. It is easy to install a computer program—changing people and entrenched systems is difficult. However, to the extent that entire courses, curricula, libraries, and other learning opportunities can be implemented on software, wholesale change is possible. We may not convince every biology teacher in the country to try our methods, especially when there is a standardized test waiting at the end of the road, but we might convince a school system to implement a computer-based biology course that is radically different from existing courses (assuming that it was endorsed by experts and, more importantly, by students).

COMPUTERS HELPING SCHOOLS ADDRESS NATURAL LEARNING

Schools are hampered in their ability to leverage natural learning because of the amount of individual attention it requires. The shortcuts schools take are partially the result of a lack of knowledge about how learning is accomplished, but more the result of economic necessity. It is expensive to get students involved in goals they care about and then to coach them on an as-needed basis.

Computer technology can make individualized attention a real possibility. Computers have the ability to present students with tasks they are interested in doing. They offer students the possibility of becoming inquisitive, the possibility of exploration, and the possibility of recovery from failure that is free from embarrassment. Computer systems can free schools to follow the course prescribed by the processes of natural learning.

The Niche for Software

When I taught a class in cognitive modeling, I tried to get students to think on their own, ask their own questions, and pursue their own hypotheses. The class worked well, but not as well as it could. Some students in it were inevitably frustrated because they could not get their questions addressed, or because we did not have time to pursue the argument they wanted to build.

To help them develop their thoughts (as well as develop the ability to develop their thoughts), I had the students turn in brief papers each week describing their positions. But these papers pale in effectiveness compared to one-on-one conversations. By the time the students got the papers back a week or more after they had written them, they often had forgotten what they were thinking and why. They were on to other concerns. The paper-writing cycle has just too thin a bandwidth for communication to offer much of the benefits of interaction.

The educational computer systems I describe in this book are intended to help solve the shortcomings I faced in my cognitive modeling class. I am often asked why I think it is important for students to sit down with automated teachers, and why I wouldn't rather have them sit down with real teachers. The answer is that, of course, I would rather have students be able to rely on real teachers. But that is rarely an option. The experts we have captured in our programs have only so much time to spend educating others.

IF YOU ARE NOT INTERESTED IN COMPUTERS

Even if you aren't interested in computers, even if the thought of having a computer be a teacher leaves you apoplectic, I encourage you to look seriously at the examples presented and compare them to current teaching methods. The teaching architectures can illustrate how to better utilize current manual methods of teaching. Each of the teaching architectures is focused on some segment of the cycle of natural learning. Each is appropriate in a limited set of situations. By understanding the strengths and limits of these architectures in relation to natural learning, we can understand how to analyze the strengths and limits of other teaching methods as well.

Using the teaching architectures as a way to understand manual methods of teaching is not the only reason for looking at them. The teaching architectures are often superior to manual methods for teaching the same material. I subscribe to the view that learning should be fun. Computers can allow us to make learning a great deal of fun. You may question this assertion—after all, many people who have used computers have had some frustrating experiences with them. However, frustration with computers is the result of poorly designed, difficult-to-use, and pointless software. Good software has the potential to open worlds that were previously off limits, impossible, dangerous, or simply avoided by school systems. Computers provide a key opportunity that manual methods cannot offer: one-on-one instruction on an as-needed basis, specifically tailored to each student who is in control of his own learning process.

5

Learning By Doing

LEARNING BY DOING

There is really only one way to learn how to do something and that is to do it. If you want to learn to throw a football, drive a car, build a mousetrap, design a building, cook a stir-fry, or be a management consultant, you must have a go at doing it. Throughout history, youths have been apprenticed to masters in order to learn a trade. We understand that learning a skill means eventually trying your hand at the skill. When there is no real harm in simply trying, we allow novices to "give it a shot."

Parents usually teach children in this way. They don't give a series of lectures to their children to prepare them to walk, talk, climb, run, play a game, or learn how to behave. They just let their children do these things. We hand a child a ball to teach him to throw. If he throws poorly, he simply tries again. Parents tolerate sitting in the passenger seat while their teenager tries out the driver's seat for the first time. It's nerve-wracking, but parents put up with it, because they know there's no better way.

When it comes to school, however, instead of allowing students to learn by doing, we create courses of instruction that tell students about the theory of the task without concentrating on the doing of the task. It's not easy to see how to apply apprenticeship to mass education. So in its place, we lecture.

EXAMPLE OF LEARNING BY DOING

Let's hear from one of my undergraduates, David Geller, on how learning by doing compares to the typical college fare of courses:

I believe that professors would be much happier if they did not have to stand in front of a room year after year teaching the same things over and over again. All they do, for the most part, is lecture from the same pile of notes every year. Why can't they simply Xerox their notes, assign the required readings, and expend their remaining undergraduate-designated energy answering specific questions or even better, designing alternative supplementary forms of instruction such as internship programs and research studies?

At Northwestern University, especially, there are so many research projects in progress, I do not understand why students are not encouraged to participate. I was actually quite interested in working in an organic chemistry lab during my sophomore year, knowing that such an involvement would undoubtedly educate me in a much more efficient manner and probably significantly improve my grade as a result. However, I was told that I did not yet have enough experience at the time and that I should come back at a later point in time. In other words, I was being told that I should go play like an idiot in my undergraduate lab and do the same stupid experiment that fifty thousand other students have already done. Then I would be experienced. That really makes a lot of sense!

Instead, I spent my time volunteering at Evanston Hospital. Today, I work in the emergency room as a "nursing assistant." I do hands-on work with every kind of emergency that comes in. I have been a part of the wonder of saving lives as well as the horror of losing them. I have felt the relief, the frustration, the tension, and the happiness, which somehow all mix and mingle in the hospital environment. I have experienced these feelings and have therefore learned.

I learned not only about medicine and emergency treatment, as well as biology and anatomy, but I also learned about life. I learned about people, their fears, their beliefs, and their pain. I learned how to deal with people and how to talk to them, not as individuals on the street, but rather as the disoriented and extremely frightened people they often are during an emergency. I drew knowledge from the doctors and nurses as well, learning how they evaluate people and their problems, and seeing how they handle given situations. Their viewpoints and outlooks on medicine have certainly affected how I think today and will undoubtedly continue to influence me as I continue my education.

Quite honestly, I have learned more from my year of working at the hospital than from my two and a half years of classes at Northwestern. Northwestern has not provided, nor has it facilitated my experiences. The hospital has.

STUDENTS LEARNING BY DOING

Sometimes it is not practical for students to learn every skill they need to know by actually performing it. We can afford to allow somebody to be a nursing assistant in the emergency room, but we cannot afford, in Groucho

Marx's words, to allow that person to be an "amateur brain surgeon." Many tasks involve either too much expense or too much danger to actually let novices perform.

Furthermore, simply placing students in realistic situations is not enough. Such situations let students "try things out," but there are two kinds of trying things out to consider. The first is where one learns by fiddling around and seeing what happens, and the second is one in which a teacher, advisor, or colleague is available who can "look over your shoulder" as you take on a new role. This latter form allows a student to gain from the experiences and observations of others. It allows others to interrupt him and give perspective on what he is doing, sharing with him the experiences of those who have preceded him. In such "mentored role play," the student might never need to ask a question. His actions will precipitate answers. His mentor will wait until the right moment to tell the student what he needs to hear.

One drawback to real-life situations is that they often do not have mentors, in which case they leave out both teaching and history. Trying out a new role without the advantage of a mentor can be a slow, frustrating way to learn. It can lead to bad habits or failure to synchronize actions. Teachers provide challenges, encourage risk taking, correct errors, and provide context. Apprenticeship requires the expert as well as the apprentice.

REALISTIC LEARNING SITUATIONS

In situations where it is too expensive or dangerous to allow students to actually try out the roles they want to learn, we can provide realistic experience through simulations. The single best piece of educational software ever invented was the air flight simulator. The best way to learn to fly would be, of course, to simply do it, so the natural course of action would be to put you in a DC-10 and to send you up. This course of action is rather impractical, however. Learning from failure does not occur when the failure is fatal, which it might well be in this situation. So the best course to train pilots is to build flight simulators.

Modern flight simulators are phenomenally real. Inside, they look like cockpits, down to the last detail. They bounce and rattle and jolt, and what you see out the window are pictures that accurately portray whatever airport you select from whatever perspective your airplane would be putting you in at the moment. It looks like the real thing. It feels like the real thing. You can take off and land at will, going in and out of your favorite airports. You can try things out and see what happens. You can crash and try to figure out what you did wrong. After enough time, you can teach yourself how to fly. Of course, if you want to learn faster, it helps to have someone sitting next to you whom you can ask for help. It helps even more if that person is not in a panic about his own imminent demise because of your inadequacies as a pilot.

I speak from experience here. As a student, I have flown a DC-10 (courtesy of United Airlines' training facility in Denver) and crashed it. My instructor seemed rather pleased at my performance. I have also had the experience of being a piloting instructor myself when I taught my two children to drive a car. Since this was no simulation, I did not take failure quite so complacently as my flying instructor did. In fact, I remember sitting with clenched fists about to pop a blood vessel each time I went out with either child. Simulation is a far better alternative.

Teaching Architectures and Simulators

The reason why simulations are so effective is that they give students a way to learn by doing. By using computer-based simulations, we can vastly broaden the range of things students can learn by doing. The teaching architecture that results is Simulation-Based Learning By Doing. The opportunity this architecture promises is to convert the learning of every possible skill into learning by doing. When it's not feasible to create real-life situations in which learners can engage in the tasks they want to learn, and be coached while they work, simulations must be created that effectively mimic those situations so well that they prepare the student for them without actually having to be in them.

The Advantage of Simulators

Even when it's practical to place students in real-life situations so that they can learn by doing, it's not always preferable. Simulations offer two key advantages over real life. The first is that real life tends to keep marching on by. Simulations allow students to play with time in ways the real world does not permit. Often, the real world moves so quickly that students do not have time to think things over as much as they would like. However, in a simulation, if a student wishes to sit and ponder his course of action, he can freeze the simulation and perhaps even ask an expert some questions. If a student is unclear as to why things turned out the way they did, we can allow him to loop back in time and review the course of events. If events are moving too quickly, the student can slow them down. Students can even decide to back up time so that they can try a different approach.

Simulations also provide teachers with better access to students. Simulations can be instrumented so that teachers can monitor students, waiting until students get into a jam that indicates that they are ready to hear something the teacher wants to convey. In computer-based simulations, the teachers themselves can be automated, thereby making one teacher's knowl-

edge available as needed to many individual students. In the full implementation of this idea, the entire corporate memory of an organization, or all the
experts in a various field, can come to the fore, ready to tell their stories, in
response to a situation that has occurred in practice within a simulation.

Different Simulators for Different Skills

Tools such as the flight simulator pave the way for a natural, effective way to
learn physical skills. The physical world is indeed complex, but we understand it well enough to build complex physical simulations. The world we
live in is social as well as physical, so to teach social skills in a similarly
effective way, we need to build social simulators. Unfortunately, the social
world in which we live is not all that well understood. This is unfortunate
because the main province of education is learning how to function in the
social world of humans. This is what history is about, this is what literature is
about, this is what psychology, economics, foreign languages, and nearly
every subject except science is all about. In fact, even some of science is
about this, too.

Learning Software

Because students learn better when they have the benefit of individualized
coaching, any software for learning should contain one or more embedded
teachers. The air flight simulator, for example, should have videos of famous
pilots. At key moments in the simulation, these pilots should pop up to tell
stories targeted to the student's situation, suspending the simulation and
beginning a dialogue with the student until he understands the point the
"pilot-in-a-box" wants to make. Now, of course, this could be done with
human instructors as well, but such instructors are not always available, nor
are they all knowing. Embedding teaching in a simulation allows for the
potential of publishing the expertise of multiple teachers, making an array of
experts available as needed.

   History is also an important component of teaching software. If a student
pilot happens to do something that was the very thing that caused a historically famous crash, wouldn't it make sense to stop the simulation and talk in
detail about that particular crash? History can be a real guide in learning,
especially if it is presented when it is relevant to a learner's current goals,
rather than as a dry series of historical vignettes.

Simulators as Complete Teaching Systems

A simulator alone is not a complete teaching system; it needs to be aug-
mented with an instructor (or, better yet, many instructors). Just as a flight
instructor might interrupt a simulated flight to remind the student of some

important principle or to share a real-life experience, a good learning-by-doing environment contains teaching modules that monitor the simulation and interrupt with stories, commentary, and other guidance in the course of the student's activity.

Teaching someone to perform a complex skill is quite a feat. To become truly expert in a field, a student must learn both the abstract principles at work and how those principles apply in practice. Schools often teach abstract principles but neglect their application. Businesses, conversely, often leave out abstract principles altogether and teach their students by rote. As anyone who has had a frustrating conversation with a car rental agent or fast food cashier trained in this way knows, rote training produces students who cannot adapt when faced with novel situations.

ILS Simulations

We have built a number of social simulations at ILS that provide learning by doing environments. Dustin is an example of a simple simulator built to help students learn a foreign language through learning by doing. Dustin (named after Dustin Hoffman because its goal is to allow you to act your part as a foreign language speaker by teaching you to know your lines) was developed for use by foreign employees of Andersen Consulting. As in any good acting situation, the scene must be set, and the scene for Dustin is a training center in St. Charles, Illinois. The business instruction classes held at St. Charles are conducted solely in English.

Dustin

Dustin is designed as follows:

1. Present an interesting situation for the student to try out.
2. Allow him to fail.
3. Show him an example of a successful interaction.
4. Allow him to use the knowledge in the example when he tries again.

Along the way, Dustin allows the student to choose the level at which he wants to try things out and gives him a variety of help tools.

This program is intended to help the student remember what to say in different situations and to understand what is said to him. It lets the student practice the English he will need to perform day-to-day tasks, as well as business skills, in the same environment he will be in when he actually visits St. Charles. The situation in Dustin looks a lot like real life.

The simulation sets a stage so that the student can verbally participate (in English) in a variety of different scenes. The technology provides a tutor and various tools (e.g., dictionary, transcript) to help him through the process.

An Example Scenario With Dustin.   Dustin offers its user a series of tasks, each of which requires the user to employ language to accomplish some concrete goal. Dustin begins at O'Hare International Airport, where the student must go through customs. From there, his first job is to find transportation to St. Charles and then check in at the hotel. At each step along the way, the student is interacting with simulated people who appear in video clips and respond to what he says.

The receptionist at the front desk at St. Charles speaks only English. She greets him, as she will in real life, except that here the student is interacting with a video (Fig. 5.1). He then types his responses in English and tries to check in. If the student succeeds, the system sends him off to do other things, such as meeting his roommate. If he fails, then Dustin takes remedial action by either showing him examples or breaking down the task at hand into smaller parts.

The student can be in total control of the learning process. He can ask what to say; he can ask what to do; he can ask to hear again what was just said to him; he can ask for a translation; and, most importantly, he can control the difficulty of the lesson depending on his needs. In Fig. 5.2, the user is getting advice on what to do next while checking into his hotel.

FIG. 5.1. Checking in at the hotel in Dustin.

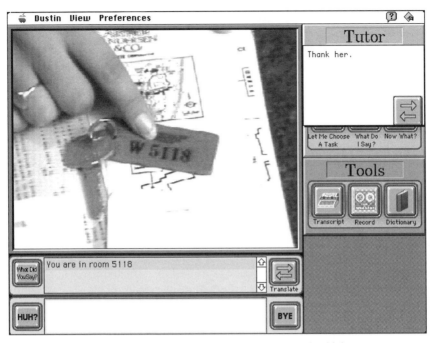

FIG. 5.2. Dustin can offer guidance on what the user should do next.

In this case, the word "lesson" has different connotations than the normal use. Dustin allows the student to play a role and to learn that role. The student can take as long as he likes. The lesson does not go on without him. If he needs to hear what was just said 50 times, the computer will oblige. It does not get annoyed. It is not on a timetable.

Education Elements in Dustin.   Dustin sets up situations that the student will encounter in real life and allows the student to demonstrate his competence. If the student succeeds at one task, he can skip ahead to the next lesson. If he has trouble, he can return to the beginning of the instruction. Because the student is in a simulated situation identical to the one in which he will have to function, he does not have to learn things that will be of no use to him. There is no need to learn the theory of the subjunctive.

Language is a tool people use to achieve goals; therefore, Dustin starts each scene by presenting a story in which someone uses language to accomplish some clear task like ordering lunch. Then the student is asked to play the lead role in the story he has just observed. The premise is that a student will, by practicing, index new linguistic knowledge in terms of the situations in which that knowledge is useful. The goal of the program is to put the student in the habit of saying the right thing in the right way at the right time.

Failure is also a key element in Dustin. Students realize what they need to learn in a very direct way: They fail at a task and become interested in finding out what they need to know to succeed. In some sense, then, they instruct themselves by seeking the information they need to complete the task.

Dustin allows students to learn language in realistic situations. But it will probably not enhance a student's performance on achievement tests. A Dustin student cannot be graded in the conventional sense, but what we can see is if a student successfully completed various tasks. We could determine how quickly a student completed a task, but why would we really need to know that? We don't ask someone who has successfully learned a foreign language how long it took them to do so. We are simply interested in how capable they are in that language. Ideally, schools must learn to satisfy themselves with scores like "got to level 5 in Dustin." Those measures work in Nintendo games. We acknowledge a master craftsman by what he has built, a scholar by what he has written, a businessman by the success of his business. Can't we do this in school, too? We can if the instruction allows achievement in the first place.

Dustin Methods and Other Simulators.   The simulator inside Dustin is fairly simple. One way to view Dustin is as a series of small, carefully scripted scenes in a play in which the student is obliged to figure out and then memorize his lines. The simulator tracks how well the student is following the script and triggers prespecified behaviors when the student goes off track.

The method we used to build Dustin works well with situations in which there is a prescribed path of behavior. The small interchanges of language we use to get through our daily activities tend to follow such prescribed paths. You expect the people at the coffee shop to know what to do when you say you'll take your coffee "white" just as they expect you to know what to do when they say "one eighty-five." Language is far from the only domain that contains situations that are similarly scripted. Doing your laundry, balancing your checkbook, and baking a lasagna are three scenes that could readily be scripted into a version of Dustin targeted at the new college graduate.

ChimpWorld

Suppose that we upped the ante on the Dustin program. Instead of helping students learn scripted behaviors, suppose we put them in a social environment that is far more free flowing, enabling them to act freely within it. Suppose we built a program that simulated all the players in a society by considering their plans, goals, individual relationships, and their concerns about available resources. This sounds like a formidable task, but one that has a big payoff. If we could do it, those who use this simulation would have the ability to learn something about how to function in such a society by trying out various behaviors and observing the results.

We have given this more aggressive approach a try. We started by building a system called ChimpWorld, which simulated a society of chimpanzees. In ChimpWorld one could try out being a chimpanzee. A young chimpanzee had better learn the rules of his organized society or he will not get much to eat and may well get beaten up. Although ChimpWorld is great fun to explore, we are not trying to teach people to be chimpanzees (although inferring the rules by which a society operates is important). However, the societal simulations aspects of ChimpWorld translated directly into a world where people needed to learn social skills.

GuSS

To make societal simulation a useful teaching tool, we built the GuSS system (Guided Social Simulation). GuSS is a tool that allows a programmer to use the ideas of societal simulation developed in ChimpWorld in any human business context in which he wishes to work. We have built three prototype GuSS applications to date: High Spotter teaches novice business consultants how to interact with clients on a job; Yello teaches phone company account executives how to sell advertising in the Yellow pages; and George teaches experienced consultants how to sell consulting services.

GuSS applications accomplish for a social world what the flight simulator accomplishes for the physical world of the cockpit. The key feature of a flight simulator is that it allows the aspiring pilot to practice a skill in an environment that mimics the real world in every way possible, except that in the simulated world, it is safe to fail. GuSS applications similarly offer social environments in which the students interact with simulated characters through conversations. Students move around in the simulated world; from the home office, for example, to the client's place of business, or other locations. Pictures of these scenes, and the characters found in them, provide visual realism. Students use a system of hierarchical menus to construct desired utterances or to take other actions in the simulated world. Characters in the simulation respond to the student through conversation and emotional reactions.

GuSS as Unique Training System.   Modern training regimens often divorce instruction from practice, concentrating on either one or the other. GuSS brings them together. GuSS applications are based on flexible social simulations. On top of this base, GuSS adds four different types of teachers.

Each teacher monitors the student's on-going activity in the simulation and offers a particular type of intervention as it is warranted:

Storyteller.   Stories convey the cultural knowledge of a world of practice as it is actually seen and performed by experienced practitioners. The Storyteller uses the Case-Based Teaching Architecture to deliver real-world stories when it sees they are relevant to the student's activity, situating the knowledge the stories contain in the context of the activity. In George, the Storyteller contains over 100 stories, gathered from experienced sellers and representing a wide range of selling situations and strategies.

Analyzer.   Like the Storyteller, the Analyzer is a case-based teaching module. But whereas the Storyteller tells students about the informal knowledge of practitioners in a field, the Analyzer talks about "textbook" knowledge relating to practice. Such knowledge includes, for example, rules and theories about communication styles, organizational behavior, and personalities. Even though the Analyzer contains much the same information as one might find in a textbook, it is significantly more powerful because the Analyzer can present its material "just in time," at the moment the student is likely to be interested.

Coach.   The Coach indicates what kinds of goals the student should have and tracks those goals to see when they have been satisfied. For example, when a student using the George system enters a new organization, his goal should be to find out who the buyer is. A new student is explicitly told that this is a goal worth pursuing. As the student becomes more adept at the task, the Coach gives less assistance, requiring the student to do more. This method of teaching, called scaffolding and fading, is an important technique in how apprenticeships operate in the real world (Collins, Brown, & Newman, 1983).

The Coach is implemented using what one might call a Learn-by-Being-Told Architecture. This architecture works because the student is ready to hear what the Coach wants to tell. It is an efficient way to bring the student to the point of knowing which goals to have and when to have them. Because the George application is meant for students who have limited time to use the system, simply telling them the answer is a reasonable course.

Evaluator.   The simulation itself provides feedback to the student about progress. But sometimes the feedback offered by the simulator is not enough to help students understand the effects of their actions. For instance, in the High Spotter application, a student who fails to make a sale or angers a client will know that all is not well. However, it may be difficult for that novice student to diagnose exactly what went wrong. Typically, the student will have made some error early in the interaction, and without help it can be difficult for him to retrace his steps to identify the error. The Evaluator provides feedback to help students understand the results caused by their actions.

Students and GuSS.   There are eight basic actions a student can take in GuSS. Most of these center on holding a conversation with a simulated agent. The student can:

- ask questions to gather information,
- request another character to do something, such as set up an appointment,
- respond to something another character has said, agreeing or disagreeing,
- engage in small talk,
- perform a courtesy, such as saying "hello" or "I'm sorry,"
- tell another character about something, for example, giving a recommendation,
- go to a place, or
- read documents.

George.   To illustrate the GuSS system, let's look at a GuSS application. George is a GuSS application intended for use by consultants who are experienced in providing consulting services, but with little experience in selling such services. In George, students are given the job of making a sale to a potential client. The student must get to know the client organization, come to some understanding of its business problems, identify those people within it who can buy consulting services, construct a proposal geared to these buyers' needs and concerns, and present that proposal in a convincing way. Depending on the personalities and organizational structures involved, these tasks may be easy or difficult.

Scenes from George.   One George scenario involves the Bronson and Bronson Department Stores. In this scenario, the student is given a potential client who is willing and able to buy consulting services, but who does not really know what services he needs. In addition to the student, the cast of characters defined for this scenario includes the following:

Dan Babbitt: The student's boss. A partner at a consulting firm.

Bill Bell: The CEO of the prospective client, Bronson and Bronson.

Helga Larsen: Bill Bell's personal assistant.

Wendy Erickson: The newly-hired Vice-President of Marketing for B&B.

Theodore Dahm: B&B's Vice-President of Operations.

Marianne Wilson: Ted Dahm's personal assistant.

The underlying problem at Bronson and Bronson (which the student does not know at the outset and may never completely uncover) is this:

Ted Dahm, Vice-President of Operations, is overprotective of his turf within the company. He was expecting to get the CEO job when founder Elijah Bronson died several years back, but the board hired Mr. Bell, an outsider, instead. Overtly, he wants to show that he can run a large operation as well as anybody. Covertly, he thinks that if he can frustrate Bill enough the CEO may leave or get fired. He has been resisting some of the changes Bill has proposed, particularly a centralization of marketing within the company. Currently, each store does its own marketing, which puts all the marketing within Ted's control.

A year before the scenario begins, Bill created a marketing division and hired an experienced executive, Wendy Erikson, away from one of his competitors to run that division. Lines of communication were supposedly set up between Marketing and Operations to make this new arrangement work, but so far it has not succeeded well. Meanwhile, the company has been growing and acquiring new stores. Six months before the scenario begins, Bronson and Bronson acquired another chain of five department stores in a nearby state. This acquisition has brought the marketing problem to a head. The new stores are losing market share because their customers are not getting a consistent picture of the chain as a whole and because chain-wide promotions are not always honored by local stores.

Bill is a frequent golf partner of Dan Babbitt, a partner at a major consulting firm. Dan has tried to convince Bill of the value his firm could provide, but Bill has had a disappointing experience with a different consulting firm and is reluctant. Finally, with pressure from the board of directors, Bill asks Dan to come in for some preliminary discussions. Dan, however, is involved in negotiations on a larger job and sends in one of his experienced managers (the student) to do the initial contact.

This scenario sets the stage. Let's follow a path that a typical consultant, whom we will call Joan Smith, might carve out as she works through the case. A student has the freedom to follow many different paths through a GuSS scenario. Thus, it is not possible to know exactly what situations any given student will encounter in any given scenario. There is more than one way to be successful and there are many possible ways to fail.

Each scenario starts off with a triggering event that begins the sales process. In this case, it is a memo from Dan Babbitt, the student's managing partner. In it, Dan briefly describes the sales lead at Bronson and Bronson and asks the student to handle it.

A seasoned seller would probably try to call Dan at this point to find out what the circumstances of the contact were and what other information he has. If the student were to talk to Dan, she would find out what he knows about the marketing problem and the personality of Bill Bell, important pieces of information for this initial contact. We will assume that Joan is an eager beginner and that she jumps the gun and immediately calls for an appointment with Mr. Bell. When Bill Bell's personal assistant (PA) answers, Joan asks for and receives an appointment:

PA: Hello, Bronson and Bronson.

Student: I'm Joan Smith from [a consulting firm].

PA: Yes, Ms. Smith. What can I do for you?

Student: I'd like an appointment to speak with Mr. Bell about some possible consulting work.

PA: OK. He's free this morning at 9:30.

At this point, Joan should ask for a later appointment, so that she has a chance to speak with her boss and otherwise prepare herself for the sales call. Instead, she agrees to the appointment:

Student: That sounds fine with me.

PA: OK. He'll see you then. Good bye.

Now, the student must rush over to Bronson and Bronson's headquarters. Upon entering, she finds Bill Bell's personal assistant in the reception area:

PA: Hello, you must be Joan Smith. Mr. Bell is expecting you. Please go right in.

The student goes into Bill's inner office and Bill greets her:

Bill: Hello.

Student: Hello, Mr. Bell.

Bill: You must be Joan Smith. Dan said he'd send someone over. I'm interested in hearing your ideas about our problems.

(The student doesn't have any ideas about Bronson and Bronson's problems; she doesn't even know what those problems are at this point. So she tries to turn the question around and get Bill to tell her something.)

Student: What can we do for you?

Bill: Frankly, I'm not all that convinced you consultants are going to be much help at all, but I told Dan I'd at least talk to you.

This response indicates Bill's hostility and gives Joan some hint of the existing relationship with Dan. At this point, Joan probably suspects she has not done her homework. She is ready to learn. The Storyteller module, which has been monitoring the simulation, is also ready to teach because this path will cause it to get reminded of a story of a similar situation. An indicator on the interface to the system lights up, telling the student that the Storyteller has something pertinent to say. In keeping with the idea of letting the student control her own learning, Joan can ignore the Storyteller (or any of the other teaching modules as well) and keep working through the simulation. In this case, however, she decides to take a look at the story.

The story (Fig. 5.3) describes a situation in which a consultant encounters a client who had been fired from his last job as a result of a recommendation made by a previous consultant. The new consultant uncovers this information by noticing that the client is hostile to consultants, and by asking questions to determine the source of the client's hostility. Using this strategy, the new consultant is eventually able to win over the formerly soured client. Because the student has read this story, she continues her conversation with Bill as follows:

Student: Is this your first experience bringing in outside consultants?

(It turns out that Bill has had experience with consultants and tells the student about it.)

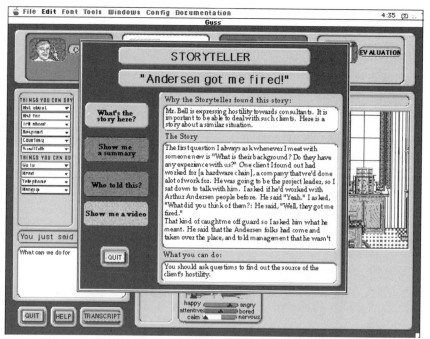

FIG. 5.3. The Storyteller in the George program offers advice in the form of memorable stories.

Bill: Well, I was at Competitive Footwear a few years back when some consulting firm put in a distribution system. It sure seemed good on paper but none of my people could make heads or tails of it.

(The student recognizes Bill's complaint as a common complaint and responds.)

Student: Any new system requires a lot of adjustment and that means training.

Bill: I hire consultants to make my life easier, not to load my employees down with extra work.

Bill becomes irritated that the student seems to be taking the side of the previous consulting firm that he disliked. The student's response is seen by the program as attempting to change Bill's mind about the value of training and indirectly his evaluation of the previous consultant's work. The Storyteller recognizes this situation as similar to another of its stories and provides the student with the opportunity to view the story "Clients have fixed impressions," a story about a client who had made up his mind and couldn't be convinced to change it (Fig. 5.4). The student takes the advice of this story, attempting to offer a more congenial statement to Bill:

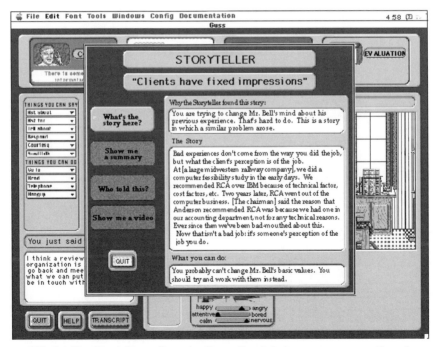

FIG. 5.4. The Storyteller continues to offer pertinent stories as you progress through George.

Student: At our firm, we ensure that every client gets substantial business
benefit from every project.

Bill takes the bait and calms down. By turning the conversation from the
costs of implementing business solutions to the benefits, the student has
deflected Bill's objection to the extra effort involved in installing new
systems. The Evaluator recognizes this as a successful answering of this
objection and tells the student that she has shown some competence in this
skill.

The student can carry on a conversation with Bill for some time. By
asking some good questions, she can find out about Mr. Bell's concerns with
respect to marketing and his disappointment with Ms. Erickson. When these
revelations are made, the Analyzer responds with information about the
problems encountered when establishing new positions, notably, problems
with the boundaries of work groups. Figure 5.5 shows the initial Analyzer
screen. Because the student hasn't prepared adequately for this interview,
however, there is a limit to what she can accomplish during it.

After talking with Mr. Bell, the student returns to her office and goes in to
talk to Dan:

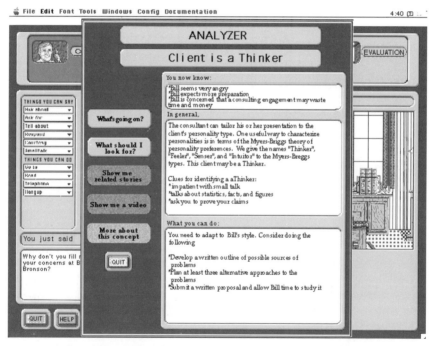

FIG. 5.5. The Analyzer offers more abstract "textbook" advice just when it is relevant
to your situation.

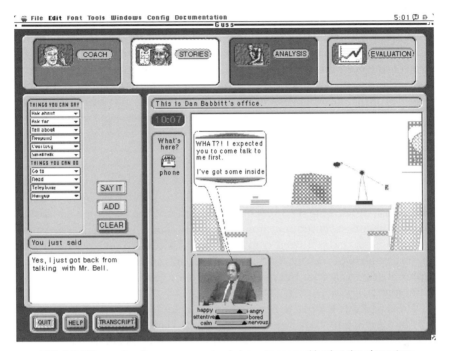

FIG. 5.6. When using George, you not only have to cope with what the characters say, you also have to deal with their emotional states.

Student: Hello.

Dan: Hi, Joan. Did you get my message?

Student: Yes. I got it.

Dan: Good. I wanted to talk to you a little about Bill and his organization.

Student: I just got back from talking to him.

Dan: What !?!

As Fig. 5.6 shows, Dan is very angry to find that the student has gone unprepared to talk to Bill. So now Joan needs to deal with calming her manager as well as making the sale. To make the sale, she needs to meet with the other important characters in the company at least once. In the process, she must develop some rapport with them and find out something about the sources of the company's problems. Joan would probably meet with Dan several more times for advice and, with his help, develop a proposal and a presentation for a final meeting with the CEO to try to close the sale.

There are many different ways for a student to approach the Bronson and

Bronson scenario, but whatever course the student takes, she will have to gather information about the company's business situation and the individuals within it and use the knowledge gained to plan a strategy for making the sale. Throughout this process, she would receive relevant stories and analyses, tailored to the situations she encounters. The real key to GuSS' presentation of principles and lessons is that the teaching modules instruct the student in small doses with each dose coming at just the right time.

Conclusions of the Learning-by-Doing Teaching Architecture

The notion of learning by doing has been with us for a long time, at least as long as the time-honored tradition of apprenticeship. Nevertheless, learning by doing is an underutilized concept in today's educational system. There are an amalgam of reasons for this, ranging from outdated status distinctions (apprenticeships are for the working class, books are for the upper class) to economics.

When a business looks to hire someone, one of the first questions asked is whether applicants have relevant experience. This reflects the company's need for people who have already learned by doing. Schools, however, do not help students get experience. Instead of having students do the tasks we want them to learn about, schools often tell students about such tasks. They then break down those tasks into pieces that they teach in isolation. When teaching a foreign language, for example, they do not typically start by throwing students into a situation in which they must understand and use that language. Instead, they teach them pronunciation for one unit, how to conjugate verbs for another unit, and how to form grammatical sentences in yet another unit. Students then become enmeshed in the mechanics of the language without really getting a sense of how to use those mechanics to communicate. When it comes time to actually use the language, they have difficulty putting the pieces together.

The major obstacle to implementing Learning by Doing is one of economics. Learning by Doing works best when a student has a bevy of coaches looking over his shoulder, ready to offer suggestions when asked. It is clearly not feasible to assign 5 or 10 (or, really, even one) experts to look over each student's shoulder in the mass education system. Computer-based Learning-by-Doing systems have the ability to relieve this economic bottleneck. To a useful degree, they are able to "put the expert in the box." The GuSS system illustrates how a range of coaches may be packaged with a complex social simulation to offer a rich educational environment.

COMPLAINTS ABOUT SIMULATIONS

One complaint against simulation-based approaches is that they can never be as rich as the real world. Simulations are necessarily abstractions of reality; they cannot capture all its intricacies. This is a valid criticism against simulations. When a student moves from doing a task in a simulator to doing that task in the real world, he is going to have to map his experience from the simulation to the real world. The better the simulation, the easier this mapping task. In a really good simulation, the mapping task is so simple that the simulation feels transparent. It feels like the experience in the simulation applies directly to experience in the real world.

From experience, I can tell you that simulators can be quite realistic. When I piloted the United Airlines' flight simulator, I really had the sensation that I was flying. It may be difficult, but we can build realistic simulators. Over time, many simulations have been built on computers of one kind or another. Some of these have been very good simulations of various physical objects and their use and effects. There are also simulations of various types of social behavior that tend to be based on statistical models of the effects of decisions. Often, one finds simulations of voting behavior, or games, or other basically statistical events. On occasion these simulations are interesting to work with, but for the most part they are not especially useful in education.

The reason is that these simulators have usually been designed to be an object of study. The user of such simulations remains "outside" the simulation, setting up its controls and observing its results. In learning by doing, however, simulators are not the object of study but the means of study. Users of learning-by-doing simulations live inside the simulated world. And this simulated world must react to the user in ways which traditional simulations do not. In particular, lessons need to be designed that ensure that a student falls into well-known traps and thus needs to reason his way out of them. If a simulation does not have this aspect to it, it may well be fun to play with, but it will not have a profound effect on the student.

SIMULATIONS AND THE LEARNING WATERFALL

Learning-by-doing simulations attack the first two stages of the natural learning waterfall. They allow students to adopt goals the students care about. And they raise questions in students' minds. As students work through a simulation and experience failures, they see where they need to improve. Learning-by-doing simulations help students gain knowledge in the same context that they will use that knowledge. Many teaching methods provide knowledge like the hints provided by the experts in a learning by doing simulation. But learning-by-doing simulations not only provide the opportunity to want knowledge, they allow for the possibility, if they have been built properly, of providing the knowledge on demand as it is needed.

Another reason learning-by-doing simulations are effective is that students enjoy using them. These simulations allow for a return to the strengths of the apprenticeship method. They provide a guiding context within which students can integrate what they learn. Students learn details in the context of a larger task—they are never faced with decontextualized facts that seem to have only a puzzling relationship, if any, to the goals students have. In the end, students feel they have accomplished something, they have landed the plane, invited Marie to lunch in French, or sold an advertisement to a roofer. The sense of accomplishing something is more of a reward than any grade.

6

Incidental Learning

INCIDENTAL LEARNING

In each area a student pursues, there will be facts that are quite important to know. But teaching students a fixed set of facts within that chosen area is harmful. It creates the illusion of knowledge without providing a context for that knowledge. Teaching these facts directly makes learning dull, difficult, and irrelevant.

Fortunately, there is an alternative to such an approach. The trick is not to teach the facts at all, but rather to have the facts be along the way to getting to something the student naturally wanted to know in the first place. Using the Acquisition Hypothesis, we assume that how one learns a fact is as important as what fact one learns. Thus we should have students learn facts while engaged in a process similar to the one in which they will use the facts. We should use students' natural interest so they come across such facts incidentally, in the course of pursuing their interests.

HOW YOU KNOW THINGS WITHOUT TRYING

Many of the facts we know we pick up in passing without really trying. We learn new vocabulary, for example, by attempting to imitate someone who uses words we do not know. Although schools do attempt to get their students to memorize vocabulary words, and students can learn to memorize them for the test, there is scant evidence that it is easy to retain or even use words learned that way. Similarly, we can force children to memorize state capitals (in alphabetical order, no less!), but did you ever doubt that the way you learn geography is by traveling? When you learn geography by traveling, you remember it better. No one taught me about the geography of New Jersey as a kid; I just went there all the time.

People learn astounding amounts just by making note of the world as it goes by. When we watch a movie, we pick up information about accents, topology, occupations, and other aspects of foreign lands. Everyone knows about singing gondoliers in Venice; chances are they learned it from movies or postcards, not necessarily from travel, and probably not from school. We pick up such things without effort or explicit instruction.

Reading teaches us things, but we also learn a great deal through experience. We learn physics by playing baseball or driving a car, without knowing that those activities have taught us something about physics. We may not be able to explain why $F = MA$, but we probably know that a batted ball can knock a person down, or that cars can skid on ice. We tend to assume that learning is bound up in the ability to articulate the theory behind these phenomena, but an important aspect of learning is simply being able to predict what will happen next, on the basis of experience.

USING INCIDENTAL LEARNING

The phenomenon of incidental learning can be exploited as an approach to teaching that works better than the way schools traditionally have students learn facts about the world, namely, memorization. Memorization has problems. It's not fun and it doesn't lead to well-indexed knowledge. Incidental learning offers a way to have students learn facts that overcomes memorization's shortcomings.

Not everything is fun to learn in and of itself. Some information is dull to learn. The incidental learning architecture offers a fun way for students to learn those boring things so that they will then come to mind when they will be useful.

FAILURE OF EXTRINSIC MOTIVATION

One alternative to forcing children to memorize facts is to bribe them to do it with prizes, candy, grades, and so on. Educational psychologists call this "extrinsic motivation." Extrinsic motivation has been used in some schools for years, although there is evidence to show that it undermines learning. Extrinsic motivation addresses the first stage of the natural learning waterfall: It gives students goals. Students want to get the prize, so they are willing to play by the rules of the game the teacher sets up. But, unfortunately, it fails on the second stage. Students learn to see the knowledge the teacher wishes to convey as a way to win the prize rather than something interesting to know on its own. They do not see it as something useful in its own right. So they do not generate questions about it. And once the prize has been achieved, students no longer have any motivation to retain what they have learned.

Students who are naturally curious when faced with an extrinsic reward do generate questions, but those questions have little to do with the content the teacher wishes to convey. Instead, the questions are of the nature of "How can I bend the rules to win the game?" or "What's the least amount of effort I can put in and still satisfy the teacher?"

A better way to motivate students to learn dull material is to give them the opportunity to achieve some goal that satisfies two conditions: One, that students have had a real interest in the goal, and, two, that the uninteresting information is "intrinsically" related to the goal; to achieve the goal, one sometimes must use the uninteresting information. Having the goal and the facts occupy the same turf helps a great deal. Not only does it make the facts seem less trivial; it allows students to properly index those facts. They learn them in a context in which they can later use them.

Premise of Incidental Learning

The important premise behind incidental learning is that when a student is doing something that is fun, he can be learning a great deal without having to notice it. Learning does not necessarily have to be jammed down a student's throat. Rather, students should be allowed to adopt goals and be given materials that will cause them to pick up the desired information "in passing." It is up to course designers to construct situations in which factual knowledge can be naturally acquired. This is the basis of the Incidental Learning Architecture.

The first trick in employing the Incidental Learning Architecture is to find things that are inherently fun to do on a computer. This could be any good video game for example. The second trick is harder. What the student naturally wants to learn in the video game ought to be worth learning. The problem is to change the skills to be learned from hand–eye coordination tasks to content-based tasks, where one needs to know real information to accomplish one's goal on the computer. This will work well if there is a natural correlation between the content-based tasks and what is inherently fun.

Because it emphasizes the importance of getting students engaged in interesting tasks, the Incidental Learning Architecture can be seen as a version of the Simulation-Based Learning-by-Doing Architecture. The emphasis of the task in the Incidental Learning Architecture is different, however. Typically, in learning-by-doing exercises, we want the student to learn the skills involved in the task. But in the Incidental Learning Architecture, the emphasis is on the facts involved. The student's task is constructed so as to bring him into contact with the facts in a natural way.

Interesting Subjects

Let's suppose that we want students to know the state capitals. Let's further suppose that a student has a real interest in baseball. Wouldn't it be possible for a student to achieve some baseball goal and learn some geography at the same time? If we wanted a student to know where Boston is, and he was a fan of the Yankees, who happened to be playing Boston, and we gave that student tickets to the game, plus a car and a map, don't you think that he would learn sufficient geography to get himself to Boston?

Because this approach is too expensive to achieve on a mass scale, we developed the Road Trip program, which does the next best thing. It teaches U.S. geography to grade-school students by allowing them to take simulated car trips around the United States. When the student arrives at a destination, he can watch exciting video clips that are particular to where he is and match his interests.

Although Road Trip has turned out to have strong appeal to a surprisingly broad range of students, our original intention was to target the least motivated students. Students who do not have an extraordinary love of learning for its own sake become bored when they are explicitly required to study. Road Trip is designed to reach the student who would rather be home watching TV than be in school.

Road Trip: The Geography Un-Lesson

Road Trip does not present itself to the student as a geography lesson. Instead, the program presents itself as a vehicle (pardon the pun) for watching TV clips. On the introductory screen, the program tells the student the following: Road Trip contains many different kinds of videos. You can watch whichever ones you choose. All you have to do to watch a clip is to get to the location where the clip is set.

After an initial introduction, the program presents the main Road Trip screen, which has three principle components: (a) the main map area, (b) the big-picture map area, and (c) the video catalog.

The main map area takes up the lion's share of the screen. Initially, the main map area contains a map of the United States, with the state boundaries drawn in (Fig. 6.1). The student can "zoom in" on a particular state by clicking on that state. The state maps look like a typical road atlas; the cities and the major roads are visible (Fig. 6.2). When viewing a state map, the student can zoom in further by clicking on a city. The student can zoom back out at any time by clicking on the big-picture map area, which always

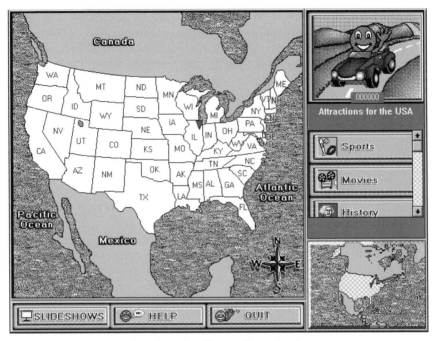

FIG. 6.1. The initial map in Road Trip.

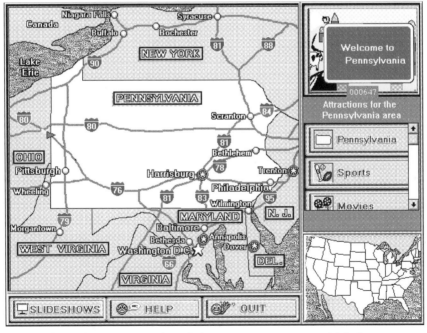

FIG. 6.2. As you progress through the program, you see more detailed maps.

displays a map that is one level broader than the one in the main map area. When the main map area shows a city map, the big picture is a state map; when the main map is a state, the big picture is the U.S. map. The student's current location is always marked with a red triangle on both the main map and the big picture map. The maps are linked to a searchable index, so that a student who wants to go to a particular city, but doesn't know where it is, can look up the city in an alphabetical list and have the system highlight it on the map.

The student can travel from city to city along the interstate highway system by zooming into the state where he is currently located, and then clicking on a road that is accessible from his current location. When the student travels along a road, the map animates to depict the student's motion in much the same way that old movies (like the opening sequence in the movie *Casablanca*) depict travel routes through animated maps. In addition, the student sees a driver's view video of a car traveling along a road, through terrain that indicates the student's current location.

Road Trip's Video Collection

Different children prefer different kinds of videos. So Road Trip contains a variety of clips. The current version of the program contains five categories of videos: sports highlights, movie clips, music videos, amusement parks, and historical footage.

The child begins browsing the video catalog by selecting one of the categories from the icon menu. When a category is selected, all destinations where a video of that type is available are highlighted on the map, and a menu of the video-clip titles is presented. For instance, the menu of movie clips in Pennsylvania currently includes a clip from the movie *Witness*, and one from *Rocky*. The program's sports titles include "Mets defeat Red Sox" and "Pete Rose Sets Record."

The video catalog is sensitive to where the student is in the program. If the main map area is currently showing the top-level U.S. map when the student browses the video catalog, then all the program videos in the chosen category will be listed. If the student is currently zoomed in on a particular state of local map, then only the videos within that locale will be listed.

The child can see a synopsis of a particular clip by either selecting it from the list or by clicking on its location in the map. When a clip is selected, its location flashes on the map, and the child is shown a teaser paragraph that advertises the clip. For example, if the student chooses "Pete Rose Sets Record," then Cincinnati will flash on the map, and the student will see a blurb that reads: See Pete Rose thrill the crowd in Cincinnati, Ohio, by surpassing Ty Cobb as baseball's all-time base hit leader with hit number 4,012.

If the student does not read well, he can hit a button to have the blurb read to him. When a child finds a blurb that sounds appealing, he can keep track of it by hitting a "mark as destination" button. The program will make a special mark on the maps to identify each destination that the student has so marked.

The student can browse the catalog as much or as little as he wishes. Some kids like to browse extensively, marking many potential destinations before doing any traveling. Others like to browse until they find one appealing video, travel there, and then browse again. Some children never browse, preferring to just set out traveling, stumbling across interesting destinations as they go. The program does not attempt to enforce one style over any others. It simply tries to get the student as excited about as many different destinations as possible.

Videos in Road Trip

Road Trip's videos entertain, advertise, and educate, but the main purpose of the videos is motivation. In the real world people often travel to see the sights; travelers in Road Trip travel to see the videos. Therefore, much of the success of the program rides on how entertaining the videos are. For this reason we spent a lot of time acquiring and producing video; experimenting with different content and different production styles; and testing it on kids. Some of the videos in the current, experimental version of Road Trip are MTV style—fast-paced, with shortcuts, and rock music. Other videos are more narrative. Different kids have different tastes.

In addition to entertainment, Road Trip videos provide two other functions. One is to encourage students to visit other destinations by advertising other, similar videos that they can see there. For instance, at the end of the video about the Indy 500, the announcer exclaims, "and if you don't want the racing action to stop, head southeast to Daytona Beach, Florida, to see the Daytona 500!" Students who watch Pete Rose break the major league hit record in Cincinnati are told they could also go to Atlanta to see Hank Aaron break the home run record.

The other function is for the video to be educational in and of itself. We have found that even clips from feature films can be informative. For example, students who watch the Amish in *Witness* or the Civil War scenes in *Glory* often learn about people and events with which they were not previously familiar. We are currently building a learning by exploring module called an "ASK system" into Road Trip to help students learn from the videos. The ASK system will allow students to ask questions about the videos they watch.

Road Trip's Route

Road Trip does not force a student to stick to his original travel plans, or to visit any particular set of destinations. Because the student has usually already learned about the location of a city if he has chosen it as a destination, the system does try to distract the student with other possible destinations the student may not even know exist, rather than encouraging him to actually arrive at his intended destination.

Road Trip uses every possible opportunity to advertise new destinations. For example, whenever the student crosses an interstate, a road sign appears announcing the junction. When the road sign appears, the program offers the student an opportunity to find out what destinations he could get to if he turned onto a new road. Similarly, when the student enters a new state, a road sign welcomes him to that state. By clicking on that road sign, the student can find out what things are available to see in that state. In this way, students often are enticed to spend time exploring a state that they originally planned to just travel through. Students often find that traveling (which they may originally have viewed as a mildly unpleasant chore to go through to get to a chosen video) is a fun opportunity for exploration.

When the student leaves a state in which he has stopped and watched videos, he is asked to identify where he has been, which videos he saw, and, out of those videos, which ones he most enjoyed. This information, in conjunction with film stills the student can choose from the videos he watches, is used to construct a slide show documenting the student's trip. This part of the program serves three purposes. First, it serves as yet another way to advertise destinations to students—the students advertise to each other. Second, by forcing the student to think back on where he has been, the program helps the student remember where places are. Lastly, students enjoy having a memento of their journey and have fun sharing their slide shows with others.

Road Trip Teaches Geography

Road Trip teaches United States geography in an unusual way. Rather than have students study maps, Road Trip has students use them. Using maps is a fairly common activity among adult travelers but is somewhat out of the experience of young people. In our tests of the Road Trip program, there were no students who required more than a couple of minutes of instruction to understand the maps. Although Road Trip was designed so that maps must be used to get to the "good parts," we found that children enjoyed the maps on their own. Some students even told us that they "liked driving the best." We had one student who didn't stop to see a video through an entire 30-minute session (despite our frequent suggestions) and, at the end, told us, "It's a really neat game."

The lesson to be learned here is that using incidental learning leads naturally to nice side effects. Our original goal was not to teach the skill of map reading. However, once we decided to have students actually do something that would require them to know geography, map reading came naturally.

Fourth Graders Don't Drive!

In one sense, it is highly unnatural to target the Road Trip program at fourth graders. Fourth graders do not drive. They do not plan vacation trips. The notion of giving a fourth grader simulated keys to a car seems artificial. But from the perspective of incidental learning, it is fine if the simulated situation is constrained or artificial. It is not the situation that must be natural, but the learning. When we only want students to learn facts, we need only make sure that the desire to know those facts be student initiated and the facts themselves be intrinsically related to the student's goals.

This goal contrasts with the goal in the Simulation-Based Learning-by-Doing Architecture. In learning by doing, we not only care that a student gets appropriate facts and cases; we also care that the student can do the task that the simulation requires. In the George application, for example, we care that the student learn how to sell consulting services. Therefore, in George, the simulation must be as natural as possible so that the student feels as if he is actually selling consulting services. However, in Road Trip, we do not care if the student learns to navigate a car. So the simulation does not need to be as realistic. Its role is to help the student become interested in knowing the facts we wish to convey.

Evaluating Road Trip

Besides testing Road Trip to see if it helped students take traditional geography tests, we also looked at something we consider more important: whether students can plan a trip, an activity they will have to perform often in life.

Road Trip does not have students study maps; it has them use maps. We have some idea of how children think about geography while using maps from the comments they make as they are using Road Trip. We overheard children saying to themselves, "Which direction is my destination?" and "How am I going to get there?" This is what you would expect from someone who is thinking about geography in terms of real-world application. Because they are thinking about geography differently, students using Road Trip may not learn the same information as students studying a map would. Although this information is certainly embedded in their plan of action, it does not necessarily mean that they would do well on a traditional test.

To test whether they could plan trips, students were given a list of possibly interesting sites and an atlas and asked to pick three sites and plan a road trip from Chicago to visit all three. To do this, students must find the state map for the site, as well as each intervening state. Then they must determine which highways will lead to the desired locations. Of nineteen students who used Road Trip, one student stopped after planning two of the three legs of the journey. The other eighteen had no problem at all using the atlas and planning a road trip, including the names of all the highways and directions to turn.

Students Like Road Trip

The students we worked with liked Road Trip. They thought it was "fun" and "cool," that it "had great graphics," and that the "video was great." More than that, Road Trip helped students who knew little geography to significantly improve their scores on geography tests. The children who knew more geography still liked the program, although their test scores did not increase much. However, these children did learn to do something that some adults seem to have trouble with—they could plan a road trip using an atlas.

The evaluations we have performed of Road Trip are extremely encouraging to us. Our major challenge in this program was to take material that is typically treated in a dull fashion and make it fun to learn. We wanted to take a dry list of facts and make that list come alive to children. The attitudes of the children who have used the program tell us we have been successful. Students who are taken out of class to use the program under formal observation have sometimes even returned during their free lunch or recess time, asking if they can "play" with the program some more.

The Opportunity of Incidental Learning

The Incidental Learning Architecture is a particularly powerful architecture for young children because they have been using it naturally as a way to learn. It's almost unfortunate for children when school begins at age five or six. At that point, incidental learning is thrown out of the window and replaced with a "sit-in-your-chair-and-do-what-I-say" architecture.

We are concerned with allowing children the right to continue to learn without "studying"—without artificially forcing the process. To accomplish this, we need to provide situations in which exploration is encouraged, rather than enforcing a rigid "teacher's agenda." Any agenda we do create must insure that the student wants to continue learning. The task of the course designer (as long as there are schools, there will be designers) is to find situations that allow for exploration, and that enable incidental learning to take place.

7

Learning By Reflection

CHILDREN AS TEACHERS

Sometimes students can be their own best teacher if they just have someone around to listen to the ideas they are coming up with. Of course, schools tend to allow very little time for such student reflection and even less time for teachers to just listen. Students rarely try out their thoughts on teachers because they know there is no possibility that the teacher would have the required time, the patience, and the ability to reserve judgment. But when students are allowed to devise and pursue activities in which they are interested, they naturally generate ideas, hypotheses, and questions. They are ready to learn from their own ideas if we can find a way to help.

INSIGHTFUL QUESTIONS

Insightful questions indicate that the student has an idea or a problem on which he is working and wants to learn more about it. The student wants to explore and broaden his ideas. Exactly what is it that such a student wants to learn? Facts are not usually what he wants to learn. More typically, he wants to learn about implications and alternatives, suggestions about his planned approach, different ways of looking at a problem, and so on. He wants someone to help him think through his ideas or problems on his own.

When these problems are personal, some people go to psychiatrists. But where do we go if the problems are technical or managerial, or everyday (but hopefully non-neurotic) in nature? Well, then we go to a friend, a colleague, or, occasionally, a teacher who is a good listener. When students come to teachers with half-formed ideas they want to flesh out, the role of a good teacher is to ask questions, not tell answers.

The role of the teacher during the questioning process is to help the student see the shortcomings in his thinking. It is to open his eyes to alternatives, erroneous assumptions, and eventualities he has not considered. It is, most of all, to challenge the student to develop a deeper understanding of his own knowledge. For the student to gain such an understanding, he must experience expectation failure. A teacher should aim to provide the questions that will lead the student into the understanding cycle.

Asking questions at the right time is a critical role of a good teacher. This statement summarizes what we call the sounding board model of teaching. When teachers adopt the role of sounding boards, they should allow students to speculate, wonder, imagine, and be creative. However, it is rather difficult for teachers to be effective sounding boards. Teachers like to tell the correct answers to students. Teachers do not have the time to sit with students and encourage them to pursue the implications of what they are thinking. Additionally, teachers often fall into the trap of thinking they are asking questions when they are really only delivering answers using the syntactic guise of a question.

Students Need to Ask Questions

Despite the fact that we now know that the asking of questions and the generation of self-explanations are critical if students are to learn anything more than isolated facts, school is oriented toward telling children answers and rewarding the repetition of answers, rather than rewarding them for good questions and allowing them to figure things out for themselves.

Dillon (1987), for example, found that students ask information-seeking questions less than 1% of the time when they are called on in class. When students do ask questions, the questions are about how to behave in the classroom rather than requests for meaningful explanations. They ask these questions because classroom discussions do not encourage better ones. It's not that they do not know what to ask about. Students, if given the opportunity, can identify deficits in their knowledge and ask questions that would serve to remedy those deficits. It's just that they don't get the opportunity. That's too bad. When students are encouraged to ask good questions, their ability to understand and remember material is enhanced (Palinscar & Brown, 1984).

Students Need To Explain Things to Themselves

Chi, Bassok, Lewis, Reimann, and Glaser (1989) found that the more students explain examples to themselves, the more they learn from those examples. This, obviously enough, suggests that students should be encouraged to explain things to themselves or others as they are working on a problem. But to have this happen in a natural way would interfere with the normal way students are tested and treated in class. If students were tested on the reasons for their answers they would learn more from the test, but learning from being tested is not what testing is all about in the schools.

Sounding Board Model of Teaching

People often need to bounce ideas off others, using their friends and family, bosses and peers as sounding boards. Properly programmed computers can serve admirably as sounding boards. What computers lack in empathy they make up for in patience. One has to be extraordinarily patient to be a sounding board. One must be willing to follow long lines of errant reasoning just to allow a student to abandon a fruitless line of reasoning on his own. Computers are easily programmed to allow a student to create detailed representations of his thinking, and to allow him to pursue or modify that line of thinking. One must be willing to allow students to pose their own answers and investigate their own thoughts. Computers can exhaustively capture whatever options students generate, letting the students pursue them as they wish. Computer systems acting as sounding boards serve as design tools for thinking. They can enable a student to capture the structure of his thought, help him focus on some part of the structure, and prod him with critical questions about that part.

Permitted to speculate with someone who is making helpful comments or suggestions, students can become, in effect, their own teachers. This goal underlies the Learning-by-Reflection Architecture.

The Premise Behind Sounding Board

The basic premise underlying the Sounding Board program is that the student will know more about the problem he is working on than his electronic teacher. The philosophy we have adopted is that the program should supply initiative but that the user should maintain control. The program supplies questions that it believes are appropriate to pursue next. A passive user may elect to follow the path suggested by the program. An active user may choose to change the course of the questioning at any point.

Generally Useful Questions

Tailored versions of the Sounding Board can contain some questions that are quite specific to the problem the program's user is expected to face. However, that does not mean that a developer needs to start from scratch when customizing Sounding Board. Even tailored versions of the program find it useful to ask a variety of general questions of the type the program already contains. Some examples are:

Questions about objects:
- Where does one usually find items like X?
- Who usually uses items like X?
- What are items like X usually used for?
- What problems do items like X cause?
- Why do people want items like X?

Questions about actions and events:
- What usually causes X to occur?
- What does X usually cause?
- Who performs actions like X?

Questions about Agents:
- What motivates X to act as he does?
- How does X get the resources to act as he does?
- Why didn't X do action Y instead of action Z?

Questions in Sounding Board

When faced with a problem that does not succumb to the standard fixes, people need to be creative. Although people are generally pretty good at banging their heads against the wall trying to force their standard approaches to work, they often need help with standing back and trying to figure out a fresh approach.

1. Attention-focusing questions (i.e., "What do you offer that your competitors do not?"): These focus the user's attention on parts of the problem he may have been taking for granted.
2. Barrier-busting questions (i.e., "What vacation would you take if price were no object?"): The idea of these questions is to eliminate some barriers from consideration long enough for the user to realize what he really wants.
3. Reminding-facilitating questions (i.e., "Who would be really good at solving problems like getting Motorola's business?"): These questions get the student to think more deeply about solutions he may already know.
4. Context-switching questions (i.e., "What recreational activities are you good at?"): Sometimes it is helpful to completely forget about the problem at hand for a moment, bringing a new context to bear on the old by asking a question about how they relate, such as, "How

could you use your chess skills to help you land the Motorola account?"

5. Domain-level problem-solving questions (i.e., in the domain of computer science: "Is there some way that parallel processing could help here?"): If the program knows questions that are particular to the specific problem the user is facing, these questions can help point out when standard solutions might apply.

The program also asks two classes of questions that are primarily for its benefit, not the user's:

1. Problem-classification questions (i.e., "What problem are you working on?"): These help the program figure out what kinds of questions are appropriate.
2. Slot-filler identification questions (i.e., "Who are your competitors?"): These help the program instantiate the follow-up questions with specifics appropriate to the user's problem.

A Dialog with Sounding Board

Here's an excerpt from a sample dialogue with Sounding Board (Fig. 7.1). In it, a sales manager named Sarah discusses with the program a challenge she is facing: She is having a difficult time landing a new account. The

FIG. 7.1. The primary interface of Sounding Board encourages you to focus on one question at a time.

program asks questions, and Sarah provides responses. As the questions help her generate useful ideas, Sarah is able to makes notes of them, which the program records. She exercises control over the flow of the questions in a number of ways, including starting on a new problem, backing up to a previous question, and canceling a current line of questioning.

When reading the dialog, keep in mind that what you are seeing is just a transcript of the conversation. The user interacts with the program through a full-screen graphical interface that presents the questions one at a time:

Question: What problem are you working on?
Response: I'm trying to land the Motorola account.

Question: What larger objectives would getting Motorola's business help achieve?
Response: It would get our foot in the door of the industry.

Question: Should we start by focusing on the SPECIFIC problem you've identified or the more GENERAL one?
Response: Getting Motorola's business.

Question: Is getting Motorola's business a matter of maintaining the status quo, or of achieving something new?
Response: Achieving something new.

Question: How would you categorize the goal of getting Motorola's business?
Response: Selling professional services.
            [The program provides example categorizations such as selling, managing, organizing, designing, or fixing.]

Question: Who is currently doing the business with Motorola that Sarah wants to be doing?
Response: An internal shop.
Response: SciTech.
Response: Some of it isn't getting done at all.

Question: Why should Motorola do business with Sarah rather than SciTech?
Response: We have more experience in the industry.
Response: We have more general business sense.
Note: I better make sure that I read up on all the latest innovations in chip manufacturing before I make my presentation.

Question: How can you impress upon Motorola that your advantages are important?
Response: Tell them stories of less experienced competitors.

Question:	What success stories could Sarah tell Motorola?
Response:	None.

Question:	What success stories could you MAKE relevant.
Response:	There was the time we reduced Apple's inventory needs by 20%.
Note:	Be sure to have Joe get me the write-up of the Apple engagement.

Question:	Who is really great at solving problems like getting Motorola's business?
Response:	John Smith—the boss where I used to work.

Question:	How could Sarah get John Smith's help?
	[Sarah indicates that the Sounding Board should skip this inappropriate question.]

Question:	What would John Smith do in this situation that Sarah could do?
Response:	Tell a lot of good success stories.

Question:	What might keep Motorola from appreciating the advantages Sarah offers?
Response:	Our staff is young.
Response:	They might think that we are too expensive.
Response:	The MIS manager there is kind of threatened by me.
Note:	Make sure they realize that our solution is less expensive in the long run.

Question:	Who else within Motorola might be better to deal with?
Response:	Maybe the operations manager.
Note:	Make sure the operations manager is contacted about the presentation.

Question:	What recreational activities is Sarah really good at?
Response:	I'm really good at chess.

Question:	How could you apply the skills that make you good at chess to getting Motorola's business?
Response:	Maybe I should do more complex strategic planning.
	[Sarah indicates a desire to work on a new problem.]

Asking the Right Questions.   The key to solving hard problems is to ask the right questions about them. In Sarah's example dialog with Sounding Board, she comes away with ideas for what research she needs to do before making contact with the client, who within the company she should contact, what points she should try to make, and what stories she might tell. The reason why this "structured brainstorming" session is so productive is that Sounding Board is able to pose fruitful questions for Sarah to pursue.

The program actually knows next to nothing about Sarah's particular problem. All it knows about are what types of questions are useful to ask when facing various types of challenges and how to present those questions in a sensible order. In some sense, Sarah does all the hard work in her session with Sounding Board. The program merely serves to shine a light on areas that are valuable for Sarah to mine for ideas.

Sounding Board and Learning by Reflection

Sounding Board shows how learning by reflection can be helpful when someone is trying to create something, in this case a sales strategy. The Learning-by-Reflection Teaching Architecture is not limited to only those cases where a student is trying to build something. It can also be valuable when a student is trying to understand something. For a student to really understand something such as a book, a design, or a period in history, he must be able to adopt different perspectives on that thing and tie it into his previous experiences. Again, interesting questions provide guidance. By asking good questions, the student cannot only develop a flexible understanding of whatever he is trying to understand; he can also create indices in his memory to store the understanding so that he can recall it when it is relevant.

Programs that Assist Learning by Reflection

The Sounding Board asks questions to help its users be creative. Questions are not only useful for processes like creativity that are often considered to be at the pinnacle of human intelligence. They are equally useful for more mundane mental processes like those involved in understanding stories. We applied learning by reflection to the task of helping children learn to read in a program called Movie Reader.

Johnny Can't Read

Why do many children have trouble reading? It may be that reading is not taught very well. Part of the problem is that schools focus on teaching "reading" but not "understanding." What's the difference? It is rather difficult to imagine what it would mean to teach reading without teaching understanding. It doesn't even seem possible. And, if you want to succeed, it isn't. Still, this hasn't stopped the schools from trying. Reading instruction in school tends to revolve around the mechanics of reading like syllables and prefixes. Learning how to decode individual syllables is different from learning how to understand. Understanding is the reason we read. We read because we want to learn something or be entertained. But, if we don't understand what we read, there is no point in reading.

Reading and Understanding

Not only is understanding the raison d'être of reading; learning to understand is the fun part of learning to read. The reward of reading for young children is the ability to make sense of those squiggles on the page. So teaching reading should mean teaching understanding. Once a child knows how to build an understanding, the mechanics of reading come quickly because the child knows what the goal is.

If we want to teach understanding, we are not limited to teaching reading. We can equally as well choose to have conversations with students, perhaps to discuss movies. "Reading" a movie, after all, is much like reading a book except that movies do not pose the language decoding problems that books do. In a movie just as in a book, following the action entails figuring out who is doing what and why. Such details are not always spelled out in a movie because doing so would make the movie tedious. The viewer is assumed to be intelligent enough to fill in the details about some of the actions and motivations himself. He also is expected to make some assumptions about what is going to happen next. A good movie often violates those assumptions.

Part of understanding a movie, then, involves a process of thinking. The more complex the movie, the more thinking is involved. The same is true of reading. Books that spell everything out and make all future actions obvious from the start do not constitute great literature, although they may well make the best-seller lists. Reading, or at least intelligent reading, the kind that involves thinking on behalf of the reader, requires understanding of the most complex kind. To children who do not already know the mechanics of reading, we can effectively teach understanding, for example, by having students watch movies.

But, alas, that's not how things work now. When we teach reading, we teach the mechanics of reading. Separated like this, the mechanics of reading make reading dull, whereas understanding, which is the fun part, hardly gets any attention. No wonder Johnny can't read; he didn't know the words meant anything!

Important Aspects of Reading

Schools typically teach reading in two stages. First, they teach children to associate a sound with a given set of letters. Children already know how to associate sounds with words, so this step allows children to be able to recognize words on a page. By second grade, most children can read simple words in isolation.

From that point on, many school systems invest most of their effort in the second stage. It is hard to put a name to this second part; many schools call it something like Language Arts. Lumped together under this rubric are such diverse items as spelling, syllabification, alphabetization, and other skills pertaining to the mechanics of language.

At this point, children, no matter how well (or how poorly) they have done in learning to decode the symbols that represent words on the printed page, begin to get bored with reading. Learning the mechanics of reading just isn't very fun. Learning to understand better would be fun, but that is not what we teach.

Decoding Letter Combinations

To see how much of reading has nothing to do with the mechanics of language, read the following vignette: John went to Lutece last night. He had the lobster.

What did John eat last night? The answer is obvious. But, interestingly enough, the story never says a word about eating. It doesn't mention restaurants, nor does it mention that John was hungry. Somehow, we just know that the answer to the question is obvious. And, we know as well that had the story said "He had the car" instead of "He had the lobster," we would not think that he ate his car. How do we do all this?

Good Readers

As good readers read, they ask themselves questions and make predictions about what will happen next. These predictions make it easier to understand what comes next and significantly add to the enjoyment of reading. It is rewarding to anticipate where the plot may lead and then watch it unfold. Often an author will purposely lead the reader to a false expectation, so that the reader can enjoy the surprise of a different outcome. The reader will never have surprises if he has made no predictions. Getting new readers to trust their predictions, and to recover when their predictions are wrong, is a critical part of empowering students with the skill of understanding.

Teaching a Child to Understand.   To see how to teach children to understand, we must first ask: What is one doing when one is trying to "understand" something? Much of what we are doing is trying to make explicit what is implicit in a sentence or, more generally, in a situation. What matters in understanding is inference making. Inference making is the process of making best guesses about what a speaker must have meant, apart from what he said explicitly. When actions or goals of a character aren't stated, we need to figure them out for ourselves. When we are told that someone wants to do something, we must ask ourselves why, if we want to understand what is going on.

When adults read stories, they make inferences automatically and unconsciously. But when 6-year-olds read, they often do not do this. What does an adult know that child of 6 does not? On the face of it, this seems like a silly question. An adult has a sophisticated knowledge of the whole world; a child understands only a small part of what is present in his immediate environment. To rephrase the question, then: What does an adult know that enables him to read that a 6-year-old does not know?

Obstacles in Reading.   For children, the problems of predicting and understanding plans are the biggest obstacles in reading. They are also big obstacles when children watch a movie, and when they observe what their parents are doing. Adults have developed the ability to follow complex plans, and they have learned cues by which to identify each other's plans. Without information about the kinds of plans there are, how can a child understand that when a character in a movie goes to the perfume store and he is in love, it means one thing, but if he is very angry and goes to the liquor store, it means another?

Main Task of Teaching Reading.   The main task in teaching reading is to teach understanding. To assess the problem of what to teach when teaching understanding, we must try to determine what is likely to prevent a child from comprehending a given text. Or, to put it more positively, what must a child know, beyond word recognition, to read a story?

Let us consider an actual story and use it as a guide to the problem. The story is from an edition of *Treasure Island,* which bills itself as being appropriate for 8- to 14-year-olds. We will take seven passages and attempt to indicate the kinds and sources of trouble a child might have in reading those passages.

1. Awkward Expressions

   I remember . . . when the brown old seaman took up his lodgings at the Admiral Benbow.

One problem children have in reading stories is a lack of familiarity with certain idiomatic usage, or modes of expression. Here, the problem is obvious because the expression "took up his lodgings" is an out-of-date phrase. The child may well know, or be able to figure out, what each word is, but he may still be confused. He will not be able to understand what plan the seaman is following. One aspect of learning how to track characters' plans is learning the cues that indicate when a character is pursuing a given plan.

2. Script Instantiation

   . . . lodgings at the Admiral Benbow.

Adult readers now realize that the Admiral Benbow is a kind of hotel (or inn, as we are later told). But how do we know that? We know it the same way we know that, in "Sam ordered a pizza at Luigi's," "Luigi's" is a restaurant, probably an Italian restaurant. We, as adult readers, know when we are in a script, and how scripts are referred to in texts. Children, however, have difficulty in making this association. They are often unfamiliar with the "stay at a hotel" script. Even if a child is not thrown off by the awkward phrase "took up his lodgings," he will not be able to figure out that the Admiral Benbow is a hotel unless he is familiar with the hotel script.

3. Plan Assessment

"This is a handy cove," the seaman said to my father, "and a well-placed inn. Do you have much company here?"

Here, in the context of the story, an adult reader will recognize that the seaman has a plan to stay at the inn if it is quiet and secluded enough. We assume he is hiding, or that perhaps something even more sinister is occurring. We wait for the reason why. But does a child? A child must be taught to look for the plans of the characters he meets. He must learn to question their motives and see the larger picture. This is a very difficult thing for a child to learn. It involves a new point of view for him. Young children tend to accept the people they meet on face value. They trust everybody. They do not see or look for sinister plans or plots. They must learn to ask questions like "What is odd about this picture?" and "What if the sailor is not someone to trust?"

Most, if not all, plots are based on the interaction and blocking of some characters' plans as they strive to achieve their goals. Tracking such things in detail is often beyond a child's experience. He must learn how. Movies can be an aid here. Children who watch movies will learn something of plot development and sinister plans.

But there is a great difference between processing text and processing pictures. In reading, many more inferences must be made about what characters actually have done. In movies, actions are spelled out in visual detail. Understanding that a character has a plan, and inferring the details of his plan is easy when watching a movie because we just watch the plan develop. We see every detail of a character's actions in front of us. In reading a story, we can assess the plot, but we must infer the details.

4. Background Knowledge of Characters

Though his clothes and manners were coarse, he did not seem to be an ordinary seaman. . . .

Would a child recognize an ordinary seaman from an extraordinary one? What comparison is being made here? Without some knowledge of what a seaman does, looks like, wants, and so on, it is difficult to understand this sentence.

Two things are important here. First, if we want to help a child understand this story, we should give him stories that have the relevant background knowledge. Second, we must also teach the child to wonder about the implications of the details of the story. A child must be taught to assess the traits of the characters he meets (i.e., what kind of person is being talked about?).

5. Plot Development

One day he took me aside and promised me money if I would keep my eye open for a seafaring man with one leg.

The plot thickens. We know that, but does a child? He must understand something of what a plot is, how stories develop, and so on. Again, this understanding is based on tracking plans. Who is doing what? What does it mean? How do I know? How might I be wrong? These are questions worth reflecting upon.

6. World Knowledge

His stories were what frightened people most of all. Our plain country people were as shocked by his language as they were by the crimes he described. My father believed that the inn would be ruined by the captain's tyranny; that people would stop coming because he sent them shivering to their beds.

To understand this passage, you need to know something of the values and morals of an English town in the 18th century. Further, it is most important to know about businesses, inns in particular, and how they are run. A basic knowledge of commerce is needed here. This story can be understood effectively only in the presence of the appropriate background knowledge.

7. Tracking Props and Goals

"He's a bad one, but there's worse behind him. They're after my sea chest."

This line is the turning point of the story so far. It indicates that there will be a fair amount of plot associated with the sea chest. As it turns out, the content of the sea chest is the crucial issue in the story. How is the child to know this? How do we know it?

We know it because we know about valuable objects, greed, likely containers for valuable objects, and story structure. When we see a particular prop in a story, we expect it to be used in the story. The child must be taught to look out for props, and to track the goals associated with those props.

8. Inferences, Beliefs, and Reasoning
    When I told my mother all I knew, she agreed we were in a difficult
    and dangerous position.

Why are they in a difficult position? For adults, it is obvious. Our heroes
possess objects of value that others know about and will want to steal. But
this is not necessarily obvious to a child. A child must be taught to construct
chains of reasoning based on beliefs derived from what he has heard so far,
and from what he knows of life. But what does the child know of life? Some
of that kind of knowledge is taught by stories. Much of it must be taught
when, or preferably before, a story is encountered. The child must learn to
figure out what is going on.

Understanding to Read Well

A child must have a well-developed sense of the world around him to
understand stories. In particular, the child must know about the kinds of
plans people adopt, when they adopt them, and how they pursue them. This
indicates that a great deal of what must be taught to enable reading is not
language per se. It is, rather, world knowledge, and the processes that utilize
the knowledge that constitutes the key issues in reading comprehension. We
can teach the facts necessary to understand through incidental learning. But
how can we teach the processes that utilize that knowledge?

Movie Reader. Movie Reader is a program intended to remedy the
problems in reading instruction. It is intended to serve as the rough equivalent
of a parent who is educated, aware of what his child does and does not know,
and who has the infinite patience to question his child about anything he
thinks the child might not understand during the course of a movie. The idea
is to have the child learn to understand by learning to ask the right questions.
When pursuing a question, the child should be able to pick up relevant
background knowledge incidentally, as needed, with the help made available
by the instructor who has prepared a film using Movie Reader.

Reading Method of Movie Reader. The model for how children should
learn to read upon which Movie Reader is based is quite different from the
model often found in today's schools. The usual method sounds very scientific. First, some educational theorist breaks down the skills involved in
reading into a set of detailed subskills. Then students master those subskills
one at a time. Finally, having mastered the subskills, students are allowed to
try to put them all together and actually read. Children usually enjoy the
initial stages of this program because it allows them to play with books, an

activity that may seem quite adult to them. But as more time is spent on mechanics, their motivation drains away.

Using Movie Reader.   When using Movie Reader, a student watches a movie on a computer monitor. At times determined by the teacher, the movie pauses and the student is asked to complete an exercise. Currently, Movie Reader provides five types of exercises for a student, each with several variations and optional enhancements, which together constitute a rich set of interactions. The exercises in Movie Reader are designed to facilitate the high-level skills needed for reading with understanding. For example:

- If the teacher feels the student might misunderstand the literal meaning of something, he programs Movie Reader to stop and either asks the student if he understood or has the student demonstrate his understanding. If there is a misunderstanding, the student is given a text explanation, shown the pertinent part of the movie again, or both.
- If the teacher feels the student might fail to make an important inference, he programs Movie Reader to help the student reason out the implications of what is happening in the movie.
- If the teacher feels an event in a movie should cause the student to

FIG. 7.2. Movie Reader encourages the learner to think about who holds which goals.

FIG. 7.3. Movie Reader also encourages the learner to think about how the plot might develop by asking how the character's goals might conflict.

develop an expectation, he can wprogram Movie Reader to stop and ask the student to predict what will happen next.

These exercises serve as models for the kinds of questions the student should be asking himself as he works through the movie. They provide a "scaffold of questions upon which students can construct their interpretations of a story" (Holum & Beckwith, 1993). The exercises encourage students to formulate and answer their own questions, help them reason through the questions the teacher poses, and provide them with the information they need to make sense of the movie. The exercises are not used to test the students' skill at understanding, they are used to help build it.

A Session with Movie Reader.   As an example, we'll use the Disney film *Cheetah,* which is one of the movies on the Movie Reader program. At the beginning of this movie, two teenagers arrive in Kenya, where they join their parents who arrived a month earlier to set up their new home. The boy, Ted, has expectations of adventure and encounters with wild animals, while his protective mother hopes to keep him close to their safe, suburban-looking house. If the viewer does not understand the conflict that develops between Ted and his parents, the remainder of the film will make little sense. Thus, a teacher might have Movie Reader pause the movie and ask the student to complete the "Drop Box," shown in Fig. 7.2.

The student attempts to match the goals with the characters who have them. In this variation of Drop Box, the characters have conflicting goals. After matching "wants to see exotic animals" with Ted (Fig. 7.3), the student then must find the conflicting goal.

Continuing in this manner, the student explores potential conflicts between characters. Sophisticated viewers and readers continually engage in this process of interpreting characters, evaluating their goals and plans, and considering possible outcomes. Movie Reader's exercises are designed to assist the student in developing these same skills.

Movie Reader and Questions.   Besides modeling the types of questions that students should be asking themselves, Movie Reader also illustrates how to pursue those questions. It gives hints that don't directly reveal the correct answer but instead provide additional information or focus the student on information already in the film. This not only helps the student arrive at the appropriate answer; it helps him learn how to go about answering the question himself.

Movies and books, of course, are often a matter of personal interpretation, and sometimes there is no correct answer. Several Movie Reader exercises can be configured so that there is no right answer, or several correct answers. Giving feedback in these situations is difficult, but perhaps what is most important in such cases is simply having the student stop and think for a minute. This strategy works especially well when two or three students use the program together, allowing the exercises to serve as the starting point for discussion.

Criticisms of Movie Reader.   One potential criticism of the Movie Reader program is that interrupting a movie with questions distracts the viewer from the movie. More generally, the question is whether any system that implements the learning-by-doing architecture will interrupt the users' train of thought, distracting them from their primary task. We have stated that students get bored by studying the mechanics of reading. But do they get similarly frustrated by the questions suggested by a learning-by-reflection system?

In experiments we have run on Movie Reader, we have found that 75% of the students who used the program did not find the questions distracting. Moreover, 80% of those students believed that the questions helped them to better understand the story. These results provide a preliminary indication that students find that learning by reflection fits in with and furthers their natural processes of understanding.

Movie Reader Teaches Comprehension.   The proposal underlying the Movie Reader program suggests that students should learn how to understand first and then let the mechanics catch up later. And to learn to understand, students need to learn to ask good questions. They need to be able to strike a "critical distance" between themselves and what they are reading, asking themselves, "How well am I following what I am reading?" and "Where is my understanding weak?" They must also learn to wonder about the implications of what they read, asking questions like "Why did the character take that action instead of an alternative?" and "How will the other characters react?"

Conclusions about Movie Reader.   When students are able to understand and enjoy the stories in books, they will be motivated to learn the skills required to read those books. We do not need to teach children to read in order to teach them to understand. We need to teach them to understand in order to read. Teaching children to understand movies is an easy way to get at the important issues of prediction, inference, and the use of world knowledge in understanding. When a child feels confident that he understands why people do what they do in various situations and confident that he knows how to recover when he is confused, he is ready to become an avid understander of the world in which he lives. He is then prepared to find out more by whatever means are available.

8

Case-Based Teaching

LEARNING FROM FAILURE

People learn by failing. Yet when people associate failing and education, they tend to remember the agony of bad grades in school or being embarrassed in front of their schoolmates rather than the thrill of learning. Failure can certainly be agonizing. It might even be catastrophic. Most failures, however, aren't catastrophic; they are merely "expectation failures"; that is, when you expect one thing and something different occurs. It is easy to see how such expectation failures lead to learning.

Consider a teenager's experiences with the opposite sex. When a boy takes a date to the circus and they have an especially fun time, he'll generalize from that experience. He may try going to the circus again when he wants to have an especially fun time with a different date. If it does not work out, the boy will think about why and modify his behavior in an attempt to do better next time. Generalizations provide expectations and when those expectations fail (in this case, when the second date falls flat), it signals an opportunity to learn. As children become adults, they form minitheories of the opposite sex by building such generalizations and repairing them when they don't work.

This is the understanding cycle at work. We label our experiences with respect to their outcomes. When the outcome matches our expectations, we don't learn a great deal; we just continue the same behaviors or actions. When the outcome fails to match our expectations, we need to recover from the failure so as not to repeat the same behavior next time. Thus, we can learn a lot by failing.

Even what we typically call "success" often involves expectation failure. For instance, you may not particularly like squid. However, it may be that you go to a restaurant where you are served squid you really enjoy. Although you would label this meal a success, your expectation about squid actually failed and you learned something as a result.

You might not only learn that you like squid, but you now might want to try other foods that you had previously avoided. In situations like this when we recall experiences and use them as a guide to future behavior, we are using case-based reasoning. Case-based reasoning is the predominant way in which people think about their worlds. In deciding what to do in a given situation, we rely upon our memories of the most similar experiences we've had and use them as a guide. Because this type of reasoning is so fundamental, it makes sense that we should tailor teaching to it.

EXPERTS TEACHING FROM CASES

Real experts reason from entire libraries of cases. Sometimes these cases are in actual libraries. Doctors and lawyers regularly consult archives of important or prototypical cases to make a medical diagnosis or construct a legal argument. But people in general are very good at recalling prior cases without having to consult a library. Most experts not only remember the cases of their experiences; they love to tell their favorite ones as "war stories." The educational value of war stories has been grossly underestimated.

One company for which I consult owns elaborate training facilities, manned by experts who dutifully teach the course material each day. At night these experts gather in the bar at the training facility and swap "war stories." When trainees happen upon these stories in the bar, they always make the same report: They learned more from the war stories told at night in the bar than from the classes held during the day. They found the classes dull and tedious, of no obvious relevance for their actual jobs. In contrast, the war stories were alive and vivid, describing situations the trainees were constantly experiencing at work.

It might seem obvious that this company should change its teaching method. Both faculty and students would agree that the students could learn significantly more if they could just listen to war stories. Change, though, is often difficult to achieve.

TEACHING WITH CASES

Given that students are natural case-based reasoners, how can teaching be arranged to reflect this model of thinking? To help students leverage their ability to reason from cases, teachers must play three roles. Obviously, students cannot reason from cases if they have no cases to begin with. You can't make analogies to the Roman Conquest of England if you never knew about it in the first place. The first role of teachers should be to provide students with applicable cases at the time they are required.

Moreover, students cannot use cases properly unless they know how to label them and understand what the cases mean to them. We cannot find what we have not properly labeled. To label a case so that we can find it when it's relevant, we need to understand its significance, to see what points it makes. Thus, a label like "Roman Conquest" is less likely to be useful than the label "One of the greatest military blunders of history caused by lack of training." The second role of teachers should be to help students explore and draw out useful generalizations from cases.

To learn a new case, a student must experience an expectation failure. So the third role of teachers should be to place students in situations in which they will face failure.

This last role sheds a different light on the goal of education. The question that most often guides teaching is "What is it that we want students to know?" But the in-the-trenches question teachers should ask daily is "What experiences do we want students to have and how can we facilitate learning from those experiences?"

THE CENTRAL ISSUES OF CASE-BASED REASONING

Some cases are more important than others. In most school systems, the importance of a case is a function of its centrality in some ideological doctrine. We teach students cases so they will believe certain things about their country, their religion, or their background. The reason for teaching a case from this learning perspective has to do with whether a case is paradigmatic. However, the reasons a case should be important should not come from ideology but from the case's ability to help students think. A case should be important because it contains important facts (perhaps it changed history), it is unusual (there is little to which to compare it), or it is paradigmatic (it represents a class of things that occur repeatedly).

The second issue is labeling. We cannot find what we haven't properly labeled. The significance of a case is an important part of the labeling of that case. Labeling determines what case will be found to be most relevant when we might need it, so how we label what we experience is critical to any future reasoning. We label in terms of the use of a case. Thus, a label like "Roman Conquest" is likely to be less useful from a teaching perspective than the label "One of the greatest military blunders of history caused by lack of training."

Case-Based Reasoning in the Real World

Given the constraints of today's classroom, it is next to impossible to use case-based teaching. Case-based teaching requires that teachers sit one-on-one with students, swapping stories and probing into them. It requires that teachers have concrete war stories to tell. It requires that teachers be able to get reminded on cue during class. These are substantial hurdles.

Little wonder, then, that curriculum designers shy away from case-based teaching. Instead, they settle for the known, dictating what teachers should talk about, with the hopes that when the course is over, every student will have learned the prescribed material. These hopes are in vain. The "forgetting-the-day-after-the-test" syndrome seems to prove that life doesn't work this way at all.

In real life, when we are having difficulty with a task or a situation, we tend to seek advice from someone who might know about the problem at hand. If this someone does know the answer and tells us, we not only benefit directly from what they tell us; we acquire a new case. Because our problems are usually not so clear-cut, and answers are not so directly applicable, this process is not as simplistic as it sounds. We might discuss our problem with someone who is not exactly an expert but can offer good advice. He or she might respond with a story from his or her own life, and if the story is well told and seems germane to our problem, we will take the added step of adapting it to make it relevant to our own lives.

This is how learning takes place in the everyday world, and its ubiquity is the reason so many people say they learn more from work or from just living life than they ever did in school. And, of course, they are right because receptivity to relevant cases encountered in daily life is the basis for the human understanding cycle and for the learning process.

THE CASE-BASED TEACHING ARCHITECTURE

One of the most valuable types of learning conversations that can occur is when a student with a problem describes his situation to an expert, and the expert is reminded of and reciprocates with an applicable story. In such a situation, the student can make the story his own, labeling it and applying it to his current problem.

Although such case-based teaching is common in the world outside of school, it is rare in today's classrooms. To overcome the obstacles that block schools from adopting case-based teaching, we developed a method of using computers to help, called the Case-Based Teaching Architecture. The Case-Based Teaching Architecture exploits the basic capacity for students to learn from stories, and the basic desire of teachers and experts to tell stories that encapsulate their experiences. This architecture starts by placing the student in an inherently interesting situation. It then monitors the student as he works through the situation, teaching him what he needs to know at precisely the moments he wants to know it. By noticing when the student is blocked or has experienced an expectation failure, the program can know when the student is ready to learn. Timeliness is crucial. Stories need to be made available to the student. Students should be able to ask for advice when they want it. But they should not always have to ask for advice to receive it. Advice should be offered in response to actions taken by the students, or good stories should be told in response to ideas proposed by the students. The more relevant the stories, and the more compelling and visually appealing the stories, the better case-based teaching works.

The Case-Based Teaching Architecture naturally complements the Learning-by-Doing Architecture. Learning by doing provides the interesting task. The task should satisfy two constraints: (a) It should be inherently appealing to students (e.g., there would be no problem in getting them interested in the task), and (b) it should lead students into expectation failures so that they can develop questions. The Case-Based Teaching Architecture can then provide cases that provide answers to those questions.

The Creanimate Project

How can the Case-Based Teaching Architecture be used with schoolchildren? Let's consider the domain of biology. Most children enter school with a great fondness and curiosity for animals; yet by the time they reach junior high school, most have decided en masse that science is dull and dry. The problem is, of course, that science is barely taught at all, and when it is taught, it is too often presented as a set of facts to be memorized rather than a choice of open-ended questions to be explored. With this problem in mind, we set out to build a biology tutor that takes advantage of children's natural affinity for animals by allowing them to explore on their own the ways in which animals survive in the wild.

What we had in mind was something as vivid as a *National Geographic* television special. However, instead of seeing footage of animals in the wild according to the order that some director imagined was right, students would be able to explore it themselves based on their own interests. We didn't want the students to wander through video clips aimlessly, though; we wanted their journey to be organized in a way that would provide them with general principles to help them think about biology in a sound way. The solution was to provide students with an interesting task and enable them to see video clips that helped them as they worked.

Teaching Science with Creanimate

When schools teach science, they often leave out many of the elements that make it compelling. The Creanimate project is designed to put the fun that accompanies real scientific inquiry into an effective educational experience. One element of science that makes it so exciting is discovering and exploring what was previously unknown. Scientists think about difficult, unresolved questions, develop possible explanations, try to make those explanations fit the data, and revise their explanations. During this time, they are working with other scientists, listening to their ideas, trying to convince them of their own theories, or allowing others to try to change their minds. Creanimate allows elementary schoolchildren to perform these kinds of activities on a level that makes sense to them, and that connects with their natural fascination with animals. In the course of a session with the Creanimate program, a pair of students (we have found that students work well in pairs, interacting with, and encouraging each other) have the opportunity to generate creative hypotheses, consider the ramifications of their hypotheses by examining open-ended questions, and practice the vital skill of reasoning from cases.

Using Creanimate

Creanimate invites children to create their own animal by taking an existing animal and changing it some way. For example, students might ask for a fish with wings or a bear that can dance. In response, the program engages the students in a dialogue in which they consider the ramifications of their changes. It might ask how the fish will use its wings or what value a bear might get from the ability to dance. Creating a new animal is an inviting task for children because it offers them the opportunity to be whimsical and imaginative. Unlike most school activities, it rewards their natural inclination to push beyond the limits that are constantly imposed on them. As odd as it seems, creating their own animal is a way of bringing authentic scientific practice to a level that connects with children's natural inclinations for learning.

When scientists study a phenomenon, one of the first things they do is disturb the system under study from its natural state and observe the effects of the disturbance. The effects of modifications on a natural system can reveal a great deal about that system in its natural state. Thus, an atmospheric scientist learns about the atmosphere by releasing gases and observing what happens to them. Creating a new animal performs the same function for students. It provides them with an opportunity to learn about the animal before it was modified and about the modification itself through the consideration of relevant, open-ended questions.

Schools typically teach science under the guise of open-ended inquiry, but they actually desire to convey a collection of specific, predetermined answers. Teachers present science as a set of achieved results, not as an inquiry into unanswered puzzles. Creanimate not only allows students to imagine their own animals; it responds to their creations the way a naturalist would if he encountered this animal for the first time in the wild. It raises open-ended questions and discusses possible answers with the students. For example, suppose a pair of students ask for a bee with a big nose. The program might respond by asking how the bee would use its big nose. In the ensuing discussion, the students could propose answers, (e.g., to suck up honey), or the program might provide suggestions. Resolving a question usually gives rise to a new question. The role of the computer in this situation is to allow students to team up with the computer in pursuit of an ongoing dialogue in which the students propose changes, the system raises questions, the students resolve those questions with new changes, and the system raises new questions about the new changes.

To take this further, let's suppose a pair of students ask for a fish with wings. The system might ask how the fish would use its wings. After considering several possibilities, the students decide the fish should use its wings to help it fly. The addition of the act of flying raises yet more questions, and the student now must deal with what else his fish needs in order to fly, as well as how flying could help the fish to survive. This might be a good time to talk about flying fish, or dolphins, or why birds fly. In any case, the students should be in charge of the discussion, determining the direction of the computer/teacher. Giving the students control over their own learning allows them to take advantage of Creanimate's capacity to show video clips of actual animals. Students see what they want to see and are, therefore, immediately interested.

A Sample Session with Creanimate

Figure 8.1 shows a sample screen from the program. The top portion of the screen is devoted to the program's output. This text can include explanations, invitations to view video, and questions posed to the students. The middle section of the screen is used for student's input. The students click on the options provided to respond to the system. If they select a partial sentence containing an ellipsis (". . ."), they have the opportunity to complete the sentence by typing in their own text. At the bottom of the screen are "user control" buttons that allow the student to exert control over the interaction, (e.g., "skip this," "change animal") or to ask for assistance (e.g., "What's the point?", "Big Picture").

The following sections describe a recorded session of a fourth-grade boy using Creanimate.

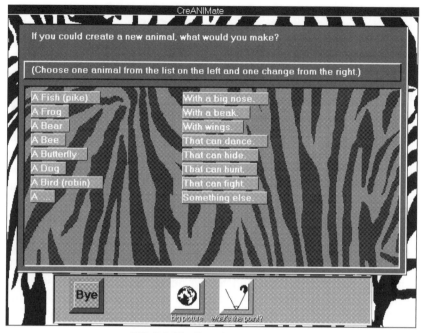

FIG. 8.1. The Creanimate program.

Choosing an Animal

The first step in the program is to select an animal from a list of options on the screen. These animals and modifications were selected by the designers according to the interests of children as determined by surveys and matched according to available video sources. The students are free to type in anything they like if they choose the last options, "A . . ." and "Something else":

Creanimate:

If you could create a new animal by taking an existing animal and changing it some way, what would you make?

(Pick one animal from the list on the left and one change from the list on the right.)

A Fish (pike)   With a big nose.

A Frog   With a beak.

A Bear   With wings.

A Bee	That can dance.
A Butterfly	That can hide.
A Dog	That can hunt.
A Bird (robin)	That can fight.
A . . .	Something else.

Student: A FROG THAT CAN FIGHT

Posing a Question

The system immediately responds to the student's proposal by posing a question about that animal. In this case it selects the question "Why fight?" after determining that the video library includes clips showing reasons that animals fight. The questions the system asks are intended to teach students the basic relationships that underlie animal behavior. In this case, the question emphasizes that animals do not engage in behaviors unless they help the animal to survive:

Creanimate:

That's a good idea, is there a reason why you want your frog to fight?

So it can . . .

Give me some suggestions.

Student: SO IT CAN PROTECT ITS SELF

The student clicks on "So it can . . ."and then types in "protect its self [sic]" (the parser corrects the misspelling).

Example Cases

The computer is able to determine from its knowledge base that "protecting itself" is a reason for fighting, and that it has a video that illustrates that. The student asks to watch the demo:

Creanimate:

That's a good idea. Bees protect themselves by fighting enemies. Would you like to see that?

Yes.

No.

Student: YES

(The student watches the video titled "BEES EXPEL WASP.")

The system has another video that shows a very different animal doing the same thing. This helps to show commonalties across the wide spectrum of animals:

Creanimate:

> Bees are not the only animals that fight enemies. For example, jawfishes fight enemies. I have a good video about that. This has battles in it. Would you like to see a video about that?
>
> Yes.
>
> No.

Student: YES

(The student watches the video titled "JAWFISH DEFENDS TURF.")

Committing to an Answer

Once the student has seen examples that illustrate the answer he has proposed to why his frog might fight, he has the opportunity to commit to that answer. If he commits, he goes on to other questions about his frog. Otherwise, he can consider additional answers to the current question:

Creanimate:

> So your frog can fight to protect itself.
>
> You can commit to that now, or we can look at some other reasons why animals fight and you can decide later.
>
> Why would you like your frog to fight?
>
> To protect itself.
>
> Show me more reasons.

Student: TO PROTECT ITSELF

Creanimate: OK, your frog will fight so that it can protect itself.

A Second Question

Now that the student has decided why his frog will fight, the program raises a new question: How will it fight? This question emphasizes the fact that the high-level behaviors of animals are composed of more basic actions. In this case, there are several things animals can do to fight:

Creanimate:

How you would like your frog to fight?

By . . .

Give me some suggestions.

Student: BY JUMPING UP ON HIM

The student clicks "By . . ." and types "jumping up on him." The system does not know the action "jumping on an animal," so it interprets the student's input as "jumping." The partial sentence "By . . ." helps the student to understand what type of answer the system is looking for. In this instance, an action would be appropriate, but a physical feature would not. However, within that constraint, students have the full range to express themselves.

Cases for Incorrect Answers

The program does not know of any animals that jump in order to fight. In the absence of knowledge about animals that jump to fight, the computer takes the opportunity to show the student some reasons why animals do jump. In this way, students learn from their incorrect answers even more than they do from their correct answers:

Creanimate:

I don't know any animals that jump to fight, but I do know why some animals jump. Salmon jump. Do you know why salmon jump? (I think this video is funny.)

So they can . . .

Show me a video.

What other videos can I see?

Student: Skip this.

In the preceding outpu, the system introduces a video with a question. It does this to help make the students active viewers of the video. They watch the video looking for the answer. It also helps them to focus on the aspects of the video that are relevant to the question under consideration.

Instead of watching this video, the student asks what other videos he can see. So, the program displays pictures of four animals. The pictures are labeled with the animals' names. Each of these corresponds to a video that shows reasons that those animals jump. The student clicks on a picture to select a video. The student clicks on the picture of the whooping crane:

Student: WHAT OTHER VIDEOS CAN I SEE

Creanimate:

Which would you like to see next?

salmon

squirrel

grass frog

whooping crane

Student: WHOOPING CRANE

To help "advertise" the videos to the students, they are labeled in the system's memory with information about what makes the particular video appealing. In this case, the video has been labeled with the attribute "Contains: frantic dancing":

Creanimate:

Whooping cranes jump to attract their mates. I have an interesting video about that. This video is for people who like frantic dancing. Is that something you would like to see?

Yes

No.

Student: YES

(The student watches the video titled "CRANES DANCE.")

This video shows cranes dancing to attract their mates by jumping, flapping their wings, and stretching their necks.

Creanimate: Case-Based Education

Children are fascinated by animals. When they find themselves in a forest, they will discover a tremendous amount about how animals interact, where they live, and how they survive, all without formal guidance. Place the same students in a classroom, however, and suddenly this excitement turns to distaste. This happens because schools remove the elements that make the forest experience compelling: Self-guided exploration where discovery of something unexpected is possible.

Creanimate's combination of asking open-ended questions and providing interesting video cases at well-timed intervals helps shift learning about biology from a passive task, with lists of facts to be memorized, into an exciting activity in which students engage in the exploration and explanation cycle. Open-ended questions are used within Creanimate to create an investigatory dialog between the student and the computer. As the student proposes a trait change, Creanimate raises questions about the impact and reasoning of those changes. When the student resolves those questions with new changes, the cycle begins again with Creanimate presenting new queries. This cycle closely resembles a dialog the student would have with an actual biologist in a one-on-one discussion.

Creanimate also takes advantage of the fact that people are natural case-based reasoners. When a novel problem arises, people quickly look to similar situations in the past for solutions. Creanimate capitalizes on this fact by providing videos of animals acting naturally when they relate to a student's current goals. By viewing different animals behaving in a variety of ways, students are able to consider methods and motivations of animal survival that differ from their original rationale.

The Students Who Used Creanimate

Different students have different cognitive styles. They learn in different ways. Most classroom exercises only support a single style. Because we designed Creanimate to allow students to control their own learning, students using the program are able to tailor the interaction to suit their own style.

We noticed that students using Creanimate tend to exhibit one of five styles of interaction (Cleave, Edelson, & Beckwith, 1993):

Model Users:	These users "play by the rules." They are compliant and earnest. They completed dialogues and stayed on track.
Rebels:	These users refused to engage in dialogue, gave flip and offbeat answers, and got easily frustrated. They frequently pushed the button labeled "What's The Point?"
Dominators:	These users were single-mindedly goal directed. They were interested in building their design. They were interested in pursuing their own topics, rather than letting Creanimate guide the dialogue.
Writers:	Writers were expressive and cooperative. Like Dominators, they avoided suggestions and entered long answers. Like Model Users, they completed dialogues and watched the videos the system suggested.
Video Hoppers:	These users were video oriented and passive. They wanted to see videos whenever possible. They avoided entering their own answers, depending instead on the suggestions provided by the system.

Students did not develop these styles when they sat down with Creanimate; they brought these styles with them. Creanimate simply gave them an environment in which they could let their styles come to the fore for us (and them) to see. These styles will emerge in any educational environment that puts control in the hands of students and offers a wide bandwidth of communication between them and their teachers/coaches/advisors.

The existence of these disparate styles shows the importance of individualized instruction. If we do not allow students control, their styles will not surface. And, if their styles do not surface, students cannot learn to manage and refine them. Instead, those styles will remain buried under the surface and will then emerge raw and unfinished outside of school.

Cognitive Styles

Whenever someone says there are five types of some thing, it's natural to ask, "Which is the best type?" But this question is too rough to be applied directly to the styles we have isolated. Like teaching strategies, these styles of interaction are not intrinsically good or bad. Rather, they are appropriate or inappropriate. A better question might be, "Which of these styles is good for what purposes?" But even this question does not start where we should: with the student. We need to ask instead, "How can we use what we know about students' styles to help them learn better?"

One of the most important things we can help students learn is an awareness of their natural cognitive style, and the strengths and shortcomings of that style. This implies that not only should we give students a learning environment in which their styles may be allowed to surface, but also that we must have this environment react to those styles. We must lead students down paths that show the shortcomings of their style so they can strengthen it. We must provide students with coaches who can tell memorable stories about others with similar styles and how those styles helped or hindered them.

CASE-BASED TEACHING IN ACTION

Expertise is often thought of as a large body of facts. Knowledge of facts, however, is only one component of expertise. What sets an expert apart from a novice is the ability to deal effectively with new situations within his or her realm of expertise. When confronted with a novel situation, an expert knows the right questions to ask and how to go about answering them. The cases and facts the expert commands help him or her to resolve the questions, but questions come first. Creanimate attempts to teach students what questions to ask when confronted with new situations.

Creanimate not only illustrates the Case-Based Teaching Architecture; it also shows one method for restructuring a dull domain into an exciting one. The students who used Creanimate had fun. They would have liked to spend more time with the program. What was the secret to how the program sparked students' interests? It helped that Creanimate deals with an area most children are already interested in: animals in the wild. From there, we made sure that the program focused on questions. We did not present students with a list of terms used by scholars. Rather than telling the student about "mammals," for example, we asked the student, "How will your animal achieve the behaviors it needs to survive?" These questions are grounded in the task the student is performing. They don't seem like the kinds of arbitrary questions teachers often ask; rather they seem like natural parts of the task. Creanimate does not ask questions simply for their own sake (or as a pure assessment strategy). Instead, it suggests questions that push students closer to their goal. The Creanimate program considers the students' interests first, and then it concerns itself with how to convey the cases it wishes to cover. Because students recognized that the program was helping them toward their own goals, they liked it.

THE SINE QUA NON OF CASE-BASED TEACHING

A word of warning is in order about Creanimate. It is easy to outline some ideas about case-based teaching and then show some examples. We have found, however, that it is possible to turn even these ideas and examples into bad software. Even when a designer starts with a good set of cases and an interesting task, a good case-based teaching program will not necessarily result. The tendency is for course designers to attempt to turn everything into a "page turner" style. Thus, they set up situations and tell whatever story they were going to tell when the situation has run its course, regardless of the user's interest.

Good case-based teaching systems, regardless of whether they are implemented using computers or not, must have three characteristics. They must have lots of cases, a complex task in which students can pursue individual goals in individual ways, and flexible indexing so the user can choose just the appropriate case at just the appropriate time. A large panoply of experts, with hundreds of stories indexed in such a way as to get nuances to matter, connected to a program in which many different kinds of actions and failures are possible, is the sine qua non of case-based teaching. Or, to put this another way, if it isn't possible to fail in a variety of different ways and get a variety of different kinds of individually tailored instruction, it isn't case-based teaching.

9

Learning By Exploring

LEARNING BY EXPLORING

Learning by Exploring means allowing students to pursue their own interests. Many students may not be interested in the curriculum, but everybody is interested in the parts of the world that they believe relate to their own existence. This basic self-interest, if it is allowed to flourish intellectually, can lead to a wide variety of discoveries motivated by curiosity based on internal needs.

If we want to allow students to pursue their own interests, we need to provide them with a way to get their questions answered. Many of the teaching architectures are, in fact, specifically designed to bring students to the point that they want to know something. How are we to help them?

One teacher cannot possibly know the answers to all questions a student might develop. The idea that any one teacher knows all there is to know is ludicrous. The 1-to-30 model of learning should be exactly the other way around—30 teachers to 1 student. Students should have access to a variety of experts. They should be able to access these experts easily and quickly and should have the opportunity to compare and contrast the different opinions of the different experts.

DIFFICULTIES IN IMPLEMENTING LEARNING BY EXPLORING

Although giving students ready access to a range of experts would certainly help them learn, its practical implementation seems unrealistic. Consider what happens today. When we want to know something, we usually ask the person who is easiest to access, as long as there is some hope that she or she has the information we want. Whom can we ask? A student has a teacher. A professional has a colleague. An employee has his boss. A child has his parents. An adult has his friends and neighbors. The situation couldn't be worse.

This arrangement keeps most people seriously misinformed. Usually when we try to access experts, what we really get are "local experts," the nearest person who knows the most. This is a real problem in daily life. We may want to find the best restaurant or the best tax advice, but we have to settle for Uncle Henry, who "knows about these things." We don't normally view schoolteachers this way, but how can they help but be officially sanctioned versions of Uncle Henry? Teachers can only know so much.

Even if we were to develop a race of omniscient teachers, we would not solve our problem. No teacher has the time to answer every question that every student has. In the business environment, in which we substitute "experts" for "teachers," the time problem is even worse. One might think that in a large organization the experts might be available to the people in that organization who need their expertise. But this is usually not the case. The people who really need the expertise, who have the most to learn, namely, the newest and least important employees in the organization, have the least access to the experts.

This argument can be taken one more step. Even if we were to have enough omniscient teachers to assign to each student, our problem still would not be solved. The problem with this "one question, one teacher" arrangement is that, even if the teacher knows the answer, he can only present his own point of view. Interesting questions often have a range of answers about which even real experts disagree. When a student asks "Should we have free health care?", do we want them to receive only one point of view? It's not clear that hearing too much of either Bill Clinton or Bob Dole would provide the best education. Instead of settling for one expert per topic, we should enable our students to formulate their own opinions by giving them access to a range of experts.

EXPLORING IN TODAY'S SCHOOLS

Learning by exploring is usually implemented in today's schools by giving "research assignments" to students. Students are asked to go to the library, research a topic, and write a report. This is a good concept: Give students the opportunity to discover what they might find interesting and then have them organize what they find into a coherent report. When students are able to research a topic they genuinely find interesting, this method works quite well. But students often are denied the right to pursue topics that might interest them and instead are told what books to read, or worse, what point of view to take. The topics they pursue are frequently assigned to them because of the content to be learned despite the fact that the act of discovery and reporting is itself the important issue.

Allowing students to discover and report has its flaws, but if it is employed correctly, it can be quite effective. However, the difficulty in accessing information is something that should be pointed out. For years, children were taught to memorize the Dewey Decimal System, as if the object of study were the library itself. Research methods are taught so students will become good at finding what they need. There is a place for this lesson, of course: Finding what you need in a world where information in books is classified according to bizarre enumeration schemes is a tremendous undertaking. But why do you really need to know this?

We don't need new teaching methods to help students find obscurely classified information. We need to make information available, readily and simply. We need to create easily explorable video or text databases. The idea is to get information to students in such a way that they can consider lots of ideas and not have to learn anything about the art of finding those ideas.

THE LEARNING BY EXPLORING ARCHITECTURE

The computer-based implementation of learning by exploring is called, appropriately enough, the Learning-by-Exploring Architecture. The goal of this architecture is to provide easily accessible and available question-and-answer interactions with experts. Learning depends on good information being available at the time one is ready to hear it. To make computers useful information providers, we must create learning environments that allow each user to follow his or her own interests. We must make use of the members of our society who have important things to say, who can provide corporate memory, who are experts on a given subject, and who have had important experiences that decision makers should be aware of.

The aim of learning-by-exploring programs is to provide an accessible database, in which one can enter and retrieve information successfully with no more than two lines worth of nothing-to-learn typing; that is, if you have to memorize commands, or learn a new language of some type, or go through multiple lines of inquiry, your database isn't accessible. The goal is to come as close to "ask a question, get an answer" as possible. If this is achieved, it will be possible to make two important strides in having experts as available teachers. First, it will encourage experts to make themselves available for recording (via video or other means), so that their answers will be generally available. Second, multiple experts can be made available for the same set of questions.

Video Databases

There is a tremendous amount of information available on video. Go to any video rental store and you can see what is commercially available to the general public. In addition, a tremendous amount of footage exists in the archives of television networks, including, for example, the important news events of the world in the last 30 years, interviews of important leaders in every field, or studies of animals in the wild. However, don't imagine that those who possess these archives are especially good at finding what they have. To find what one needs in any archive, one must have that information classified by content—by an understanding of what information it contains—rather than by characterizing its title or area in some way. This kind of classification is necessary for everyone, not just students.

Imagine if all the video material that exists were available to any student who wished to view it. The idea sounds impossible but it isn't. It is merely massively difficult. Nevertheless, it is important to begin the effort.

Children who have grown up on television are more receptive to video than to print. And, in many ways, video is more powerful than print. Although print authors can analyze a subject very effectively, nothing compares to seeing it for yourself. The trick is not only to make what someone wants to see easily accessible, but also to offer natural follow-ups, alternatives, contradictions, different viewpoints, and so on, to what has been viewed.

Making a Database Accessible

The challenge in building an accessible database is one of organization. It does not help anybody to make thousands of hours of video available without an organization scheme that would allow users to find what they wanted. Furthermore, this information is of no use if the organizational system cannot tell users what is available that they would not have known to look for at precisely the moment when they might become interested in that information.

Programs that Help with Learning by Exploring

At ILS, we have designed two types of computer systems to implement learning by exploring. Both systems are based on the notions that students must be free to follow their own path, and that they should have multiple experts available to answer their questions. The difference between the systems has to do with how wide a domain of material they attempt to cover. The first type is called an ASK system. ILS has already implemented and delivered a number of these systems; they provide students with one-on-one (and, in several systems, one-on-many) teaching in a specific domain. The second system type, called Searching Agents, has more ambitious goals. These systems work with a large repository of stories, called the Story Archive, which is currently under construction at ILS. Unlike ASK Systems, Searching Agents are not restricted to a limited domain. Instead, they attempt to delve into the Story Archive to retrieve answers to specific types of questions across many domains.

ASK Systems

ASK systems are a form of hypermedia based on the metaphor of having a conversation with an expert (or a group of experts). In this conversation, the user provides questions and the ASK system provides the answers. In a real conversation, both participants influence the flow of discussion. In an ASK system, the same holds true. The user influences the flow by selecting which questions to pursue, and the ASK system influences the flow through the answers it provides.

An ASK System for TRANSCOM.   When the Gulf War broke out, it presented designers of ASK systems with a terrific opportunity. The key problem in building the kinds of teaching systems we are proposing is in the acquisition of expertise. It is easy enough to get experts who are great storytellers to talk to us so that we can put their stories into an ASK system. But to make real ASK systems, there needs to be a real user at the other end. We need to know who will be asking the questions of the ASK system, why they will be asking the questions, and—a significant question—who will be paying for all this.

The military certainly wants to learn from its experiences in the Gulf War. New planes, new allies, new weapons, tremendous distances—all contributed to the new problems and solutions the military needs to keep on file. The military is, of course, well aware of the need for these kinds of records but does not currently have a good way of capturing and using them. Like many businesses, it writes lists of "lessons learned," but these are usually either too abstract to be of much value or too detailed to wade through. It also employs historians who write lengthy reports, but it is difficult to get the right information buried in these reports to the right person at the right time.

We proposed building an ASK system, TransASK, to fill the military's need. The Advanced Research Projects Agency agreed to fund our idea, and in a few months, work on the TransASK system had begun. TransASK is designed to serve as a job aid, training tool, and reference aid for officers assigned to the United States Transportation Command (TRANSCOM). TRANSCOM is a joint military command that carries the responsibility of planning, coordinating, and scheduling military transportation in wartime and, more recently, in peacetime.

One of the interesting aspects of the TransASK system is how challenging its charter is. Our goal with most learning-by-exploring software is to build systems that students will be able to tap into to answer their questions. TransASK, however, was built for practitioners. Practitioners may pose some of the same questions as students, but many of their questions will be more advanced and detailed. Nevertheless, the structure of this domain and the process of building the ASK system for it are similar to those used in building other ASK systems.

The Role of TransASK.   During a fast-breaking crisis, a military command must accomplish a tremendous amount of planning and coordination in a very short period of time. The TRANSCOM Crisis Action Team (CAT) is a special entity within the command that takes over such functions during crises. CATs face a severe training problem. Because of the short term of many military assignments, many of the action officers who are assigned to the CAT have little experience in their current jobs, and, in the frantic atmosphere of a crisis, their co-workers do not always have time to give them much help.

The basic job of the TRANSCOM CAT is to determine what materials and personnel the commander-in-chief wants shipped, to verify the accuracy and priority of those requirements, and to schedule transportation that meets the commander-in-chief's timetable. Much of this job requires interacting with a complex military planning system, and following up on questionable data by directly contacting people who can explain and verify it. Newly assigned officers have many problems within this structure, which requires them to:

- know the standard procedure for doing a particular task;
- know how to use the automated systems;
- identify suspicious and conflicting data;
- know who to call for additional information and verification and how to contact them; and
- handle the stress of CAT operations during a crisis.

The role of TransASK is to provide guidance on these and other similar issues on an as-needed basis, as an officer is accomplishing his mission either in a crisis or during a training exercise.

TransASK captures the expertise of transportation planners at TRANSCOM and other commands in the context of their experiences during Desert Shield and Desert Storm. Twenty-five experienced people, ranging from generals to noncommissioned officers, were interviewed. Their expertise is most often conveyed in the form of first-person stories (quite literally "war stories") that are vivid and memorable to a viewer. Trainees find these stories easier to apply to their current problems than the decontextualized advice typically contained in "lessons learned" documents.

TransASK is designed with the officers' jobs in mind. The challenge in designing the human interface was to make it rich enough that a user could easily find the answers to specific questions, but simple enough that he would not be overwhelmed. To make it easy to find information in the system, the interface gives the user a set of graphical displays organized around the situation that brought the user to the system in the first place: The user is filling a particular role in the CAT, he is engaged in a task required by that role, and he is having a problem accomplishing the task. Selecting a role, task, and problem from the displays brings the user to a story relevant to his current concerns.

The Development of ASK Systems. The first ASK system ILS built was ASK TOM. It was a "proof of concept" system intended to demonstrate the value of video-based ASK systems. The idea was to record one expert so well that anything you might think to ask him would be readily available. Tom was an expert in bank trust consulting who gave us two days of his time, allowing us to build a fairly extensive system. But, alas, although Tom knew more than two days worth of stuff about banking, we were not able to get access to him again.

To test the idea of a solely text-based ASK system, we built ASK MICHAEL, an ASK system totally constructed from an existing text. *Business Week* found that Michael Porter's (1990) *Competitive Advantage of Nations* was full of good stories, but that it did not hang together all that well as a book. Books are, after all, linear: One page follows another. However, because Porter's book contains a series of stories connected in complex ways not readily captured in the linear form of the book, it was better presented as an ASK system.

ASK Systems and Books. Will ASK systems really change how we get information? I have often been asked if it isn't nicer to curl up with a book rather than a computer. When people first encounter ASK systems, they see them as a beginning of the end of the book. And, indeed, they may well be. But it is important when considering whether computers may yet be the end of the book, exactly what kind of book we are talking about. In this case, we need to specifically consider the reference book. The real question is: Will computers replace encyclopedias, textbooks, dictionaries, scholarly compilations of data, and technical reports?

My answer to this is an emphatic yes. Whether ASK systems are the ultimate replacement for these types of books is a question that cannot yet be answered, but some alternative is certainly needed. No one curls up with the D through F book of the encyclopedia, or if they do, they don't last long. After we read about Paris in the encyclopedia, it is possible we will want to know next about Prague, which is in the same volume, but we are just as likely to want to know about London or Amsterdam, which are not. More important, while reading we might get curious about Napoleon, or about the making of Bordeaux wine, or about city planning. Encyclopedia indexers try hard to help with all this by trying to point you in the right direction. The most notable of these attempts is the Syntopicon of the Encyclopedia Britannica, an enterprise in indexing done by the very clever Mortimer Adler. But as clever as this index is to topics of knowledge, it is still limited by its static nature. Knowledge is dynamic and ever changing, and users have independent, idiosyncratic needs. This means that, ultimately, every user wants his own "specially-constructed-because-of-my-needs-of-the-moment-encyclopedia"; one that changes as if by magic. This is the goal of our ASK systems. If they replace the reference books, few will mourn their loss. What counts with reference books is the speed and ease of access.

The Story Archive

In today's classrooms, teachers have difficulty making knowledge from a broad range of sources available to students. Few experts are readily available in the school. Students do not have access to experts outside the school either. In fact, it's even a special event whenever an outside expert comes to visit even though those experts are often not really all that expert (Captain Dan the traffic man comes to mind as an example from my experience).

In today's schools, access to knowledge largely means access to books. But it's time-consuming and difficult for students to locate the specific parts of the specific books that contain the information they want. Most students have had the experience of finding a source that gives an interesting lead, but then they have to dig up three other sources to pursue that lead.

To make computers really useful information providers, we must give them a memory full of experts saying relevant things. Then we must build systems that can access relevant parts of that memory instantaneously, allowing a student to concentrate on the content of the subject at hand, rather than digging through card catalogs and searching through library shelves. The Story Archive is a long-term research project currently under construction at ILS that is intended to pull together video-based stories from many different experts about many different domains. Searching Agents are one of the forms of programs we are developing at ILS to navigate the Story Archive for users insuring that the Story Archive qualifies as an accessible database.

Searching Agents link together stories in the Archive. Each agent has a particular realm of expertise; a particular way it looks to link together stories. To have a flexible system, then, we need to have a range of Searching Agents. The Searching Agents make the Story Archive easier to use. When users have a certain type of question in mind, they know they can go to the Searching Agent that handles that kind of question. This is how people typically get their questions answered—they go to the local expert. But the local experts of the Story Archive (i.e., the Searching Agents) have an advantage over the local experts you might go to for tax advice or with a car problem. The Searching Agents do not have to answer your question—they only need to refer your question on. They have at their disposal the knowledge of true experts. The job of a Searching Agent is to go into the Archive to locate the most relevant knowledge from the most relevant expert.

Agents in the Story Archive

We currently have eight types of Searching Agents in mind for the Story Archive:

The Scientific Agent
The History Agent
The Economics Agent
The Psychology Agent
The Dramatic Agent
The Logic Agent
The Thematic Agent
The Description Agent

These eight agents are responsible for searching for related information for any given story that is discovered in the archives. When set in motion, it is their job to find other stories to tell, and to alert the user to the existence of those stories. Thus, they can be seen as a kind of dynamic index, telling the listener of the story about what else there is to know, given what he has just found out.

Each agent can behave in two different ways, looking either for general principles or specific examples. When looking for general principles, agents attempt to find stories that include perspective, theoretical discussions, principles, and lessons. When looking for specific examples, agents attempt to find interesting stories rich in relevant concrete detail. These behaviors seem different enough to users to give each agent two distinct personas. Accordingly, we have given each agent two names, one to reflect each persona.

The Scientific Agent

The Scientific Agent seeks good science stories. The difference between the general principle (Einstein) and the specific example (Edison) personas of the Scientific Agent is the difference between theory and technology.

Using the Gulf War as an example, there are two very different lines of inquiry possible upon finding out about stealth bombers and scud missiles. Inquiring about theory leads to one line of questions. How do these things fly? What had to be known to build them? How does one calculate their trajectories? How does flight work anyhow?

Inquiring about technology leads to different questions. What is the advantage of these planes and missiles over others? How were they developed? What are their effects? How might they be improved? What new technologies are under development?

Both are reasonable lines of inquiry, and both start with the same index in the initial story, namely, technology employed in this war. But, they answer different questions about that technology and thus search for very different stories in the archive. These lines of inquiry are encapsulated in the following two basic questions that the personas of the Scientific Agent strive to answer:

- Albert Einstein: "What are the underlying scientific principles in this story?"
- Thomas Edison: "Please explain the technology that is important in this story."

The History Agent

We can, in an historical search, be interested in events that are in some way like the current event and can shed light on this type of event. Alternatively, we can choose to focus on specific antecedents to an event, asking "What are the events I need to know about to better understand how this event came about?" Here again, we have two very different types of searches going on.

Heroditus, the general principles persona of the History Agent, looks for analogous cases that, although they have nothing to with the current case as far as historical cause, contain lessons that apply to the current case. Thus, we might expect the Vietnam War, Germany's incorporation of the Sudetanland, and the U.S. invasion of Panama to be brought up for consideration by the user.

In the case of the Gulf War, Tacitus, the specific examples persona of the History Agent, would certainly want to tell us about the Arab–Israeli situation, the Iran–Iraq war, the British domination of the Middle East in the early 20th century, the Iraqi invasion of Kuwait, and so on. This is the causal aspect of the History Agent that is charged with presenting the context in which this war fits.

If the History Agent is to be able to do its work, the Story Archive must provide it with appropriate raw material. Taking the example of the Gulf War, the Archive would need to contain information about the event's historical roots directly, and information about the characteristics of the players (large, rich, powerful, aggressor, imperialistic, etc.) in the Gulf War that would enable similarity searches to be made.

The personas of the History Agent pursue these guiding questions:

- Herodotus: "When has something like this has happened before?"
- Tacitus: "What is the historical background of this story?"

The Economics Agent

There are two different aspects of economic issues. One has to do with the theory of economics, and another with straight business issues. Seen as a war for oil, the Gulf War had a lot to do with issues of how countries control their own economic destinies, the self-sufficiency of nations, cartels, and free enterprise. It is relatively easy to launch into a discussion of basic economics as a result of hearing a story about this war, just as with the science agent it was rather easy to link up to a good physics lesson.

On the other hand, there are also specific, concrete issues of business. What would have happened to the price of oil if Iraq had kept Kuwait? How does a billion-dollar-a-day expense affect the economy of the United States? What business interest stood to gain the most from the war? Who was hurt? What are the long-term effects?

Here again, we see the distinction between the large and the particular. We might need to understand the war from the perspective of the economic theories involved, or from the set of business cases it created. Either should be made available via the two personas of the Economics Agent:

- Adam Smith: "What are the economic implications of this story?"
- John D. Rockefeller: "What are the business implications of this story?"

The Psychology Agent

When trying to understand their world, people naturally focus on what other people are doing. To understand the Gulf War, they want to know specifically who was involved and what were their motivations. If they are the curious type, they also want to know who else is like that and why, in general, people behave that way. It is the job of the Psychology Agent to bring to the attention of Story Archive users stories that are related on the basis of the people involved and explanations of their motivations.

The Freud persona is responsible for analyzing the psychology of the characters in a story. What is Hussein like? Is he mad? What about Bush? What is the psychology of the Germans and Japanese? Why is Mubarek doing what he is doing? A psychological analysis of these people would certainly enhance one's understanding of the Gulf War.

The Dickens persona is responsible for finding analogous characters in different stories. In the Gulf War, Hussein kept being compared to Hitler and Nassar. What were these people like, and are their lessons to be learned from the comparison?

These personas are guided by these basic questions:

- Sigmund Freud: "What are the motivations of the actors in this story?"
- Charles Dickens: "Who is this character similar to?"

The Dramatic Agent

Sometimes, we are simply happy to hear a good story because it is interesting, entertaining, and fun. To find such stories, the Story Archive needs an agent searching for good stories to tell. Again, there are two approaches for this.

The first approach is to look for a story that gives context to the current story. We might hear, for example, of the Gulf War by means of a short piece of text or video about the war. At this point we might want to see a well-put-together piece about the war, perhaps a full-length movie that used the war as a backdrop. Given the amount of news coverage dedicated to the Gulf War, finding a context piece should not pose much of a problem.

The second approach is to look for human-interest stories related to the particulars of the current story. For topics that are less well documented than the Gulf War, human-interest stories can provide a sense of what the problems are. Even in the Gulf War, such stories add depth. We might use, for example, stories from other wars to show what life in the trenches can be like, or what it is like when a family is notified of the death of a soldier.

William Shakespeare is the general principles persona of the Dramatic Agent and O. Henry is the specific examples persona:

- William Shakespeare: "Show me stories that describe the big picture, the global perspective.
- O. Henry: "Show me human-interest stories about this topic."

The Logic Agent

We are interested in why things were done. Sometimes the reasoning chains involved are fairly straightforward, and sometimes they are rather convoluted and mysterious. The Sherlock agent attempts to unravel mysteries in a given event, and the Socrates agent attempts to lead the user to the obvious answers to his questions.

These agents are therefore quite different from the agents we have described so far. Their job is to find things that answer a question in the mind of the user. To do this, they need access to causal information relating aspects of an event to aspects of other events. The Socrates agent must be aware of patterns of reasoning that are typical in a given situation and attempt to match those patterns to the current situation. Thus, for example, if Socrates knew that wars are often caused by economic issues, it might search for information about Iraq's economic situation prior to the war. If the Sherlock agent knew that one mystery of the war was what happened to Iraq's air force, it might search for situations where the strategy of hiding one's power proved historically effective in war.

- Sherlock Holmes: "What are the anomalies in this story? What are their explanations?"
- Socrates: "What are the expected outcomes of this situation?"

The Thematic Agent

Stories have points and lessons to be learned. We need to step back from them and learn about life. The Guru agent derives a point from the story and is prepared to tell you other stories that have the same point. The Rabbi agent attempts to find stories that have the opposite point or disprove the point made by the original story.

- The Guru: "Show me stories that confirm the thematic points of this story."
- The Rabbi: "Show me stories that oppose the thematic points of this story."

The Descriptive Agent

The Descriptive Agent is a kind of "how to" agent. There are, after all, lots of mundane facts associated with any event being discussed. We might want to know, for example: How did the United States get its troops over to Iraq? What was the war plan? How did it go? Where is Iraq? Where is Kuwait? What were these places like before the war?

These facts can be grouped into two clusters using the distinction between general principles and specific examples. Under the general principles cluster, the responsibility of the Knute Rockne persona, we gather links that have to do with planning. Under the specific examples cluster, assigned to the Christopher Columbus persona, we gather the myriad mundane facts that can link one story to another. For examples of links based on such facts, look at the "See Also" listing at the end of any encyclopedia article. The goal of Columbus is to find enough mundane facts to determine which ones are relatively interesting to tell and present them to the user.

These personas require that the basic facts of any situation be part of the initial representation of that situation.

- Knute Rockne: "What are ways to achieve that goal?"
- Christopher Columbus: "Show me stories about the entities mentioned in this story."

A Stroll Through the Story Archive

To give a better idea of what it is like to use the Story Archive, let's see what a session might look like. Let's assume you have selected the Civil Rights area of the Archive to begin your exploration. The Archive will start by offering you Martin Luther King's "I Have a Dream" speech. This speech touches on most of the major themes of the U.S. civil rights movement in the 1960s.

A card appears in the middle of your screen, representing the speech. Around the card are pictures (or "icons") of the 16 retrieval agents. To view King's speech, you would click your mouse on the card. To find what follow-up stories one of the agents has to offer, you would click on the agent's icon. Let's say you view the speech and then decide to follow some of the agents' "discussions."

When you click on the "I Have a Dream" card, a television screen appears, with a set of VCR-like controls underneath it. On the screen appears Martin Luther King, who says:

> Now is the time to rise from the dark and desolate valley of segregation to the sunlit paths of racial justice. Now is the time to lift our nation from the quicksand of racial injustice to the solid rock of brotherhood, now is the time. I still have a dream. It is a dream deeply rooted in the American dream. I have a dream that one day this nation will rise up, live out the true meaning of its creed: We hold these truths to be self-evident, that all men are created equal. Because I have a dream that my four little children will be judged not by color of their skin, but by the content of their character. I have a dream today. With this dream we will be able to work together, to pray together, to struggle together, to go to jail together, to stand up for freedom together, knowing that we will be free one day. . . . And when this happens, and when we allow freedom to ring, when we let it ring from every village and every hamlet, from every state and every city, we will be able to speed up that day when all of God's children, black men, white men, Jews and Gentiles . . . will be able to join hands, and sing in the words of that old Negro spiritual, "Free at last, free at last, thank God almighty, we're free at last."

At this point most of the agent icons on the screen have changed color from black to blue, indicating that they have pertinent follow-up stories. On the card that represents King's speech is a list of the concepts that are prominent in the story. You can label any of these concepts as especially interesting to you. If you were to select "Civil Rights" and "The 1960s," for example, you would find that some of the agents change from blue to pink, or even red, indicating the stories they have found are relevant to your topics of interest.

Suppose you said to yourself, "Yes, King's message of peace and brotherhood is a good one, but the 1960s were not all sweetness and light. What would an opposing viewpoint look like?" The agent you'd want to talk to in that case would be the Rabbi, whose job is to cast doubt by counterexample. You notice that the Rabbi is among those agents glowing red, indicating a close match between your areas of interest and the stories he has found. Clicking on the Rabbi's icon produces a list of stories you might be interested in. Suppose you select the one called "Brown on Violence." When you do, the old card representing "I Have a Dream" disappears, and one representing "Brown on Violence" takes its place. If you click on that card, a new video window appears. In it, you see black activist H. Rap Brown addressing a press conference:

> I say, violence *is* necessary. Violence is a part of America's culture. It is as American as cherry pie. America taught the black man to be violent, we will use that violence to rid ourselves of oppression if necessary. We will be free by any means necessary. We also say, to extend that, that if black leaders continue to aid in the genocidal attempt of America to execute and eliminate black people, that they will be considered enemies, also, of black people.

You may wonder what could prompt such an extreme position. You could ask Tacitus for a historical background story, or you might ask John D. Rockefeller for the economic causes and implications. Suppose you click on Rockefeller's icon. One story that would be available to you would be a speech by John F. Kennedy on the effects of racism:

> A white baby is born there, and a Negro baby is born next door. That Negro baby's chance of finishing high school is about 60% of that baby's. His chance of getting through college is about a third of that baby's. His chance of being unemployed is four times that baby's. His chance of owning a house is one-third as much. His chance of educating his children is how much? His chance of being a federal district judge is nonexistent—because there aren't any.

We could continue to follow this conversation by asking another agent for a follow-up to Kennedy's speech. Another possibility would be to jump back to "I Have a Dream" and see what other threads lead away from there.

The Archive keeps a list of stories you've seen to make it easy for you to jump back.

When you do, you will notice that some of the agent icons are red, indicating a high level of "excitement" on the part of the agents. What this really means, as we said, is that the stories the agent has retrieved are very relevant to your set of interesting concepts. One of the agents who is vying for your attention is Tacitus, our historical background agent, who has two stories that provide background information about King's speech.

The first is called "Color, Culture and Racism"; the speaker is the famous boxer Mohammed Ali, talking about the subtle effects of racism. Although the speech is humorous, it makes a serious point:

> The black man has been brainwashed, and it's time for him to learn something about himself. When you look at television you see White Owl cigars, White Swan soap, Kane White soap, White Tornado floor wax, White Floss toothpaste. They taught him when he was a little boy about "Mary had a little lamb, whose fleece was white as snow." Snow White. And then there's the white house. . . .

> You look at television, they have two cars, one black, one white. They put a gallon of gas in each one, and see which one can go the farthest, and every time, the black car stops, and the white car keeps going. So this brainwashes the Negro. He goes to the drug store, and orders two scoops of ice cream, one chocolate, one vanilla. And every time, they put the chocolate on the bottom and the vanilla on the top.

> And the so-called Negro, the way the educational system has been outlined, has been brainwashed. He needs to learn something about black, so when he goes to the grocery store . . . and sees that the angel's food cake is the white cake, and the devil's food cake is the chocolate cake. . . .

> Everything bad is black, so he's been brainwashed. So now he needs to be taught something about himself, so he can be proud, and quit worrying you, and pushing you out of your neighborhood, quit running with your daughter, and quit chasing you out of your schools, and every day you've got a headache with this Negro, that has been brainwashed by your kind.

> So now it's our job to re-brainwash him, to teach him that rich dirt is black dirt, don't feel bad. Strong coffee is black coffee—you understand? You make it weak, you integrate it. So now he feels proud, now he's not begging no more. Now he wants to be himself, he's not worrying you no more. So he needs some black history, and he needs some black culture so he'll know who he is and be proud to be who he is, and quit worrying you so much.

The second story Tacitus wants to show us is called "History and Racism." The speaker here is Stokely Carmichael:

America cannot tell the truth about herself. If the history of this country were written, you would have to say that this country is a nation of thieves. It began by stealing this country from the red man. If I said to you that Christopher Columbus discovered America in 1492, you'd say, "That's correct." So how come there are already non-white people living here, and they don't exist until this honky comes and "discovers" them. Ain't that something? . . . All their heroes have been white. They make you bow down to George Washington. Did they ever tell you that honky owned slaves? Did they ever tell you that? Not only did he own slaves, he sold a black woman *for a barrel of molasses!* And he's supposed to be our hero. Some hero.

At this point, you might be wondering about George Washington. Maybe you hadn't known that he was a slave owner. Suppose you want to find out if any of the follow-up stories to "History and Racism" involve George Washington. You could do this by removing "Civil Rights" and "The 1960s" from your interesting concepts list, and then adding George Washington. The agent icons have once again changed color. This time, only one icon—the Rabbi—indicates any interest.

The Rabbi's job is to cast doubt on the underlying themes of the previous story, by showing counterexamples. Here, the Rabbi counters the negative view of Washington expressed by Carmichael, by highlighting Washington's role as a hero of democracy. He does this by showing a videotape, made at ILS, of Irwin Weil telling the following story. Weil is a professor of Russian history and literature. His introductory course is perhaps the most popular course taught at Northwestern University:

As you may know, probably the first modern type of democratic revolution that took place in Russia took place some years after the Russian soldiers came back from Paris—By the way, having given the French the name for one of their cafes, *bistro.* That means fast food in Russian. . . . Well, in Russian, *buistra.* In French, *bistro* —And sure enough, these officers, infected with these French ideas, put on a kind of revolution in December of 1825. Perhaps some of you have heard of the Decemberists. These were the famous Decemberists in Russian history. Of course, they had no idea of what it meant to have popular support or anything like that. A whiff of grapeshot and it was over. But it's interesting that one of the two societies—there was a Northern and a Southern society—one of the two societies that was most active in this . . . movement were people who almost worshipped—and you'll never guess!—George Washington.

And you know why? Because Washington refused to become emperor. Remember, his officers wanted to make him emperor, so they could become, of course, magnates. They wanted land, and Washington got into a big fight with his officers, so big in fact that my native city is called, after their society, Cincinnati. They were the society of the Cincinnati. They wanted land, he said, "All right, all right, already, I'll give you land, take it on the damned Ohio

River, out in the wilderness." That turned out to be my native city, named after the Cincinnati. To the Russian mentality, this was something wonderful. Here was a great military leader, who, after all, had fought the British to a standstill, who rejected the title of Emperor. This was what true democracy meant, and through George Washington, they had a very good idea of what the Americans did.

This story is a suitable place to end our tour of the Archive. It captures the essence of why we use stories to teach. It is rich with detail, it is intimate, and it ties together a great deal of information. A textbook lesson would give you some dry facts about French ideas spawning a failed revolution, which you would probably forget immediately. In this story, you see Russian soldiers in French bistros, talking politics with the natives. You see idealistic young officers learning a quick lesson in reality. You see greedy American generals pressuring Washington.

Most importantly, these events are now tied together for you in an interesting way. This is how historians, as opposed to history students, think about history. That's why historians *like* history. In teaching like this, we have the opportunity to help people think about history like historians, about science like scientists, about literature like critics and writers.

Student Interests

It's worth emphasizing the small size of the "chunks" of information students receive when they use learning-by-exploring environments. The clips typically run from 30 seconds to two minutes long. This small size keeps control in the hands of the student. If they are interested in what a clip has to say, they can pursue it. If not, they can back up and pursue something else. Learning-by-Exploring environments are able to track students' interests in ways that environments built around lengthy narratives are not. When a teacher shows a 30–minute filmstrip about the history of the American Revolution, if a student is uninterested, all he can do is fall asleep. In an ASK system, he can change direction to maintain his interest.

Learning-by-exploring environments not only allow students to maintain their interest; they allow students to act on that interest. A 30-minute filmstrip on the American Revolution will cover a lot of ground. If a student finds the material discussed in minute twelve to be particularly interesting, tough luck. He will get but a taste of it. However, in a learning-by-doing environment, a student can investigate a topic that interests him. He can look at it from a number of perspectives, linking in other clips that are related in a variety of ways. The power of learning-by-exploring environments is in their ability to organize the knowledge they contain, bringing up clips only when they are relevant and portraying them in a way that makes their relevance clear to the student.

The Technology of Accessibility

What ASK systems and the Story Archive offer is a way to open up the walls of the classroom. They give teachers a way to bring in outside help. One of our systems contains clips from Jimmy Carter, Ronald Reagan, and Gerald Ford. When a student develops a question concerning how a President might react to a proposal, such systems allow a President to give an answer. When a student wants to know about the implications of an historical movement, a world expert on history can suggest an answer.

Such resources have been available before, of course, in books and filmstrips. But they have not been accessible. Libraries can be seen as enormous passive buckets of content. They contain many answers but those answers are tough to get to. To find an answer, you first need to physically go to the library. Then, you need to state your questions in terms the library's systems understand, such as Dewey Decimal System. Using Dewey Decimal-ese you locate a number of "content units" that might contain what you want. The "content units" that libraries deal in are complete works (books, movies, articles). So, you go to the stacks, pulling out these content units and thumbing through them. If you are lucky, you find what you need.

Small wonder few students are known for the depth of their library research. Librarians can help, of course, but only so much. They cannot know which parts of which books are relevant. They cannot have the stacks of the library immediately at their fingertips. Learning-by-exploring environments offer a different vision, one in which the place of research is no longer different from the place of activity. Rather than a passive library, they provide active accessible databases. When students are working through a problem in the classroom, they should be able to immediately access an ASK system, without interrupting what they are doing. They should be able to access the world's experts and have something like a conversation with them, trading off the experts' points of view while developing their own. With this possibility, the idea of a self-directed education becomes just that much more reasonable to consider. Why not have a collection of Nobel Prize winners as your own personal physics teachers? Technology makes this possible.

10

Goal-Directed Learning and Creating the Software We Need

GOAL-DIRECTED LEARNING

Life can be described as a process of setting goals. People attempt to acquire new abilities, attain certain positions, acquire various objects, establish various relationships, ensure certain feelings, and acquire specific types of knowledge. They come to have these goals quite naturally; many of them are simply part of being alive. Others come from being part of a particular society. Still others are highly idiosyncratic and individualistic. Whatever their source, goals drive what we do. When we hear about something that reflects, complements, or could advance our goals, we are eager to learn more about it. All teaching should respect this simple point. When teaching relates to students' personal goals, rather than to those goals imposed upon them by school, students are eager to respond.

To leverage the power of natural learning using the teaching architectures, we need to provide goals that students will willingly adopt. We also need to provide a way for students to control the environment in which they learn, giving them the opportunity to adapt what is presented to them to their needs. They should be guided by their own interests and goals, taking actions when appropriate, receiving instruction on demand, and sitting back and reflecting on how the world is reacting to their attempts. Goal-directed learning shows how to tie together the teaching architectures by having them support students who are pursuing specific goals.

Why Children Need to Make Their Own Mistakes

Goal-directed learning sounds like a simple notion, but it is rarely employed in schools. Instead, educators fall back on the predominant notion that you should simply tell people what you wish them to know. Parents, too, want to tell their children how to live and are even more upset when they won't listen. Yet children insist on "making their own mistakes." Teachers have not only the desire but are encouraged to lecture students about what they should know, especially in universities. In this approach, knowledge is a commodity that can be sold for the price of tuition like a bar of soap. Knowledge, however, is not a commodity. Most people are hardly aware of what knowledge they have, how to find what they do have, or how to lose what they don't want to know. Knowledge is more like air, there when you need it but hard to detect unless you know what to look for.

Schools and Students' Goals

It might be very difficult to teach students trigonometry, in part because it seems so irrelevant and pointless. If those same students really wanted to design a house or construct a model bridge, however, they might very well be eager to learn trigonometry when it became clear to them that they needed to know it. With this idea in mind, we can begin to see that the problem with school as it is currently constituted boils down to this: The order in which information is presented in school is more or less the direct opposite of the natural order in life. In life, individuals have goals, they formulate plans they believe will help achieve those goals, and then they decide what actions will advance those plans. Having determined the actions they must do, they ask themselves if they have the necessary skills and resources to carry out those actions. If they do not, they begin to acquire those skills and resources. This may in turn entail formulating new goals, plans, and actions just to get to the point where the original plans and actions can be executed.

Schools tend to reverse this natural order. Well, actually that's too kind, because in the attempt to reverse the order, schools often skip the most important part—making sure the knowledge that is covered is relevant to students' lives. Consider mathematics instruction. First we teach the skill of arithmetic, then we teach algebra, then geometry, trigonometry, and, finally, calculus. But what is all this for? No one really ever says.

How Goals Direct Learning

Schools have always been designed to teach skills before actions, and actions before goals. Is this reasonable? The school's way of doing things is so ubiquitous that it clouds our thinking on areas of learning that have nothing to do with school.

For instance, imagine that you wanted to take the pictures at a friend's wedding because he couldn't afford a photographer. Your friend is willing to supply all the materials you need, and he is able to borrow a camera and a darkroom for a few days. You are eager to help, but know nothing about photography. How do you proceed?

Your goal to take pictures of wedding guests would probably lead you to begin taking pictures of people, discovering in doing so how to operate the camera, how to recognize mistakes in lighting or composition, and how to remedy problems. If you wanted a more thorough understanding of photography, you might seek help from professionals or from books and keep practicing until you felt you knew what you were doing. You might, depending on how serious you got about all this, try to learn more about optics, or chemistry, or art. But, and this is the key point, what you would initially want to learn would be in service of the goal of doing the best job you could at the wedding.

Courses in photography do exist, of course, and you could take one. These courses are in no way as bad as most courses offered in school because they do indeed assume a common goal; namely, everyone wants to take good pictures. Even so, students might want to take different kinds of pictures, have varying initial abilities, and want to learn varying amounts of detail. Students would not, however, first be required to enroll in an optics course, or a chemistry course, or an art course. Why not? The people who run these commercial courses know that students wouldn't take courses if the natural learning order were reversed and they had to take optics courses first. Only schools, with a captive audience (such as our children), could get away with such perverse ordering.

Sickle Cell's Learning Environment

Perhaps the most important point that underlies the educational software built at ILS is that by applying a little creativity we can convert what might seem like inherently passive learning situations into active ones. The challenge is to figure out how to offer learners a chance to pursue interesting goals. A new opportunity of this kind arose in a project designed for the Museum of Science and Industry in Chicago. The museum was interested in teaching visitors about Sickle Cell disease, a genetic blood disorder found predominantly in people of African descent. Rather than merely designing a passive display featuring animation or a quiz, we decided to take a different tack and build an active "workbench" with which museum visitors could do something fun. Our approach was to train the visitors to be genetic counselors.

Now, of course, the visitors to the museum have no intention of becoming genetic counselors. But by presenting them with a challenging problem, we could capture their natural motivation to learn. Users advise a couple who are worried about having children because they suspect their children may be at risk for sickle cell.

The interaction in Sickle Cell Counselor is organized around a simulation that provides four activities: asking experts, doing lab tests, calculating risks, and advising the clients. Each activity is available to be visited and revisited, in whatever sequence the user desires. The program provides visitors with access via video to experts with whom the visitors may have simulated conversations. Four human experts offer videotaped advice:

- a guide serves as the voice of the tutor, offering help and suggestions regarding about how to navigate through the program, what to look for, and what to try next;
- a doctor who offers medical information;
- a geneticist who supplies genetics expertise; and
- a lab technician who helps the user with the mechanics of the blood lab.

A simulated blood lab is available because an important step in determining clients' risk factors is identifying their hemoglobin types. The blood lab gives the user a chance to draw samples from each client, view them under a microscope, and perform a conclusive lab test. Users can see what red cells (both healthy and sickled) look like and can identify hemoglobin types by their differing electrical properties. The user's goal, though, isn't to "learn about red cells and hemoglobin," but to identify the clients' gene types. It is only through pursuing this goal that a user acquires some level of understanding of these concepts.

A Session with Sickle Cell

The Sickle Cell Counselor takes a subject that students typically find boring and brings it alive in an active learning environment. The following is an example of an interaction with the Sickle Cell Counselor. In the text shown, a button pressed by the user is indicated by a labeled button icon, the questions available to the user appear in a box, and video clips are paraphrased. Figure references appear in parentheses. The example begins immediately after the user has selected a client couple (who appear in video):

Zeke: Help me out here. Our first child is healthy—real healthy. And then out of nowhere, my niece is born with Sickle Cell.

Denise: I think we should stop having more children—I think we should be happy with the one healthy child we've got.

Zeke: But that's the point—William's healthy. That means we don't have Sickle Cell, right?

This client introduction sets the scenario. The couple isn't sure whether or not having a healthy child the first time means a second will be born healthy as well, and their uncertainty serves as the focus of the user's inquiry.

Guide: Hi. I'm here to help you with your activities as Sickle Cell Counselor. At this point, you can advise the clients, talk to experts, or do lab tests.

The visitor here decides to talk to the experts and uses the mouse to click on the appropriate selection.

Guide: On this screen you can choose an expert and select a question to ask that expert. Dr. Cynthia Boyd is a physician and can answer questions related to the medical aspects of Sickle Cell. Dr. Eugene Pergament, a geneticist, can answer questions about genes and how people inherit Sickle Cell. And Dan, our lab technician, can help you learn how people are tested for Sickle Cell characteristics.

Now the visitor decides to talk to Dr. Cynthia Boyd (see Fig. 10.1) and is faced with three questions she can answer:

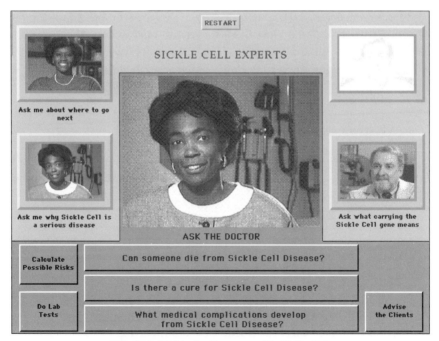

FIG. 10.1. "Talking" with an expert in Sickle Cell.

> ## Can someone die from Sickle Cell Disease?
>
> Is there a cure for Sickle Cell Disease?
>
> What complications develop from Sickle Cell?

The visitor decides to ask the first question and a video of Dr. Boyd comes up:

Doctor: Sickle Cell Disease and Sickle Cell Trait are both diagnosed using a laboratory test called hemoglobin electrophoresis. This gives us a breakdown of the kinds of hemoglobin a patient is carrying in the blood.

At this point, the visitor decides to hit the button labeled "Do Lab Tests." The guide pops up to introduce the lab:

Guide: This is the blood lab. Here you can perform tests normally done by a lab technician; you can take samples of your clients' blood, view them under a microscope, and perform electrophoresis testing.

The visitor can manipulate tools provided in the interface to draw samples of the clients' blood and view them under the microscope. Having put a sample under the microscope, the visitor can ask the following questions:

> ## What am I looking at?
>
> What do sickled blood cells look like?
>
> What should I do now?

The visitor asks the first question and a video of the Lab Technician pops up to reply:

Lab Tech: The red blood cells you're seeing look healthy. But since Sickle Cell Trait doesn't normally cause red cells to sickle, you can't tell by looking at the sample whether or not the client carries Trait. To do that, you'll need to run the electrophoresis test.

Figure 10.2 shows the visitor performing electrophoresis testing and determining that both members of the couple have AS hemoglobin. This means that they each carry the Sickle Cell Trait. Having made this deter-

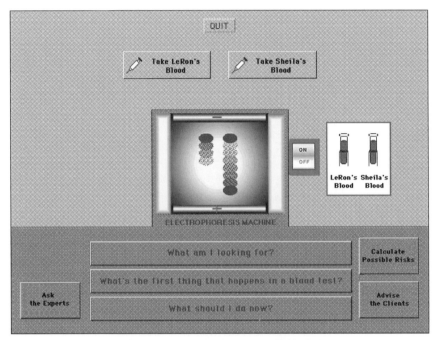

FIG. 10.2. Running a blood test in Sickle Cell.

mination, the visitor decides to leave the blood lab and talk to the geneticist. The geneticist presents the visitor with three questions that she may ask:

> **Is there a way to calculate the possible risks?**
>
> Is the Sickle Cell gene a recessive gene?
>
> Can parents have more than one child with Sickle Cell?

At this point, the Punnett Square shown in Fig. 10.3 is displayed. The geneticist describes the square:

Geneticist: Using the Punnett Square, recognizing what the genotypes of the parents are, one can easily figure out what the gene makeup of their offspring will be.

Seeing that there is some chance that the couple's children will have Sickle Cell, the visitor decides to advise them that it is too risky for them to have children. The couple responds:

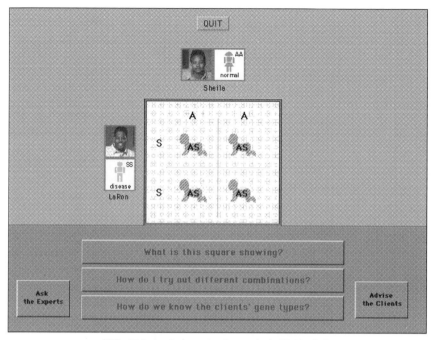

FIG. 10.3. Analyzing a test's results in Sickle Cell.

Zeke: What are you talking about? How did you decide that?
Denise: Yeah! What are our risks?

At this point, the guide offers the following questions to the visitor:

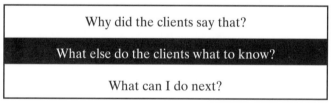

The visitor selects the second question and the guide responds:

Guide: Finding out your clients' hemoglobin types was an important step.
           But they don't know their own risks of having a child with Sickle
           Cell.

The visitor then asks to calculate the possible risks. In response, the guide
brings back the display of the Punnett Square but tells the visitor more about
it.

Guide: Here is a Punnett Square. This shows you what the odds of each possible outcome are for two parents with the hemoglobin types you specify. Because you've found out your clients' gene types, the square is already filled in to show your clients' possible outcomes.

Earlier, if the geneticist had tried to describe how to use the square to calculate probabilities, the visitor would likely have been uninterested, because the visitor had no direct reason to care about probabilities. Now, however, the couple has specifically asked the visitor to tell them the risks they face, so the visitor is ready to hear about how to calculate them. After describing the square, the guide offers two more questions for the visitor to ask:

> ### What is the square showing?
>
> How can I try out different gene types?
>
> How do we know the clients's gene types?

At this point, the guide hands off to the geneticist who is the proper expert to answer these questions. When the visitor asks the first question, the geneticist replies:

Geneticist: The Punnett Square shows that three different types of offspring are possible. There is a 25% chance that the child will be born with SS-type hemoglobin and will have Sickle Cell Disease. There is a 25% chance that the child will have AA, or normal hemoglobin. And there is a 50% chance that the child will have AS hemoglobin, meaning the child will carry the Sickle Cell Trait.

The Punnett Square may also be used like a spreadsheet to try out various genotype combinations. The visitor may play with the square, trying various experiments, talk with the experts more, or decide to go back and talk with the couple again. Let's assume the visitor decides to try advising the couple one more time. This time, the system offers to tell the client what the risks are, advising them to do as they think is best given that they understand the risks.

After giving this advice, the guide returns and the couple gives some feedback to the visitor:

Guide: About a year has passed, and your clients have come back to tell you what choice they made, based on the information you gave them.

Denise: Well, after our counseling session with you, we talked everything out and decided to have another child, and, -

Zeke: we had a girl—Elizabeth—a beautiful girl.

Denise: and we found out she has Sickle Cell Disease . . .

Zeke: but we knew the risks.

Denise: It's hard sometimes . . . but when I look at her I know we made the right choice. Thanks for helping us.

Because this visitor gave the clients the essential information, they are grateful. Conversely, if the visitor does not address the couple's principal concerns, the couple reacts with anger or frustration.

Testing Sickle Cell

Sickle Cell has proven to be a popular exhibit at the Museum of Science and Industry in Chicago. We were told that it's difficult to get museum-goers to spend even two minutes with a typical exhibit. But we've found that some children stay for 30 minutes with Sickle Cell and that patrons often find themselves waiting in line to use it. By using the idea of goal-directed learning, we made what was an initially passive idea (to get information about Sickle Cell disease into the minds of the general public) into an active experience and, as we had hoped, people like it.

We have also done some formal testing of Sickle Cell and found the results encouraging (Bell, Bareiss, & Beckwith, 1993). The most obvious result of using Sickle Cell was, simply put, the users felt they knew more after using the system. They could answer more questions about the condition and they had fewer misconceptions.

Learning begins with a goal, even in a science museum. Rather than teach a set of decontextualized facts about genetics, Sickle Cell Counselor gives people a compelling reason to explore the underlying knowledge. The context to the user, counseling, is used as a framework from which users can hang newly acquired concepts. This framework serves as a point of integration. All the coaching and instruction the user is given is in service of the counseling task. Because users are eager to help their "clients," they want to learn what they can to give better advice. To teach counseling per se was not our primary aim. But we constructed a program where completing the counseling task meant acquiring the skills we wanted people to learn. This is the principle behind goal-directed learning. The users' goals serve to organize their experience.

The Challenge in Sickle Cell

The challenge for software designers is to figure out how to find active learning regardless of the situation. As is evident in the Sickle Cell Counselor, the user is presented with a challenging problem to capture his or her natural motivation to learn. This reinforces the idea that learning begins with a goal. Rather than teach a set of decontextualized facts about genetics, Sickle Cell Counselor gives people a compelling reason to explore the underlying knowledge. Because users are eager to help their "clients," they want to learn what they can to give better advice. This is the idea behind goal-directed learning. The users' goals serve to organize their experience.

Broadcast News

One of the most comprehensive programs built by ILS to date, incorporating many of the teaching methods discussed in this book, is Broadcast News. This program teaches high school students about social studies topics, such as political science, international affairs, economics, and current events by inviting them to produce their own TV news show. Students using this program work with real news sources for a day in the recent past. The stories engage students in important social studies issues. The tasks the students perform require them to understand those issues. Subject-matter experts are available to answer the students' questions about the stories, and to challenge decisions the students make.

Broadcast News supplies students with all the tools and materials needed to put together a news show. These include the following production facilities, which closely mimic those typically available to a real local news show:

- facilities for editing text and video;
- wire service copy and video feed;
- background material, including old articles and newscasts, and a library of reference works; and
- a teleprompter, video camera, and computer-controlled VCR, which allow students to anchor the show they develop, and produce a tape of it.

Learning with Broadcast News

Students who use Broadcast News learn something about journalism, but that's not the point of the program. The point is to use journalism as a vehicle for teaching about the content of the news. The nightly news touches on a broad range of important topics, but one doesn't necessarily learn much simply by watching the show, because the activity of watching is too passive. Nothing about the task of watching a news show challenges the viewer to acquire background he doesn't already have. Furthermore, it is not easy to get the background material even if one is motivated to do so. Nothing encourages the viewer to question the producer's presentation, or to think about what the important issues are.

However, the task of creating a news show is quite different. When students are actually developing a story, they do have to acquire essential background information. When reviewing a rough draft of a story, students are forced to think about the story to do a good job. Are the facts reported in the story accurate? Is the story clear? Is the story biased? Are the issues covered really the most important ones? Is anything important left out? These are the kinds of questions the journalism task requires students to think about and that lead them to want to know news content.

Using Broadcast News

Putting together a real news show requires a team of people, including producers, writers, video editors, and anchors. When students put together a news show in Broadcast News, they play one or more of these roles. The roles not played by the students are played by the computer.

In the earliest sessions, students are given very limited roles; the computer does almost everything. As students become comfortable with the tasks, their responsibilities are increased. Eventually the students take over all aspects of the newscast, including selecting which stories to put on the air, sequencing the stories in the show, writing them, and finally anchoring them. This gentle phasing in of responsibilities teaches students about the various challenges of journalism, so that the mechanics of the job do not distract from the students' main focus, which is learning about the subjects of the stories.

The easiest job is anchoring. The only ability anchors require is the ability to read. They don't really even need to understand what they are reading. Playing the anchor role may not be very educational, but it is fun, because the anchor gets to appear on camera. Therefore, every session ends with one student anchoring the program he or she has helped produce. During this phase the computer acts as teleprompter. A camera, connected to a computer-controlled VCR, records the student reading the story. By pressing the mouse, the student can play the video that has been selected to go with the story. By the end of each session the student/anchor has a tape of the broadcast. This is a big motivator for teenagers who have grown up in the TV age. Students can compare their shows with those of friends and can take the tape home to show to their families.

A Session with Broadcast News

During a student's first few sessions with Broadcast News, he plays the role of assistant producer, as well as anchor. The computer, acting in the role of executive producer, chooses the stories for that day's broadcast, assigns the stories to writers (a role also played by the computer at this level), and edits all the stories except one. The student's job as assistant producer is to edit the story the executive producer "doesn't have time to edit." This is usually the lead story for the day. In the case we present here, the lead story is the assassination of Rajiv Ghandi, on May 21, 1991.

The main screen for the assistant producer job is depicted in Fig. 10.4. The system presents the student with a rough draft of the story, including markers that represent when video will be shown during the reading of the story. The simulation components of the program allow the student to read the source material upon which the story was based, to watch the video clips the "writers" have selected, and to request changes to elements of the story. The teaching components of the system present the student with appropriate advice and allow the student to explore questions about elements of the story.

The rough drafts the students are given are carefully constructed to present appropriate challenges. The curriculum designers who develop the rough drafts intentionally place errors and biases into the stories, leave important things out, choose confusing video, and so on. The point is to

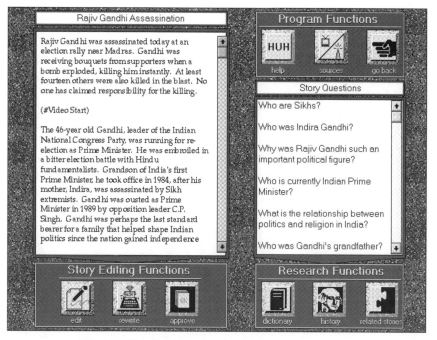

FIG. 10.4. Your first job in Broadcast News is to edit a story.

require the student to notice these problems and fix them in order to produce a good broadcast.

The student generally starts by reading the story left by the executive producer. The first sentence of the story is: Rajiv Gandhi was assassinated today at an election rally near Madras. The average secondary-school student does not understand this sentence when he first reads it. Many students do not know who Rajiv Gandhi was or where Madras is. Some do not know what an assassination is.

A student who does not understand what the story is about may click on the "history" button. This brings up a learning-by-exploring teaching module that offers a list of general background questions about the story as a whole. One such question in this case is "What makes this story newsworthy?" Selecting this question brings up video of our expert journalist explaining that Gandhi was a world leader and that news is the reporting of change, such as the death of a world leader (Fig. 10.5). At the same time the learning-by-exploring module presents the students with a list of potential follow-up questions.

Because a student who hears this answer still will not have much detail about exactly who Gandhi was, he may wish to ask a more specific question. If the student selects a range of text, the system will bring up a set of questions related to things mentioned in the selected text. If the student

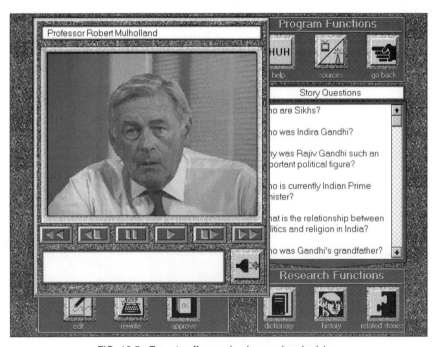

FIG. 10.5. Experts offer you background and advice.

selects the first sentence in the story, the system will bring up a set of questions about Gandhi, Madras, and so on. If he clicks on the question "Who was Rajiv Gandhi?", the student sees a video clip of a political scientist telling exactly who Gandhi was. Again, with the answer comes a new list of follow-up questions. An important advantage of Broadcast News over the typical classroom lecture setup is that a student can stop the video at any point to ask a follow-up question.

When a student listens to a lecture in a large class, he is in a bind if the teacher refers to things that the student doesn't know about; the only way for the student to get an explanation is to interrupt the teacher, exposing his ignorance to the rest of the class. Other students who already know the answer to the student's questions may get bored or may ridicule the student who makes the query.

In Broadcast News, interrupting with follow-up questions is easy and private. For instance, when our political scientist describes Ghandi as a Prime Minister, students who don't know exactly what a Prime Minister is can stop the political scientist immediately to ask the follow-up question: What is a Prime Minister? While the expert suspends his first answer to answer the follow-up, the student can at any time suspend *that* answer to ask a further follow-up, such as, "How is this different from being President of the United States?" Or the student can return at any time to hear the rest of the original, suspended answer.

When the Learning-by-Exploring module brings up a political scientist who responds to this question by explaining how a parliamentary system of government works, the student listens with a very different ear compared to how he might typically listen to a lecture. Consider the difference between, on the one hand, listening to a long lecture about different forms of government around the world, and, on the other hand, listening to a small piece of that lecture that answers a specific question you just asked because you need to know the answer to complete an interesting task. That difference is the essence of what goal-directed teaching is about.

Once the student has read and understood the story, usually with the help of the experts, he is ready to consider any changes he may wish to make. For example, a student who did not know who Gandhi was may wish to include Gandhi's title in the first sentence, so that viewers do not experience the same confusion the student did. To make changes to the text, the student would select the sentence and click on the edit button. He is then presented with the following options for a rewrite:

- correct error
- change emphasis
- add detail
- delete detail

None of the choices is intended to be *right* or *wrong* in any absolute sense. Different students will make different choices, just as different TV stations make different choices. The point is not to test the student to see if he can come up with the right answer, but rather to force him to think about the issues, and to make a decision. Of course, the fact that there is no definitive right answer does not mean the experts do not have their preferences. If the student opts for lots of gory detail about the method of assassination, the political scientist might object, saying, for example, "I think the details of the assassination are less important than what this means for the future of Indian democracy."

But the student need not agree with or accept the advice given by any particular expert. That the expert may object doesn't mean the student has made the wrong choice. Often the student will find that the experts have incompatible opinions. The student may get challenged no matter what choice he makes. The point of the challenges is to make sure the student thinks about what the important issues are and makes an informed decision.

After the student "marks up" a change, the text is marked in red until the student sends the story to the writer to have his marked changes executed. Students may, at any time, send the marked text to the writer for a rewrite. The text returns with all changes made as directed.

After receiving the rewritten text, students may make more editing changes, do more researching, or decide the story is ready for broadcast. To implement this final option, students select the "approve" button. Doing so calls up a case-based teaching module that analyzes the story and suggests potential problems. This module, like the learning-by-exploring module, uses videos of experts to comment on the story. For example, in this case, the expert makes a comment about the terms "Sikhs" and "Hindu Fundamentalists." He tells the student that many American viewers will not be familiar with these terms and might be confused by them. The student may choose either to ignore this comment and approve the story for broadcast or return to the story, ask the experts about these terms, and edit the text before approving the story for broadcast.

If the student needs additional background information to understand the issues related to the story he is putting together, the learning-by-exploring module gives him an on-line multimedia research library. It contains background stories from old news shows, as well as encyclopedia-like entries on the various people, countries, and institutions mentioned in the stories. A special section of the library includes evening news shows from the week prior to the current news day.

After the student gives final approval to a story, the educational component of the session is essentially over, but the glamour component of anchoring remains. The program acts as a teleprompter and editing booth. The student reads the story as the text rolls by. A camera/recorder setup con-

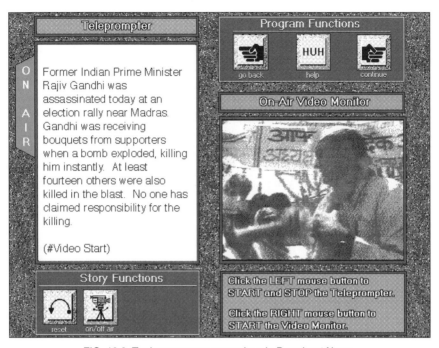

FIG. 10.6. Taping your own news show in Broadcast News.

trolled by the computer records the student and lays down the appropriate video footage (Fig. 10.6). After anchoring the broadcast the student can watch his broadcast and then, for comparison, can watch what NBC put on that night. The comparison between what the network put together and what various students put together is a good starting point for a class discussion.

Once the student masters the role of assistant producer over a series of sessions, he can move up to executive producer. The executive producer performs all the tasks the assistant producer performs (some can be delegated) and, in addition, must select which of the many stories that come over the wire services belong in the show, what order to put them in, and how much time to devote to each. This forces the student to make tough decisions about which issues are important. Here again, the experts will challenge the student's decisions. For instance, most secondary-school children find little interest in stories about aging or taxes. When they leave out these stories, it opens up a good opportunity for the experts to explain why these issues are important to adults.

After using the program for a while, students often get tired of having to get rewrites from the computer. During the most advanced sessions, the program allows the students to write and rewrite stories themselves. This gives the student more flexibility in putting the story together, but it greatly limits the amount of feedback the experts can give, because the program cannot interpret the natural-language text the student writes.

Teaching Methods in Broadcast News

Broadcast News brings together four separate teaching architectures. Although each of these architectures teaches students something different, from the student's point of view, they merge together seamlessly under the umbrella of goal-directed learning. All the student knows is that he wants to put together a news show, and the disparate elements of the program work together to help him.

The four teaching architectures Broadcast News uses are:

- learning by doing, as students learn journalism by being journalists;
- incidental learning, as students pick up historical facts along the way;
- learning by exploring, as students sit back and ask questions about the story they are constructing; and
- case-based teaching, as expert coaches provide advice.

Not only does Broadcast News use these teaching methods when they are appropriate; it satisfies a crucially important requisite for what education should be: Fun. Children like the idea of putting together their own news show. We believe it is a better way to teach history and current events than most of the methods now in practice in high school.

Don't Force Knowledge on Students

Goal-directed learning is a very straightforward concept. Take students' actual goals, and let all instruction be in service of giving them the skills to achieve those goals. Don't force on them anything that won't help them achieve their goals or that they don't want to know. This concept leads to a set of principles that guide the construction of learning environments.

When you have a clear idea of what you will do with knowledge, you will become motivated to learn. If you decided to build a house by yourself, you would quickly discover that you needed to know something about architecture, about strength of materials, about basic physics and geometry, a little mathematics, a lot of government regulations, principles of design, electricity, water, and a whole lot more.

Goal-directed courses that have intrinsic importance to students can cover large ranges of materials and go on for very long time periods. This might, of course, create havoc in the regimented schedule of the school system, but havoc may be what is needed to stimulate changes.

Principles of Quality Software

From our experiences building the programs described in this book and others like them, we have learned a core set of principles about how to design quality educational software. Interestingly enough, these principles turn out not to be specific to software but to pertain to teaching in general. As you read them, ask yourself whether you would have enjoyed school more and gotten more from it if it had followed these principles:

Principle 1. Learn by Doing: Learning should center on a task. The task should require those skills or knowledge we want to teach. The task should be challenging, but within the student's ability.

Principle 2. Problems, Then Instruction: Students respond best to instruction when they see how what they are told relates to problems with which they are struggling. Instruction must clearly and directly address the real needs of students.

Principle 3. Tell Good Stories: Students respond to well-told stories. Educational software must contain interesting cases and tell them when and only when they relate to students' problems.

Principle 4. Power to the Students: Students should be in control of the educational process. Software may recommend what path to take, but students should always be able to stray from it to pursue their own interests.

Principle 5. Provide a Safe Place to Fail: Reality is not always the best teacher. In some situations, it is unrealistic or dangerous to allow novices to practice in real situations. Computers can offer novices realistic simulations that provide a safe environment in which to make and learn from mistakes.

Principle 6. Navigation to Answers: Software that instructs but does not let students ask questions removes control from students' hands. Students should be able to ask questions of the educational software they are using and expect reasonable replies. Often, however, students do not know what question to ask. In this case, it should be possible for students to navigate through an information base to easily discover what is there.

Principle 7. The Software is the Test: Teachers want to know how much their students have learned. This is a reasonable goal, but, unfortunately, it usually leads to a multiple-choice test. Because the software we are talking about enables students to do certain things, or to discover certain answers, the test is in whether the student demonstrates a new ability or makes a discovery. As long as the program can monitor what the student has been doing, no test is necessary. Instead, software can be thought of as having various levels of achievement and various gates that have to be opened to get to the next level. To reach a given level, the student must have been able to do the tasks leading to that level. No explicit tests need ever be given if the software has been correctly designed.

Principle 8. Find the Fun: Learning should be fun. An instructional designer's single most important job is to make learning fun. No matter how well educational software is designed, if it is not fun, it will not work well.

Educational Software Now!

Did you ever wonder why there hasn't been more good software for kids? It turns out that, from an economic point of view, it is not really in anyone's interest to build good software for kids, at least not now. There are two routes that the producers of educational software have had to market their wares. One has been to team with textbook publishers. The other is to sell "software titles" through retail outlets. Neither route enables software producers to get paid to develop the breadth of software we need. Let's consider each in turn.

Who Wants Educational Change?

Who really wants educational change? Not the book publishers. They are more than happy to continue in the old way. They sell textbooks to schools and, as long as those books sell, they have no reason to change them. Textbooks are very expensive to write. So even if a textbook was shown to be wrong in some way, it is not changed unless some powerful school system, such as Texas or California, demands the change. But these states, although they are concerned about education, are often more sharply concerned about political correctness or whether textbooks mention fast food, or if the appropriate drug propaganda is present, than they are in learning theory. School boards are political entities after all.

When the educational software business began in earnest in the early 1980s, the book publishers were the first ones in. Why? They were not there because they cared about the new technology or the educational possibilities. They were there because they were concerned about protecting their textbooks. They commissioned software from educational software companies that were trying hard to stay in business. Essentially, all they did was enhance the existing textbooks, pointing students back to the book as often as possible. Alternatives to the books were not considered.

This model didn't create very innovative software, of course. It was responsible for creating drill-and-practice software and games based upon the textbooks sold by those same publishers. Schools, as a result, ended up getting stranded with out-of-date computers and irrelevant software. No wonder the educational community is down on computers.

The Limits of "Software Titles"

Educational software developers who did not sign up with textbook companies were left to peddle their own software. To do this, they turned to bookstores and software stores that sold "software titles." This is an important expression because it makes clear how these "titles" had to be marketed. Software publishers began to look for "blockbuster titles," that is, the piece of educational software that would sell millions of copies, like "Typing Tutor" or "Where in the World is Carmen San Diego?" Although these programs are nice enough at what they do, the blockbuster concept is quite an unfortunate model for education. Its effect is that no software developer can work on more than a few great titles. But how much instruction can be provided by a great title? 1 hour? 2?

One or 2 hours at $50 a title (the prices have dropped some, but not much) is not going to change the world. Here and there software will be created. It might even be good software that will entertain a child at home for a while, or provide an hour off from the tedium of the classroom. Still, nothing important can change from the creation of such bits and pieces. Wholesale production of software is needed.

Software for Curricula

Why don't the computer companies develop good educational software? The big hardware companies, IBM and Apple, have survived for years on the idea that all they had to do was make and sell computers; the programs for those computers would be developed by someone else. This model seems to have worked pretty well for them until recently.

How about the software companies? Ever since computers began to move out of the research lab, there have been companies devoted to building software for them. The large software companies build software to help other businesses run payroll systems, do billing, manage inventory, and so on. Smaller companies, often people working out of their homes, spring up to build niche business applications, such as software to run a dentist's office or yet another neat computer game.

The problem with these models for us is that neither will suffice to generate large-scale, high-quality educational software. Such software is out of the league of the lone developer working in the basement. Such software is as costly to build as the payroll systems the large software houses sell. However, the customers for these systems are other large companies that can afford to pay plenty for them. Schools cannot afford to pay large amounts for educational software. Neither can parents afford the really large variety of software required to provide a comprehensive library for their children. So hardware manufacturers and software developers are left waiting for a revolution that will not naturally occur.

Someone has to care enough to start this industry. Eventually there will be high-quality educational software in the home and in the schools. It will get developed when people who care about education get together with people who know about learning and people who know how to develop software. For now, we will have to watch as those educational software projects that are commercially viable for one reason or another get built, first in the area of business training and then in the area of blockbusters for kids and home.

Eventually, this new industry will be created, when it is in someone's interest to do it. For now, it is only in the children's interest.

How Will The Software Get Built?

If the markets will not naturally produce the educational software required to revamp the system, how do we propose that it get built?

For one thing, business training software will get built as a matter of course. Unlike software for children, software that helps businesses educate their employees offers savings to customers that can afford to invest to realize them.

But although training software may lead the way, the software for children still needs to be developed. This is a social problem and solving it will require society (in the form of government) to step in.

The role of labs like ILS goes beyond providing examples of what good software can look like. Although research labs cannot produce the required software by themselves, they can produce tools that make it easy to clone the kinds of programs they construct. In some cases, though yet not in enough, they can even make tools simple enough to use to enable teachers working on their own to produce useful applications, thereby allowing some good educational software to get produced without big investments and large project teams.

ILS and Real World Savings

Businesses find training to be an enormous expense. But by investing in good training software, they can cut that expense dramatically. To see this in action, let's consider an example.

Andersen Consulting devotes a great amount of resources towards training their employees; nearly 7% of payroll in recent years. They do so much training that it has been worth their while to purchase a defunct college in the suburbs of Chicago and convert it into a dedicated training center. Every year, they send thousands of employees from around the world to courses at this center. One of the most widely attended courses, Business Practices School, is annually attended by over 4,000 consultants. This school provides a five-day overview of business practice issues important to Andersen and their clients. Each consultant who takes the course needs to spend between 60 and 80 hours in self-guided training before even beginning the five days of formal classes in Chicago.

Andersen recognized the large expenditures they were making for this course and decided to ask the ILS, of which they are the founding sponsor, for help. ILS helped convert the Business Practices School into an interactive computer-based training course. This conversion halved the time the course required while improving its quality. This change has not only saved Andersen over $10 million in travel, lodging, teaching, and billable time lost from the time spent away from client sites but has helped business lessons to be delivered at a more individual level. By replacing the lecture-based instruction with educational software that gives students challenging goals and allows them to control their learning, Andersen has enabled its consultants to learn the underlying information more thoroughly and retain it better.

The Software We Need

Entire curricula need to be created in software that represent alternatives to the existing curricula now in place in the schools. Doing this entails creating hundreds of hours of software just for one subject for one age group. Clearly, this is extremely expensive and will not happen in today's commercial environment. The book publishers could spend that kind of money, but it is not clear why they would. There probably is a very profitable business in educational software in the long run, but that is only probable—there are hardly any guarantees. In any case, such a business would be at the expense of the existing textbook business, a prospect unlikely to excite a textbook publisher.

Clearly, the government has to intervene. The total amount necessary to build all the curricula for all the grades in software may well be about a billion dollars. It would be a billion dollars well spent, an investment in our future, which is more than you can say for many other similar-sized government expenditures.

The Need for Tools

Reforming the educational system is clearly a vast task. Just as clearly, ILS, working on its own, will not be able to produce the volume of software that we think will be required. Whereas ILS develops self-contained application systems like those I have shown you, a critical part of our mission is the development of software tools that will vastly shorten the time it takes to create similar applications in the future, and that will make it possible for those with modest technical expertise to create these applications.

Building these applications requires a variety of tools. We are currently developing six broad categories of tools.

1. Simulation-Based Learning-by-Doing Tools. ILS is developing tools that will enable people to "learn by doing" by placing them within simulated situations that replicate real-world environments. Building such simulations is a daunting task. To provide realistic simulations of social and physical environments, it is necessary to have tools that facilitate the creation of such environments.

2. Knowledge Organization and Retrieval Tools.   The potential of video in informational and teaching programs has barely been tapped. Libraries of short video clips in which experts answer questions or tell their favorite "war stories" can serve many important functions, for example, as corporate memories, or as teaching archives that make experts available on an as-needed basis. Information in such a video database can add to other information in the database, thus facilitating retrieval of opposing points of view, answers to follow-up questions, historical background, simplifications, and amplifications of the viewed material. To build such systems, we need tools that can help organize the massive amounts of video, textual, and machine-readable data required.

3. Teaching Tools.   There are many ways to teach, each of which has its own strengths and weaknesses in various situations. ILS is creating tools that will support different teaching methods that are appropriate in different contexts. For example, the existence of a large case library provides an opportunity for case-based teaching, whereas a detailed domain simulation supports simulation-based learning-by-doing. Further, ILS is creating tools that help determine which teaching method is appropriate in a student's current context. All our teaching tools are intended to help educational software designers integrate effective, diverse teaching into the learning environments they are creating.

4. Tools to Enhance Thinking.   The computer has the power to serve as a real thinking aid by asking pertinent questions that help the user clarify his thoughts. We can use this power as the basis for systems that teach thinking skills by having the computer pose problems in the user's domain of interest and help him work out solutions to those problems, illustrating in the process important ideas about thinking and problem solving in general.

5. Interaction Tools.   There are many ways to enhance the power of teaching programs that have nothing to do with teaching per se but instead facilitate the process of interacting with a computer generally. The ILS Button Pad, which provides a standard set of buttons students can use to put themselves in control of their software, is one example. Other examples are graphic tools that help produce interface designs that aid understanding or natural language-processing tools that endow software programs with a limited ability to understand English.

6. Course Creation Meta-tools.   We hope to enable people whose job it is to create educational software for business or for schools to do their job better and with less need for computer expertise or for solid grounding in a theory of learning. We want to give these designers tools that will let them build educationally and computationally sound programs by: (a) asking relevant questions about the domain to be covered and suggesting designs, (b) providing system prototypes that can be used as frameworks for the construction of new instructional programs, and (c) providing tools to help nonprogrammers customize existing software.

Through such tools, we hope to create a new generation of powerful instructional design methodologies. These tools can take advantage of the knowledge that teachers have by helping teachers themselves create new software.

11

Goal-Based Scenarios and the Open Curriculum

DIFFICULT CURRICULUM

Knowing, learning, and teaching are intimately connected. This linkage would seem obvious. Yet, for something so obvious, it has been long over-looked. One would think that the way schools teach would be in accordance with the way children naturally learn. But this seems to be an idea whose time has not yet come. Instead of beginning with how children learn, schools typically start with an externally imposed curriculum of what students should know. Students are taught according to the structure of that curriculum rather than according to the structure of natural learning. This approach is strange because the externally imposed curriculum ignores the natural interests of children and so eliminates the children's motivation. Instead of getting a child to really care about Lincoln, we tell him he has to know about Lincoln for a test. What if we made knowing about Lincoln crucial to some goal the child already had? Can we do this? We can if we ask the student to be Lincoln for a few days in a simulated docudrama, for example, or if we ask him to decide on some current issue that concerns him by citing Lincoln. Leveraging natural learning means finding a way for the child to want to know what you want him to know.

DEVELOPMENT OF CURRENT EDUCATIONAL MODELS

Our concept of what it means to be educated stems from a time when one could legitimately expect of an educated person that he had read all the books in the world. When these books were not easily found or purchased, the concept of lecturing from them made sense. Attempts to make school-rooms that would benefit the masses have always taken their cue from the model of education implied by small numbers of great books and not enough copies of them. In this model, the job of the teacher was to distill the books he had himself read into a form that would be palatable to his students. The job of the curriculum designer was to decide which books were to be covered. This job became more difficult with the addition of more books, but, for the most part, most books that have appeared in the 20th century have been ignored by these curriculum masters.

Schooling today is an attempt to make minischolars out of students by giving them doses of what was meant by scholarship in the 18th and 19th centuries. The theory of knowledge implicit here is that the educated person knows something about all the great books. This idea works when there aren't that many books in print (or at least it seems to work). But in an age when no one could possibly know something from every book that has been written, when there are enough books to go around, and when there are so many others forms of knowledge available to students, these ideas are outmoded. We must look to concepts that relate to today's world, one where there's so much to know that it is likely that students will have to direct their own education out of practical necessity.

What Kinds of Things Are There to Know?

If the goal of school is to get students to know things, then we need to understand something about what knowledge looks like. What kinds of knowledge are there?

Consider the relationship between the following sentences:

- I know that Sacramento is the capital of California.
- I know Mary.
- I know how to run for office in the United States.
- I know how to repair diesel engines.
- I know how to hit a baseball.
- I know a funny story about President Carter.

What it means to "know" is different in each of these sentences. Knowl-edge can be broken down into distinct types: facts (Sacramento, Mary's appearance), cases (the stories we know), skills (engine repair, batting), and processes (running for office). We often get confused when talking about what we know because it is difficult to say exactly what it is we know about cases, skills, and processes. We often end up concentrating on facts because it's easy to state the facts we know.

In real life, however, it's almost always more important to know cases, skills, and processes than it is to know facts, but these types of knowledge are typically left out of accounts of what we want children to know. Why? Because such things are not easily assessed.

We must be careful not to avoid teaching kinds of knowledge because they are difficult to assess. Even a quick look at today's system shows that it overemphasizes facts, underemphasizes skills, and grossly neglects such processes as communication and human relations.

What Types of Knowledge to Teach

Here are some things we would like adults to know, and therefore children to learn:

Skills (scriptlets): People who are very skilled at something often employ complex strategies, which are, in essence, combinations of scriptlets, packaged so that the understanding of how they fit together gives their user the reputed skill.

Cases: A case is a story about one or more events that comprise a whole. Cases typically serve to illustrate points about how to behave or how the world works. Each point illustrated by a case is usually of some larger significance; that is, it can be generalized to other situations. Sometimes, however, cases are simply used as reference points that are part of the common culture. The Battle of Gettysburg is a case. It might be used to illustrate one or more particular military points, or to tell us something about history, or it might simply be used as an example of something all Americans know about. Cases can typically be described from many points of view.

Processes: A process is a high-level skill we feel is especially important; they tend to have a very abstract nature. The decision to call X a process and Y a skill is inherently political because it is based on what one feels the school system should proactively support in the curriculum. The school system can successfully pursue only a few skills proactively; those we believe the school system should select are processes. Given that one can effectively pursue only a few processes, it makes sense to pick very high-level ones. The three processes we concentrate on are communications, human relations, and reasoning.

Types of Knowledge Not to Teach

Facts should be strikingly absent from any list of the types of knowledge we should teach students. Why? Because students will learn the facts they need when they need them. We do not have to teach students facts. When the schools do take the teaching of facts as a goal and teach them in isolation, students do not usefully learn them anyway.

Distorted Facts

Most facts are oversimplifications of events that, when learned as facts, lose all their interesting properties. Here for example is a "fact" that was a standard part of the curriculum in our schools throughout the 1950s and 1960s: Columbus discovered America in 1492. It is a fact that every school-child was taught and that most graduates of our schools remember. But the truth of this statement has become quite controversial recently, and it is by no means clear that this "fact" is really a fact at all. In any case, it is not the date of Columbus' voyage that is the thing worth learning about Columbus. What really matters are the concepts of invasion, religious toleration, warring empires, subjugation of weak peoples by strong people, and the establishment of colonies in the early years of U.S. history.

Or consider a fact that isn't so controversial: The Continental Congress signed the Declaration of Independence on July 4, 1776. Actually, this fact isn't quite true either. On July 2, 1776, Congress approved Richard Lee's recommendation for independence. On July 4, 1776, the Declaration was approved by John Hancock, President of Congress, who ordered that it be printed up on parchment for signatures. The Declaration of Independence was signed on August 2. A few who were not present then added their signatures later.

What difference does it make when either of these events took place? What matters is how they intertwine with the events that led up to them, and the consequences they have had for our lives. There may well be much controversy about Columbus' discovery of America, but there is less controversy over the fact that Columbus' act opened a chapter in the history of the world that had important ramifications. The Declaration of Independence has had a great effect in history, and it is nice the United States has an official birthday, but neither of these ideas is well represented by concern over any fact that a student might or might not know. Ideas matter more than facts.

The meat of history lies in understanding the motives and behavior of human beings, what they have done, the effects of their actions, and the consequences for the future.

What a Course Should Do

Education should have a pragmatic purpose. Education ought to be about building learners' abilities to do useful things. What is important to learn is whatever helps learners do things that they want to do or that they can be induced to want to do. So detailing the knowledge students need to have entails first detailing the things students should know how to do and then explaining what knowledge will be useful in each case.

Depending on an individual's situation and goals, there are many things that might be worth learning. To give a very detailed prescription for what knowledge a student should acquire, we must take into account that not every child will need or want to do the same things. A curriculum must therefore be individualized. It must be built around an understanding of what situations a particular learner might want to be in, or might have to be in later in life, and what abilities he will require in those situations.

Nevertheless, for many people the notion of mandating the same knowledge for every student is appealing. Building lists of facts that one claims everyone should know is relatively simple to do. Furthermore, there is the attraction of providing standards that can be easily measured. But from the perspective of the teacher and the student, this approach spells trouble. Each mandated bit of knowledge removes more local control and drives the system toward fixed curricula and standardized tests, which not only diminishes teacher flexibility but also student choice, and, therefore, student interest and initiative.

Better Courses

Schools are full of courses that constitute what the academic authorities feel students must learn to be "qualified" in a given subject. The French curriculum covers certain aspects of French language, culture, and history as deemed appropriate by the designers of that curriculum. When colleges say they require students to complete the math curriculum, they mean that they require study in certain particular aspects of mathematics, to be studied over the course of a certain number of years, with certain tests at the end. There is some variation in these curricula from school to school, of course, but not all that much, especially when standardized tests loom at the end of the year.

Courses, however, ought to be no more than a collection of scriptlets to be acquired; that is, if real knowledge comes from doing, and scriptlets are what are acquired in doing, then any course should be no more than, and no less than, a set of experiences that allow students to acquire a scriptlet in the natural way scriptlets are acquired; that is, by practice.

Of course, there is the issue of motivation. No one will learn a scriptlet, much less practice one, unless there is real motivation to drive what may be real work. Programming your VCR or sending e-mail are not intrinsically rewarding activities. Learning to do them comes from the results they bring. This means, to a course designer, that the results they bring need to be brought to the fore, serving as real motivation to acquire the scriptlet.

To motivate a student to learn a scriptlet, one of three things needs to be true. Either the student must find the result of the scriptlet to be intrinsically rewarding, or the scriptlet must be part of a package of scriptlets that are intrinsically rewarding.

An example of a scriptlet that stands alone and is intrinsically rewarding is the ability to use a cash station machine. Most scriptlets, however, are not so rewarding when considered by themselves. No one would sit still for a lesson dedicated to signing credit card slips, for example.

Often, however, scriptlets can be grouped together to accomplish a goal, although not one of them would naturally stand alone. Driving a car is a collection of scriptlets, including engine starting, braking, and lane changing. Playing baseball is a collection of scriptlets, including fielding a ground ball to your left, hitting the curve ball, or sliding. People don't do these sorts of activities (unless they are practicing) in the absence of a real need to do so. Nevertheless, all of them take practice. Scriptlets that are part of packages must be taught within the context of those packages. We see why this matters later on.

Sometimes, however, scriptlets are not intrinsically interesting either taken by themselves or in some natural package of scriptlets. We might all agree, for example, that being able to calculate square footage of an area is a useful skill that any adult might need. Schools would normally place such instruction in a course of mathematics. But I am arguing that the concept of scriptlet makes clear that there should not be any courses in mathematics (especially not in the early years of school). Rather, mathematics scriptlets (of which the calculation of square footage is one) need to be taught in a meaningful curriculum. Square-footage calculation is not intrinsically rewarding, nor is it a part of a package of scriptlets that depend on each other. It is a quite independent scriptlet that no one wants to learn for its own sake, and it presents a serious motivation problem.

If we believe that scriptlets like calculating square footage are indeed important, we must figure out how to devise a curriculum that will make learning them rewarding. The answer to this conundrum is, as usual, goals. To motivate students to learn a scriptlet, we can give them a goal that interests them and requires them to know the scriptlet. For example, we might embed learning how to calculate square footage within an attempt to plan and build a house. In such a curriculum, this calculation would need to be made many times and would be learned in a natural way. If no situation containing a particular scriptlet can be found that is rewarding for the student, it is reasonable to assume that this scriptlet isn't all that important for the student to learn.

The same is true in business. If we determine that reading a financial report (a package of scriptlets) is important to know, we must find a context in which that knowledge matters (i.e., whether to approve a loan to a business). For instance, giving students a decision to make in which the various scriptlets in reading a financial report come into play can make all the difference between students really acquiring the relevant scriptlets and their simply learning them to pass a test. One thing is important to remember here. It is not simply a question of finding the context in which the scriptlets come into play; they must come into play quite often. Practice is a very important part of scriptlet acquisition. This does not mean repetition of the same scriptlet again and again as is done in drill and practice situations in school. Rather, it means finding repeated situations in the curriculum in which the same scriptlet is of use so that the practice does not seem like practice. If you want someone to become a good driver, the issue is not having him drive in circles but giving him a job that requires repeated driving in a nonartificial way.

A course, then, ought to provide a means by which scriptlets can be acquired even if the scriptlets (or packages of scriptlets) themselves are not intrinsically rewarding. The situation must be structured so that students can see how and why they need each scriptlet.

Facts, Subjects, and Domains

Schools typically organize courses around subjects like art or mathematics. Why is this? It turns out that it's not because that's what is best for students. It is just what is best for the scholars who sit at the peak of the academic pyramid.

A subject is a collection of similar skills, cases, and facts that have been grouped together as an object of study. Subjects are defined by two things: a criteria for selecting which cases and facts serve as "subject matter," and a set of skills used to understand that subject matter. For example, physics is a subject that deals with interactions between matter and energy. "Doing physics" involves a set of skills that range from timing the swing of a pendulum to constructing particle accelerators. Academic researchers usually investigate a single specific class of subject matter. That's why subjects are a convenient mode of organization for them.

When teaching subjects, schools often make the mistake of separating the cases and facts (which are taught in lectures) from the skills (which are taught in labs). But teaching skills in labs apart from facts and cases tends to confuse students and kills off their motivation for learning the skill. Likewise, teaching subject matter apart from the relevant skills is a bad idea because students find it difficult to use the subject matter in a context different from that in which they learned it. Many view history, for example, as a set of cases and facts, but this view ignores the skills that history packages and drains the life and most of the value from it.

The problems with subjects, however, go far beyond the artificial distinction between lecture and lab. Subjects keep schools from effectively tying education into students' lives. Students do not experience the world as a set of subjects; they experience it as a set of domains. Some examples are politics, trucks, and animals.

A domain is, like a subject, a collection of skills, cases, and facts. Domains, however, have a much more eclectic mode of organization. Domains organize things according to how they tend to group everyday human experience. Domains have three interesting properties. First, domains tend to cut across subjects. Any of the aforementioned domains can be used as a vehicle to teach the subjects of physics, biology, or history. Second, peoples' goals and interests tend to flow along the lines of domains, not subjects. Third, apart from superficial differences, many domains tend to be quite similar to each other. This means they can serve as convenient mechanisms to negotiate between the interests students naturally have and the subjects educators want to teach. If schools want to tap their students' interests, it means they must forego the traditional lines of subjects and reorganize around domains.

Good and Bad Teaching

To see how a course can be organized around a domain instead of around traditional subjects, let's take an example. Consider learning about wine. I chose this subject both because I happen to know something about it and because it is an adult topic. As such, it is taught only to people who volunteer to take a class about it, often even paying money to attend.

Let's go to wine school. Not a real wine school, but a wine school where the instruction is done in a way similar to that done in today's schools or in many formal training programs.

Such a school would start our instruction in wine by splitting our time into four class periods and handing out a text for each. One would be a geography text, teaching about where Burgundy is, and where the wine-growing regions of the United States are; talking about Virginia and New York, and Texas wineries, for example. Next would be an agricultural text. It would teach about the various grapes, where which is grown and why, discussing soil conditions, climate issues, optimal grape-picking times, and so on. The third would be a text about the wine-making process—fermentation, storage, blending, and such would be included, as well as a discussion of the wine business, including who owns which chateaus and so on. The fourth would be a history text, answering such questions as: What kind of wine did the Romans drink? Who invented the cork stopper? How were issues of proper storage discovered? Why do the British prefer to drink Bordeaux? Which wine-growing regions of France were there in Roman times? On schedule, regardless of what we were doing, the school would rotate us from geography to agriculture to process to history and back again.

After instruction in these various areas, we would begin testing. What was the best year for Bordeaux in the last 30 years and why? Who owns Chateau Margaux? When did Mouton-Rothschild achieve first growth status? What grapes are grown in Oregon and why? What was the first French–American joint venture in wine growing? Can you identify the Chateauneuf du Pape region of the Rhone valley on a map?

What is wrong with this picture? Nothing. It is the way schools teach most subjects. Schools teach information that can be tested. How will they know if you have learned anything if they can't test you? Notice that no scriptlet (save those of memorization or reading) would really be involved at all in such a course. The goals of the student, which presumably had something to do with drinking wine rather than with the acquisition of facts, were ignored. In general, I don't think such a school would stay in business long. Students would vote with their feet and, if students in school or training programs could vote with their feet in the analogous situations, they most certainly would.

The school that would stay in business would not involve lectures about wine. Teaching about wine means drinking wine, not memorizing facts about wine. Drinking wine with some help from someone who knows more than you do means you will learn something. Being able to compare one wine to another, having many different experiences from which to generalize, means being able to create new cases (a particularly great wine would be remembered, for example) and new generalizations (seeing a common property that all wines from a certain place or year had in contrast to others from different places or years, for example).

Over time, a learner becomes curious about an ever wider range of issues. Learning entails, among other things, knowing what questions to ask. This means collecting enough cases or scriptlets that one can begin to wonder about them, to seek out new cases and refinements on scriptlets so new knowledge can be acquired. It is only in this context that the acquisition of facts is of any interest at all. Only when facts are sought after by a student for reasons of satisfaction of curiosity will those facts be usefully acquired.

As I became an experienced wine drinker, I began to wonder about Rhone wines, or the British preference for Bordeaux. (They used to own it.) I know about when Chateau Margaux changed hands because the quality has changed dramatically (down and then back up) the last two times that occurred, and I really like Chateau Margaux and need to know which years to avoid. I became curious enough to actually go visit the famous Chateau Margaux, but I would not have visited it if I hadn't liked the wine in the first place. A shrine isn't a shrine unless it means something to you. I know where Bordeaux is now because I had to find it on a map to get to Chateau Margaux. I drank Bordeaux for years without really knowing anymore about the region of Bordeaux than that it was in the southwest of France somewhere. All the new facts I learned would have been meaningless and easily forgotten had I simply been told them at the wrong time. The right time was when I wanted to know them, a time that could only have been determined by me and not a teacher.

Teachers often hope that their students will develop a lifelong curiosity about what they teach. Teaching by subject matter, though, stifles curiosity.

If we as educators want to grow students' interests, it helps if we start with things they care about in the first place. It helps even more if they can see directly how what they are learning furthers their goals.

Redesigning Courses

Much of the knowledge schools currently spoon-feed explicitly (and boringly) to students can be better taught implicitly within the context of helping students achieve goals they have selected for themselves. Given that we have mechanisms to deliver teaching on a "just-in-time" basis, we can construct courses that call for teaching to occur as the student discovers a "need to know."

Skill-centered, learner-guided courses, which we call Goal-Based Scenarios (GBSs), are quite different than what we see in today's educational system. We believe all courses should be designed in the form of GBSs. A successful GBS negotiates between the desires of students and course designers. For the student, a GBS offers a chance to pursue a clearly stated, interesting goal. For a course designer, however, a GBS is a vehicle to deliver a package of skills the designer wishes students to learn. The challenge for the course designer is to construct a course that will make the student interested in and capable of acquiring the package of skills as a natural consequence of trying to accomplish the course's motivating goal. As long as the goal is of interest to the student, and the skills needed to accomplish that goal are the skills the course designer wants students to have, we have a match, and thus a workable GBS.

Goal-Based Scenarios

To understand what a GBS is, it helps to know what a GBS contains. Figure 11.1 lays out the components of a GBS.

A designer of a GBS tends to look at it from the top down. What drives the design of a GBS is the set of target skills the designer wishes the student to gain in the GBS. A student, on the other hand, tends to look at a GBS from the bottom up. What drives a student is the context and structure of the activities the GBS offers.

Target Skills

Target skills are simply the set of skills the designer wishes to convey using the GBS as a vehicle. GBSs are always constructed around skills and processes. Facts and cases have no place in a GBS's pedagogical goals: Although they may be helpful to a student, they must not be taken as an end in and of themselves. Rather, they are taught as supporting material while the student is engaged in trying out the skills around which the GBS is built.

FIG. 11.1. The components of a Goal-Based Scenario.

Target skills must be explicitly broken down to a level at which they can be taught directly and demonstrated so that students may be held accountable for them. Processes are clearly not at this level. One cannot directly teach or assess "understanding," for example, but one can teach how to read a piece of text aloud and assess whether a student can do it.

The Mission

The mission of a goal-based scenario states the goal that students are trying to accomplish. It is the component that most immediately sets the tone and captures the nature of what they are attempting to accomplish. It is concerned with what students achieve, not how they achieve it. A number of GBSs may share the same mission, each using different cover stories, focuses, or operations to pursue it. For example, the mission of "build a house" may involve drawing up a set of blueprints, putting together a set of specifications, or actually assembling a house.

When creating a mission, the designer must realize that students need to be able to clearly judge when they have achieved the mission: to be able to recognize what achieving that goal will mean. A mission of "becoming honest" is not concrete enough to be meaningful. On the other hand, "creating a news broadcast" is a meaningful mission.

Further, students must understand that success in accomplishing the mission means they will be able to accomplish a general class of goals outside of the bounds of the specific GBS. This helps make clear the utility of the target skills. The mission must be one that allows the student to say, "If I can do this, I can also do all these other things," as opposed to, "OK, I did this and it was fun, but so what?" Learning how to drive by delivering packages in Manhattan, for example, allows a student to say, "If I can drive here, I can drive anywhere!" Navigating around cones in a parking lot might involve many of the same skills but does not convince students of the utility and robustness of their skills.

The Cover Story

The cover story, in conjunction with the mission, establishes the context of a GBS. The cover story defines the premise under which the student pursues the mission. It lays out the scenes where the action takes place, and other details that flesh out the GBS, making it more plausible and enticing to the student. The cover story is crucial in drawing the student into the task from the beginning. A boring cover story will lose the student for the entire GBS. It's just like reading a novel: If in the beginning the book sounds like it won't be fun to read, you probably won't want to keep reading to see if it gets better.

When designing a cover story, it is important to make the story coherent and realistic. The elements of the cover story should be thematically consistent with each other to avoid frustrating the student. If a given role would ordinarily include certain tools, and certain locales, the simulated setup should provide those tools, and the scenes of the GBS should include that locale. If a GBS is to tap into students' experiences, it must reproduce those aspects of the cover story that will make it real to them. If students pursue an implausible cover story, they will not be able to use commonsense knowledge they learn when they try to solve "similar" problems in the real world.

The only place in which it may be desirable to reduce realism is when providing teaching support to students. Once students assume the cover story, they should be provided with the support needed to do the job. When possible, it is important to provide help through materials that are consistent with the cover story. However, sometimes it is necessary to go outside the cover story to provide needed support. When teaching support simply cannot be smoothly integrated into the cover story, the support should be provided anyway.

The Focus

The Focus specifies what general class of task the student will learn through the GBS. We have identified four different broad classes of focus tasks. Here we use the example of a trucking GBS to illustrate the four classes:

- Design: Students might create their own truck company in the context of a simulation that places the company in a simulated economy.
- Diagnosis: Students might be hired as new chief executives of a troubled

trucking company and have the job of diagnosing and explaining the problems the company faces.

- Discovery: Students might have the task of improving the operations of their trucking company by comparing it to other trucking companies and discovering what they do that their company might learn from.
- Control: Students might run a simulated trucking company, making the day-to-day business decisions that arise.

It is important to note that using one of the preceding types within a GBS does not preclude using others. A GBS, depending on its level of complexity, might contain elements of all these types of focus. It is not crucial to identify which is the main focus. It is useful, however, to identify which focuses are used in the design of a GBS because each one raises a particular set of issues that needs to be considered. Additional focuses mean the designer needs to consider additional questions.

The Operations

Whereas the focus specifies the abstract nature of students' activities, the operations specify the concrete activities. Operations might include:

- issuing a directive in a social simulation
- answering a question
- using a tool to shape part of an artifact
- searching for a piece of information
- deciding between alternatives.

Because ultimately the student must learn the target skills of the GBS through these operations, a GBS designer must take care when selecting them. If the actions required on the part of the student are irrelevant, incoherent, pointless, or too complicated, the students' motivation and interest will wane, and the desired skills will not be learned.

Designing a Goal-Based Scenario

From a top-down perspective, a designer goes through six steps when creating a GBS:

1. Identify a set of target skills
2. Develop Missions that require the target skills
3. Choose a Focus
4. Create a Cover Story that envelops the Mission

5. Plan the Operations

6. Build learning environments to support the target skills

Identifying Target Skills

GBSs are effective because they enable students to do something meaningful. Every aspect of a GBS design—the mission, cover story, focus, and operations—rests on this. By making the pedagogical goals of the GBS explicit at the outset, the remainder of the design process is simplified.

Specifying a set of meaningful target skills is relatively easy to do in corporate training, because the focus of such training is to prepare students to fill well-defined roles with clear associated skills. In K to 12 education, it is more difficult to say what a student should be empowered to do in the future. However, it is just as crucial.

One way to produce a set of target skills is to examine the competencies of a professional in the domain. To teach about plants, focus on the work of a botanist or weekend gardener; to teach about current events, look at how an intelligent adult can "read through" a speech or form opinions about government programs; to teach business, interview stockbrokers and CEOs.

Target Skills of a Civil War GBS

To see more clearly how to design a GBS, let's take an example. Assume we want to build a GBS to help teach elementary school students how to "do history" in the context of the Civil War; that is, to explain the significance of critical events in the Civil War, predict outcomes if various conditions had been different, identify the consequences of the war, and trace the present-day effects of those consequences.

The first step in building a GBS is to lay out the target skills. What target skills might we identify for this Civil War GBS? By taking as our model the skills an historian employs, here is a set of skills we might want our students to learn:

Explaining Phenomena from the Period
- Recognize the major players in the period, and their motivations
- Know important roles (e.g., President)
- Reason from own motivations
- Describe the rise and fall of slavery
- Identify the differences between the North and the South
- Specify the relationship between geography and politics in American history
- Reason about the period using analogies from personal experience

Predicting
- Develop an argument about a failure of Lincoln's
- Suggest how the South might have won
- Relate aspects of the Civil War to current events (e.g., Super South Primary, Martin Luther King, Los Angeles riots)

Historical Data Gathering
- Read news accounts from the data
- Recognize biases
- Read maps
- Develop strategies of information gathering
- Use bibliographies, library search, reader's guide, etc.
- Find economic data
- Piece together information to form an account of a scene
- Reconcile multiple viewpoints
- Hypothesize about missing detail
- Relate specific stories to abstract principles (such as the release of the Emancipation Proclamation)

Developing a Mission

Having identified the target skills, the designer must next specify a mission for the GBS—a particular achievement that will motivate the student to engage in the GBS and require the student to acquire the target skills. An explicitly defined mission will, in turn, guide development of the remaining pieces of a GBS.

A "mission" should not be confused with a "skill." A mission is something a student achieves through application of any number of skills. In other words, a mission is a state or condition, whereas a skill is what is used to bring that state or condition about. Although creating a proposal is a skill, having the finished proposal itself could be a mission.

A Mission in a Civil War GBS

The Civil War GBS might have a variety of missions. Suppose we specify a generic mission of having the student bring about a particular state of affairs in the United States at a particular point in time: January 1, 1865. We might then offer a range of specific missions to draw in different students. Here are four examples:

- Establish Peace at all Costs (requiring the student to determine the demands of the South and powerful elements of the North);

- Devastate the South (the student must concentrate on the battlefield success and find ways to increase the size and effectiveness of the armed forces);
- Enable the South to win; and
- Get re-elected (the student then concentrates on weighing public opinion and finding out what favors to grant to allies).

Choosing a Focus

When choosing a focus, the designer must first decide whether the mission is best served by a focus on design, control, discovery, or explanation task (or some combination of these). This decision leads to the establishment of the iterative sequence for the GBS; that, in turn, dictates how the instructional elements of the GBS are to be paced and sequenced.

Each class of focus task carries with it a natural iterative sequence (that is, a natural sequence of steps that people follow when performing the task). For a GBS with a design focus, the student repeatedly generates a part, integrates it into the whole, then tests the whole. If the focus is explanation, the student might conduct a test, observe it, then produce an explanation. Observing phenomena and stripping it down to necessary and sufficient conditions is central to a discovery task. A control-based GBS inevitably revolves around decisions: Detect a state of affairs, gather evidence, then choose between alternative plans.

The Focus of a Civil War GBS

The missions of the Civil War GBS (Peace at all Costs, Defeat of the South, Southern Victory, Re-election) suggest a focus on control and management—in this case, management of national affairs. The basic unit of activity in the Civil War GBS will be points of decision: At certain times, the student will be asked to decide, for instance, whether to adopt a certain military strategy, to approve a budget, or to grant a favor, and so forth. At each decision point, the student can (a) develop a plan, (b) choose from alternative plans, (c) gather more information, or (d) defer making a decision.

Creating a Cover Story for a GBS

The cover story is the context that unites the other components of a GBS; after identifying the target skills, the mission, and the focus, the designer must decide on the general context under which skills are learned and applied in the service of the mission. Because people use context to help them recall relevant skills, the cover story must closely match the situations in which the target skills are naturally employed. If, for example, a student is being trained to fill a particular job, the best cover story is the setting in which the job is conducted.

The Cover Story of a Civil War GBS

In the Civil War GBS, the student assumes the role of the President of the United States in 1863. This cover story is a natural for the missions outlined for this GBS. Further, once it is established, it leads directly to ideas for operations our GBS could include. For example, our student might manage the various affairs of state: Meet with individuals representing differing interests, gather information relevant to an issue, make decisions, and choose issues on which to concentrate.

Planning the Operations of a Goal-Based Scenario

Once the essential components of the GBS are established—the competencies the student is to develop, the goals the student can adopt, and the context in which they are achieved—it is time to turn to the specifics of the student's endeavors, known as the scenario operations.

How will the student interact with the GBS: in one-to-one sessions on a computer, through team meetings, by using out-of-school resources, or through classroom activities? What actions can students take: Do they create documents or gather data? Does the GBS require computerization, and, if so, what parts? Will students achieve their missions individually, or as a group?

Operations in a Civil War GBS

In the Civil War GBS, students interact individually with a computer simulation, pursuing their own agendas. The simulation describes events that transpire, arriving at certain points at which decisions must be made. When a decision point is reached, students are able to (a) gather information relevant to the decision via a set of on-screen buttons, (b) isolate alternative solutions (either propose them via a natural language interface or ask the system to generate them), and then (c) commit to a plan (either one of the alternatives, or defer decision).

Building Environments in Goal-Based Scenarios

The final task remaining in the GBS design process is to determine how the GBS will help a student to achieve the mission and acquire the target skills. The designer must decide what types of support to give the student and in what ways that support will be made available. These decisions require the designer to consider the important cases to relate, the feedback to give, and the media by which information will be delivered.

If the rest of the GBS design process was completed well, this step is fairly straightforward. But a designer must take special care when laying out the cases and facts that the student might find useful. The designer must not make these cases and facts ends in themselves but rather must use them as the means by which the nature, applicability, and consequences of skills are conveyed to the student. To show how skills may be generalized, the designer should develop for each target skill both "domain-dependent" cases, which treat the skill with reference to the cover story and mission, and "domain-independent" cases, which treat the skill in a way that is independent of the context.

A Learning Environment in a Civil War GBS

Cases in the Civil War GBS fall into three rough categories. Some cases summarize and describe specific events of the period, including the first battle of Manassas, the Gettysburg Address, and the rise of the Know-Nothing Party. These types of cases are best presented using a combination of text, videotape, and diagrams. The second type of cases in the Civil War GBS involves the source material historians use to reason about the past. These snatches of data on the period include news accounts, interviews with survivors, period maps, and so on. Finally, there are cases that describe the actions the student can take, and their consequences at any given point of the simulation.

This discussion of the design of a Civil War GBS may have a dry flavor to it—discussions of designs often do. But the result is that we have a picture of how we can help a student learn to "do history" and become familiar with an important era in American history by playing President. Picture a typical student sitting in a typical mainstream elementary school listening to a typical history lesson. Would that child rather be in the class or using the Civil War GBS? Where would that child learn more? It seems clear that by interacting with the material of history, and actually using it, the child comes away with far more knowledge.

GBSs Tie Together Different Subjects Using a Single Domain

The Civil War is typical in its ability to motivate students and build the skills we want students to learn. But it does have one unusual aspect—it falls largely within the confines of a single academic subject. Typically, when teachers try to imagine GBSs, they produce such single-subject versions. This is only natural because the skills they would like to teach typically come from the subject they teach. As a cautionary note, it is important to realize that much of the power of GBSs comes from their ability to tie together different subjects, integrating them in a way that makes sense to the student.

Assessing Student Needs.   We are in an age of change. The volume of knowledge that our culture claims to be significant is exploding. Information systems are revamping our administrative organizations. It is impossible to predict what and how people will do things in the future. This "age of change" means we cannot predict all the knowledge and abilities people will need to have.

Open Curricula.   Paradoxically, less control can lead to more learning. An open curriculum is based on the idea that we should adopt a more focused way of managing students' learning. We can select a small core set of things we want students to master and not sweat decisions about exactly how and when they learn them. This idea places students in charge of their own learning, helping them find something they want to accomplish, and assuming they will learn what they need. The concept of an open curriculum goes against all notions of a conventional fixed curriculum.

Knowledge and Goals.   Although building exhaustive lists of facts students should know is a hopeless goal, there are some *abilities* that students should know that are likely to be with us for some time to come. Everyone should know how to read. Everyone should know how to approach an unsolved and complex problem. Everyone should know how to participate productively in a group effort. Everyone should be able to understand and make decisions regarding the real world and his role in it.

We need everyone to be able to engage in the same processes (vote, get along with his or her neighbor, articulate his or her point of view) but not to do the same jobs or follow the same interests in life. We must recognize this distinction when we plan out educational goals. Those who are mathematically inclined may want to study calculus because they may have use for it in life. Those who cannot stand mathematics are likely to abhor it when they are allowed free choice in adult life. If we allow people free choice as students, they can concentrate on learning what they might need in their lives. Freedom to choose what not to study implies freedom to learn more about what one cares about and freedom to explore new interests not normally covered in the curriculum.

Back to Basics Problems.   It is impossible to predict which concrete bits of knowledge will be useful in the future. Those who want to raise standards or get back to basics always try to implement their programs in terms of fixed curricula, and those curricula inevitably run into problems when they try to get very specific about just what concrete bits they specify students should swallow. The point they miss is that what matters is not how well students can retain knowledge but how well they can apply it.

Those wishing to make meaningful change cannot assume that they can progress by promulgating lists of knowledge. They must concern themselves with how students should learn. How knowledge is acquired matters as much as what is acquired. When knowledge is acquired in service of a goal, it remains forever linked to that goal.

GBS in an Open Curriculum

The open curriculum is no more than a menu of GBSs that all pertain to the same domain. Children might select a domain (and hence a curriculum) on the basis of their usual interests. Adults might select a domain on the basis of the goal they have going back to school. The key point is that curricula ought to correspond to the interests students have. Such a curricula allows us to capitalize on the notion that "an interest is a terrible thing to waste" while observing the caution that "students must control their own learning."

A Biology Curriculum of GBSs

Goal-based scenarios are useful for scientific subjects as well as liberal arts subjects. Let's take biology as an example. Bill Purves, Professor of Biology at Harvey Mudd College, reconsidered the biology curriculum from a GBS perspective. He developed GBS missions that would cover the entire set of skills he feels are most important for a college biology major to have at graduation. Surprisingly, he needed only three GBSs to do the job:

- Biology GBS 1: Feed the world. Develop a proposal to cope with the world food crisis as well as an explanation of why your proposal would be effective.
- Biology GBS 2: Pick one of the following patients. Figure out what caused his or her disease. (The student is given five patients suffering from different diseases, including a nutritional deficiency, a venereal disease, a microbial infection that is not a venereal disease, a hereditary disease, and one caused by an environmental hazard such as a radionuclide or toxic substance.)
- Biology GBS 3: Develop a mutant bacterial strain capable of producing human insulin in sufficient quantity to meet the needs of a diabetic person.

Considering that college students usually need to sit through 20 or so separate, usually unintegrated, courses in their majors, the notion that three GBSs can cover the required ground is heartening. Considering that these GBSs sound like so much fun is downright rousing.

The Basic Processes

All students, in virtually all contexts, need to be able to engage in certain processes, no matter what their particular lives are like. If there is a sine qua non of education, it must be these universal processes, not a set of particular facts. There are three processes that are more important than any others, and any curriculum must teach them. However, it is critical that these processes be taught indirectly, embedded in scenarios that are themselves primarily targeted at teaching specific scriptlets and cases. The three processes are:

- Communications,
- Human Relations, and
- Reasoning.

What does it mean to learn these processes? Clearly, learning a process is different from acquiring a scriptlet. A scriptlet can be easily described as a set of steps, and those steps can be practiced so they become routine and require little or no thought to execute. Because scriptlets are prescriptions for action, we can meaningfully talk about their execution. The same is not true of processes.

It sounds odd to say that someone knows how to do "human relations." We can say they know how to communicate or how to reason, although it is very difficult to specify what we mean when we say such things. Clearly we are not talking about scriptlets here. It would be very difficult to specify a set of procedures that form a package called "communication." Being able to get along with others or to think about a new problem may have some executable procedures, but it also seems to entail a great many more fuzzy concepts such as being nice or trying unusual solutions that are a great deal more difficult to quantify.

The word "process" here sheds little light on these phenomena in the same way that "skill" sheds little light on what it was that we wanted people to know how to do. As with "skill," the word "process" can encompass too much. There are many phenomena that can be called processes. There are political processes, economic processes, scientific processes, and so on. What these ideas have in common is that they refer to complex sets of forces that come into play and require more of their participants than a simple knowledge of how to execute certain simple procedures.

The phenomena they represent are complex and are often not given to clear procedures that can be guaranteed to work. Sending e-mail and programming the VCR are not processes because they can be accomplished using simple rote procedures. Likewise, there are known solutions to braking a car, riding a bike, or making toast. But for what we have been labeling processes, there are often no good answers or, alternatively, many good answers.

Teaching Processes

Let's look at some strategies for performing processes. Some good ones for human relations might be:

- If you want someone to like you, ask for their help.
- If you are in charge of someone, be firm but treat them as an equal.

Good strategies for reasoning might include:

- To attack a new problem, try to see it is an instance of an old problem.
- To find a solution, hypothesize a world in which the current problem wouldn't exist.

Some good strategies for communication might be:

- Never say everything you know in one speech.
- Always write in an easy-to-read, unpretentious style.

No matter what else a course is intended to teach, if it has a format that includes using a group, it will also cause domain-independent human relation strategies to be developed individually, by each participant. If the course includes open-ended problem solving, it will teach strategies having to do with reasoning simply by force of having to engage in these strategies. And, if the results of any of this needs to be communicated, strategies for communication will be developed. These three processes, and how to engage in them, should never be explicitly taught. They will be learned by the very best method of all, by having students experience the processes for themselves.

Teaching to Individuals

Communication, human relations, and reasoning capture what people would agree are the basics. Of course, we must also help students learn skills above and beyond these three processes. But we do not need to mandate long lists of these skills. It is critical that we not fall into the "literacy list" trap of proclaiming that students learn everything we decide to support. People's interests and goals vary, and it is neither plausible nor desirable to teach the same set of skills to every student. Not every student can readily learn every skill.

Students are more likely to learn a skill if it is one they have chosen, and if they have an aptitude for it. One of the primary goals of the school system should be to get students excited about and confident in their ability to learn. Allowing students to choose which interests they will pursue is therefore crucial. As long as they are choosing in concert with a teacher who can judge that what they propose to do is worthwhile, we can be confident they are not wasting their time.

We would want most students to learn the skills that are normally packaged under traditional subject headings, for example: politics, physics, economics, math, reading, history, geography, reading, design, and biology.

These are all worthy subjects, and someone who is designing part of the open curriculum should strive to include the skills these subjects package. But not everyone needs to learn any one of these particular subjects (or any one of the particular skills within them). To help the student learn anything useful without crushing his desire to learn in the process, we must be willing to sacrifice the impossible dream that the student learn everything we would like.

Although at the level of the curriculum, we should not make anything other than the three basic processes mandatory, at the level of the course, we may insist students learn additional specific skills. Thus, a segment on trucking intended for a high school student might include the requirement that the student learn how to build a budget, develop a print advertisement, or design an air conditioning unit for a refrigerated trailer. Courses may well have specific requirements for students to master. But students should not be forced to take those courses if they don't match some interest the student holds, or that the teacher can help the student develop.

These ideas pertain to business training as well as public education. It would be ludicrous to propose that every business training exercise focus solely on the three basic processes. Perhaps these processes should be part of every exercise, but clearly business training should also aim to impart specific skills. These skills must nevertheless be of intrinsic interest to employees. If they illustrate a way for employees to do their jobs more effectively, for example, they will be of interest as a matter of course. But if, as is the case in some companies, training is primarily a way of getting some time away from the day-to-day grind or fulfilling a mysterious training requirement, then it is quite likely that the training will be valueless, as is so much of the classroom teaching prevalent in the mainstream educational system.

Changing Schools for Better Education

The least we can ask of our schools is that they not destroy the natural love for learning that our children bring into the first grade. Unfortunately, it would be hard to find a more effective method of destruction than that used in today's schools: Children are placed in peer groups all too eager to ridicule differences that raise their fears about taking risks. They are drilled with facts and rules that indicate to them that there are experts in the world who know stuff, and that the student's job is to simply absorb what these experts have to say. Their interests are disregarded so that they learn to believe their interests must not be very important. They are ranked frequently enough to be instilled with the idea that they are not very smart, or they embark on a mission to seek the official approval that comes from parroting back the official answers.

12

A Look to the Future

THE FUTURE

What am I predicting for the future, once open curricula can be built around good educational software? Am I really advocating the end of the book? Do I really think there should be no more teachers? What about that favorite teacher who inspired you to be like her and whose image sustained you all these years? Shall we eliminate even her?

Actually, I am not advocating eliminating anything except a boring and irrelevant education system.

A number of the objects and structures of what we take to be normal everyday aspects of modern life are likely to change profoundly in the near future. Let's consider a few of these relevant to education and how knowledge is captured and disseminated: the book, the video rental store, and our whole concept of information.

CONSIDERING THE FUTURE OF THE BOOK

First, let me say that I like books. I write books. But that does not mean that books are the best possible way to present information. Just because it seems like books have always been here does not mean they always will be. To many people, just the idea that the book may soon disappear is so frightening that it's difficult to discuss the subject rationally.

Perhaps one way of putting this in perspective is to consider a question from last year's qualifying examination at ILS. (Yes, I do give exams; well, anyway, I do give this one each year, I can't recall any other.)

> Technology tends to influence art in serious ways. And art influences story telling. If you wanted to tell a story in some way other than simply by talking, then painting a picture, or carving a stele, there were limited options available 2,000 years ago. After the invention of the printing press, a new art form developed, although it took a few years, namely, the novel. This was an art form for storytelling influenced by the new technology of the book. Similarly, movies became a new way of telling stories when film technology was created. Your job is to outline the storytelling art form of the future. Make your idea realistic enough that, if your suggestion is good, I could ask you to build it and expect to see it sometime before you graduate. Bear in mind while doing this that there is a difference between an art form and an artist. Great painters may not have been great storytellers, and great storytellers may certainly not have been able to paint. The program you propose would be usable by an artist/ storyteller who, while facile at the technology, would primarily be a potentially great storyteller who has now found his medium.

The emphasis in this question is on how new technology can serve a specific function. As such, it frames how to think about our vision of the future. The question about books is not "will there be books?" but "can the purposes served by books be better served by other means?"

To answer this question we need to make a distinction between at least three kinds of books: reference books, treatises arguing a point of view, and novels. The question we want to ask is: Can computer technology improve on these three ways of conveying information? The way to answer this is to understand the point of each of these three types of books.

The Future of the Reference Book

A reference book, an encyclopedia, a travel book, a collection of movie reviews, or a book of art prints, and so on provide information to a user who is in either of one of two situations. Either he knows what he wants to find out and hopes that the information he seeks is in the reference book he has found, or he is leafing through the reference book, seeing if there is anything of interest to be found there. There is nothing warm and fuzzy about a reference book and I have found that, when I suggest that reference books will soon be a thing of the past, only the publishers of those books are among the mourners.

Most people do welcome the idea that reference books will get replaced by something that's easier to use. Information is difficult to find in this world because there is too much of it. ASK systems will help. The better we get at making them, the sooner reference books will disappear. If you can ask the computer a question and get an answer, or if you can leaf through information in a way that is easier, more useful, and adaptable to you, you will not think twice about getting a computer that has access to everything you might want to know.

The Future of the Nonfiction Book

Nonfiction books, or treatises that argue for some viewpoint, seem more difficult to replace than reference books. Readers usually spend hours with such books and no one really wants to read for any length of time at a CRT. We much prefer to curl up with a good book in bed or in an easy chair. So let's first get the hardware issue out of the way. The elimination of this type of book may indeed be a question of hardware in the end, but let's separate the issues. Let us assume that such book could be made available in computers that felt and looked just like books to a reader; that is, imagine you are curled up with your book in your favorite chair, but that book, which feels and looks just like a book, actually can change the information on the page by your pressing a button instead of turning the actual page. Because your book is also a computer, we can add some other functionality as well.

What additional functionality would you want? You might want to ask a question of the author at some point. You might want to see what is being described in video. You might want an alternative point of view to the one being expressed by the author. You might want additional details about what you have been reading that are not available in the book. Is there something wrong with this picture? I honestly don't see why these are anything but reasonable desires and satisfying them is anything but a good thing.

As a step in this direction, we built ASK MICHAEL, which I described earlier. By putting the text into an ASK system, we've made it easier for readers to find what Porter has to say than it is in the original book. The indexing scheme we used works very easily and topics naturally flow in a variety of directions. We chose this book because its linear flow didn't work very well. It is important to realize that books made of paper are inherently linear and one directional. Each page is supposed to follow the next. It is the form of the book that gives rise to the form of the arguments expressed in the book. Because an author knows his reader will read each page in order, he writes each page in order or at least tries to make it seem as if he were talking in a linear and orderly way.

Thoughts, on the other hand, although they seem sequential, really are not. People have their minds going in several directions at once, and they may have a variety of questions to ask at any given point, each of which would take them in a different direction. Further, it is only the economics and practicalities of book publishing that make the idea of "one author–one book" a reality. Publishers can't get antagonists to argue with each other in a book because if they are really antagonists they probably don't get along well enough to produce something together. And mixing video in with writing, even if it is technologically feasible, would be a copyright nightmare.

To put this another way, the system that sells books, the authors who write books, the readers who read books, and the critics for whom books in their current form hold a very special place all would object to my concept of this future book, hardware considerations aside. They would object because it would be difficult to package and sell the new book form, because the concept of a single-authored work would probably go away, because readers aren't used to this idea, and because critics are dependent on the art form they have become adept at analyzing.

It seems obvious to me that none of these are really very good reasons from the point of view of delivering the information readers desire when they desire it. It remains to be seen whether readers prefer this new means of expressing information, one with multiple directions, multiple media, and multiple authors, to the single direction, media, and author form of information. Still, it's important to understand that what we lose with this new concept is not the idea of single author's expressions of a viewpoint but the packaging of that viewpoint as a single salable entity. I don't think this matters at all except to publishers and authors, and both of them would be satisfied by alternative means anyway if it meant more money and more distribution of their ideas.

Will this multiple form of authorship, the type that comes quite naturally with ASK tools, replace the book? I think the answer to that is obvious. It will if it is better, by whatever definitions of better apply. It is, I believe, important to create this new kind of nonfiction medium and let readers (or users if that's the more appropriate term) decide.

The Future of the Novel

The novel is really an art form that exists because there are books. It's only one of several art forms that provide a vehicle for telling fictional, sometimes mythic, stories. Like these other forms (short stories, movies, plays), it exists to take advantage of a particular way of packaging a story, in this case using a book. It's pointless to ask whether the novel is the best way to present a story. Each of the vehicles has its own strengths and weaknesses.

When thinking about what effect computers will have on the novel, many people point to computer tools like electronic mail and word processing programs. They talk about how computers are making it easier to create and disseminate texts. Computers do make life easier for writers, but, when thought of in this light, they are only a tool for making it easier to work through a process that is still defined by its end product, the book. Under this perspective, books still provide the storyteller's guiding constraints, including the length of the end product, how readers will interact with the product, and a host of other considerations about what storytellers can or cannot do.

Too see what an impact new technology can have on how stories are told, it's more instructive to consider movies than most of today's computer software. Movies put stories into a package that is quite different from the book. Since the early 20th century, it's been interesting to note how the concerns of those who make movies have grown to be quite different from the concerns of authors. Visual cues in movies provide a world of ways in which movie makers can accent their stories that are just not available to the authors of novels. What would a horror movie be like if it didn't have heavy clouds whipping across the face of a full moon? What would a Schwarzenegger bust-em-up be like without camera cuts every split second during the good parts? Sound plays a similar role and is similarly unavailable to novelists.

If you judge by how the public likes to consume its fiction, such freedom allows artists to make movies more compelling than novels. Still, movies will not eradicate novels because novels give their authors an ability to play with language that is just not available to movie makers. That's a good thing, too, because novels have the advantage of being relatively cheap to produce. Many more artists can afford to have a shot at producing an important new novel than a new movie.

Computers, like motion photography, provide yet another way to package stories and, like movies, it needs to evolve. It's exciting today to see the first steps of that evolution. Hypermedia systems already let artists mix elements from movies with elements from texts in ways that neither form could previously support. Hypermedia systems also already provide new elements available in neither previous package. Most notably, they can contain multiple paths, so that a book can be different for each reader.

These capabilities are first steps. What might next steps provide? It might be possible to create characters who have lives that really interact with the "reader." We saw in ChimpWorld that the characters in the program reacted to each other and could react to the user who might be playing the role of a chimp. In GuSS, we saw that the user was part of an interactive system wherein he became part of a scene that involved a company, and that company changed in some way because of his involvement. One could imagine an author creating an environment like that of Hamlet, for example, and letting the user be one of the characters, literally feeling Hamlet's wrath directed at him in response to moves he might make. Going still further, it is possible for multiple authors to create environments that interact with each other. People in AI used to joke about having the well-known psychiatric interviewing program (ELIZA) try to interview the well-known paranoid model (PARRY).

Such ideas would have been fun to try, of course. In a more sophisticated computational world, Hamlet could run away to many possible other worlds; he could meet Juliet, for example. Would he fight Romeo for her? Sophisticated authoring systems would make these meaningful questions for an author to decide.

What happens as computers evolve as storytelling tools will inevitably reflect on novels and movies. Could computers allow for easy authoring of movies by taking stock-filmed characters and allowing one to create action and simulated dialogue so real that anyone could alter any film in any way he wanted? Perhaps an author could create films out of films so that none of the original films remained, leaving a new story seen in a new way.

The point is that it's too early to say exactly how the computer will evolve as a platform for telling stories. Two things are clear, however. First, authors will have more tools at their disposal, more ways to tell a story, and, hence, more stories to tell. Second, authors could involve their users in ways that are active rather than passive, creating a whole new concept of who the author is trying to communicate with and what communication really is.

The Book and the Horse-Drawn Carriage

I am not against books, but I do believe their range of usefulness will be narrowed dramatically by new technology. In time, it will probably be narrowed to the extent that the automobile has narrowed the applicability of horse-drawn carriages. I do not believe this to be a bad thing; in fact, I believe it to be an exciting proposition.

Of course, those who depend on existing forms of books to make a living may object to these notions. Many who built horse-drawn carriages probably objected to the automobile. Still, in time, they will come around and support more powerful media.

THE FUTURE OF HOME VIDEO

Remember how you used to go down to the video rental store and rent a movie? Oh. You still do that? You won't for long. Why not? Actually the answer to why not isn't as interesting as the reason why I am discussing this issue here. I can't say that I really care about how movies are rented, but the related technology that I do care about will profoundly affect that, and other businesses.

We have had to create a video lab at ILS to shoot and edit, not to mention index, large amounts of video to stock our programs with relevant material.

We have also had to arrange with the owners of various video to use their libraries. We can usually get these owners to allow us to use their video free of charge as long as all we are doing is experimenting. Still, making these arrangements isn't necessarily easy.

Little by little we are creating in our lab a world that will impact profoundly on every home. Let me explain. Suppose you want to take a trip to France. To get help, you can ask a travel agent, who will show you brochures of hotels and offer to put you on a tour. Or you could ask friends who have been there who will make suggestions, or perhaps show you the slides they took there. Or you can buy a book or two about sightseeing in France, restaurants in France, churches in France, whatever. In the world we are creating, you will have to do none of that.

Just to help you think about this, imagine Road Trip, Dustin, ASK systems, and Movie Reader. Each of these programs could be adapted to help you plan a trip to France. Road Trip could allow you to take a simulated trip around France, seeing for yourself what there is to see there. At any point where you desired more information, you could enter an ASK system. Let's say you were in Champagne and decided it looked pleasant there. You looked around the town of Reims, visited a winery and saw them make champagne and decided to find out more. You want to see the hotels in the area, ask about the history of how champagne came to be made in this region, and want to understand if aged champagne is worth drinking. A well-constructed ASK system, connected to Reims in Road Trip, makes itself available to you and you easily find your answers. You now ask to talk to the simulated travel agent. You ask questions, and a video talking head supplies the answers. You book the trip by conversing with the simulated agent.

Now you are thinking that you'll need to know some French to help your trip go smoothly. You use Dustin in a variety of situations, restaurants, hotels, wineries, clothing stores, that you anticipate you will be in. You practice with Dustin until you feel confident. Next, you are ready to watch French movies. You ask the movie expert, who after some discussion with you about your taste and language ability, puts a movie on the screen that has been adapted by Movie Reader to highlight difficult expressions and to explain things when you are confused.

Examples of each of these programs already exist, although they are not targeted to taking a trip to France. Making this exercise in trip planning real is therefore a matter of extending what has already been done. It might be a lot of work, but the path has been laid out.

Practical Requirements

In the future, it may be possible for you to have a vast amount of video available at your home. This video may be accessible in an intuitive, useful way through software like that being developed at ILS.

To make the world I describe real, you need a source of both software and video that is trivially easy to obtain. This means your computer needs to be hooked up to the outside world in some way. Imagine that instead of the cable that provides cable TV going into your TV, it went into your computer instead. Now imagine that cable was truly interactive. Instead of your just being able to tell the cable to put the one of many channels it is carrying on your TV, you were able to ask for a tour of the Taittinger winery or you were able to transmit a question about why champagne bottles are so heavy. In both cases you would be sending an electronic message back to the company that installed the cable to search its video library and send back the right video to your computer. All this would happen behind the scenes. As a user, you wouldn't and shouldn't know about it.

To make this happen, some companies, possibly the current providers of cable TV or the telephone companies who provide fiber optics into the home, would have to operate an interactive digitized video database. To put this another way, when you ask for the video of Taittinger, you don't want to hear that it is busy, or can't be found, nor do you want to wait.

If these databases are to be able to deliver customized access to particular video clips, those clips must be properly indexed. Indexing clips so that you can easily get from a tour of the Taittinger winery to a discussion of why champagne bottles are heavy requires very flexible and detailed indexing. The first commercial uses of on-demand video will likely use much simpler forms of indexing. The very first commercial use of this technology delivered to the home will, I suspect, be in the form of movies and the elimination of the video rental store. Labeling movies by title is easy enough, so it will soon be possible to dial up any movie a video library contains. What about help from Julia Child with a particular recipe? Doing that involves indexing all her answers in such a way that you don't get an entire television show in response to a question while the sauce is congealing. This kind of indexing is not all that difficult. Creating large ASK systems that link each video clip to many related clips requires more sophisticated indexing. Still, we already know how to build such systems, so commercial applications may not be so far off.

DOING BUSINESS IN THE INFORMATION AGE

We are slowly moving, I believe, into an economy where knowledge is a commodity. People have noted recently that we are moving into a service economy from a manufacturing economy. We often hear about the "information age." But I am not sure that it is very well understood what the real effects of a knowledge-based economy might be.

What would become of the travel industry as we know it? The travel agent you called up to book the trip, or to suggest which hotels to look at or which places to see, would not have to be a travel agent at all. It is easy enough to book your own reservations if you have a computer today. This ability has not killed the travel industry because not that many people have computers and because it hardly seems worth the effort when the travel agent is easily available by phone. Some companies have, in fact, become their own travel agents, but infrequent users do not spend the time to learn how to book reservations.

Deciding to use a computer to search an unfamiliar database, with unfamiliar commands, is not a decision that any but the most bold computer users take lightly. However, this situation will change and will change fast. In the future you might be able to use your computer to "travel to France," for example, and see videos about places you might visit, ask experts about what you see, and book reservations. When the accessible database you interact with grows to contain more detailed and better packaged information than any one travel agent could possible know, the travel agent on the corner will be out of business.

Some travel agents might stay in business if they provided the services available through the computer, but, as I have said, this is not absolutely necessary. In any case, the real competitive advantage in this business will be in the providing of video. The provider who makes the best video available, the best hotel expert, the best champagne expert, the best sightseeing planner, even the best language training program, would be the one who would get the computer user's attention and hence his business.

Knowledge as a Business

Knowledge suppliers will have to find out how to charge for their best stories. Eventually, selling knowledge in the guise of access to knowledge on video will become a major new growth area.

For example, when you can have access via computer to travel information about France, you are entering the domain of the publishers of travel guides. I don't know how they will choose to play their hand, but I do know no one will buy travel books anymore.

The publishers may well decide to be the first in the knowledge supply business. They are, after all, already in that business, although I must admit after consulting with many of them that most of them think they are in the business of selling objects, not knowledge.

The world of business will be forever changed by the coming information infrastructure. Owners of knowledge will sell their wares to packagers of knowledge who will sell their service to storers of knowledge who will have to work with accessers of knowledge who will, in turn, work with conveyers of knowledge. These may turn out to be, respectively, experts selling to publishers who sell to timesharing companies who deal with software vendors who deal with the cable or telephone companies. Again, I really don't know how it will play out, but if you look carefully you can see it coming.

Economic Problems with Information Distribution

There are some real obstacles to the coming age of multimedia computing. The prospect of having large, accessible databases of video raises an interesting issue. Who owns the video?

It is all very nice to suggest that you could ask a question of a computer and that any videotaped talking head that had an answer could be called upon to respond by the computer, but who pays the talent? One of the biggest obstacles to the creation of the world that I am imagining is the rights to existing video. No one really understands how to charge for the material he or she owns. NBC News, for example, owns a tremendous amount of video. It seems reasonable that they would like to make money on this asset. If a news event from the past is the answer to your question, how do they charge for the use of that event? If some text is the answer to your question, perhaps one story from Michael Porter's book is what you need, how does Porter or the publisher of the book get paid? When a talking head we have taped provides a good answer, does he get paid?

Working out the details of these arrangements will be complex, partially because the existing models are based on very different means of payment than "pay per access" or "pay for partial use of a large body of material." But these things will get worked out, I suppose.

Who Will Step Up to the Plate?

Will some company jump in and be the first to build large accessible databases of video? I don't know. It involves a major investment in a nonexistent business and assumes users will be willing to pay for access. The situation is not unlike the one that existed prior to telephones being installed in every home or the one that existed prior to everyone having a television.

Creating the necessary infrastructure and the necessary software and collecting the necessary video is a complex and expensive task. And, of course, we have the classic chicken and egg problem here. No one wanted to spend serious money on television programming until everyone had a television and until advertisers were willing to foot the bill. Similarly, no one is going to spend the money to provide what I have described until the profit possibilities are clear or until advertisers decide that this is an important new medium.

In the meantime, allow me to make two predictions. First, the company that steps up to this market will make a fortune. This is the telephone business all over again. Everyone will want one, and the first one in will be way ahead of everybody else. Second, when all this happens the education problem will be over. Once people see that the world of information is really at their fingertips in a way that is easy to access and simple and fun to explore, people will realize that school is no longer the real provider of education. Children will never want to get off these new fully video-connected computers, and their parents will be happy to see them so intellectually involved. The coming video database infrastructure will make for a more informed populace, one that finds out what it wants to know when it wants to know it.

Epilogue

LEARNING IS FUN

School should be fun. But it is quite clear that for most people their one-word description of their lives as students would probably be something quite different from "fun." One cannot read a description of any writer's time in school without hearing quite painful (and often funny) tales. For most people, school was an annoying, stressful, and sometimes painful experience. The tales that people tell when they look back fondly at school rarely have anything to do with school itself but are instead about making friends or playing on teams. When people do tell tales of school-related success, the stories are usually about cramming for the big exam, or working hard to get a grade. They are almost never about learning. Why not?

It is clear that the interesting action, the stuff that comprises a child's mental life in school, is about interaction with other children in one form or another. School is not about learning. It is about jobs, it is about winning the competition, it is about money, it is about getting other kids to like you, it is about getting the teacher to like you. None of these things are inherently bad. Most of the things that school is really about are a normal part of life, and there is no reason why kids shouldn't deal with them in school, too. But the kids should also be learning.

Mostly, they should be learning that learning is fun. They should be learning that expanding one's horizons is fun, that learning you were wrong about something is not so painful, and that taking an educational risk is worth doing. They should be learning that school is a good place to do these things. The children of today dread going back to school in September,

217

dread exams, dread receiving their grades, and are generally fearful. No wonder school is stressful. But there is no reason children cannot have intellectual fun, cannot be excited by ideas, and cannot be challenged to acquire new knowledge. Natural learning is a basically enjoyable thing to do. Two-year-olds love to learn. Many adults love to learn. Only school-age children associate learning with fear of failure. We must get the fear of failure out of the school system. Cramming for an exam or trying to please a teacher ought not to be the goal of those seeking an education. If we fail to understand this in a profound way, there will be no helping our schools or our children.

EIGHT THINGS THAT CAN BE DONE

Whereas much of this book is about the role that technology can play in revamping the schools, the ideas here do not depend on computers. The schools of tomorrow, with or without new technologies, can improve by the following simple suggestions this book brings out:

1. Doing, not Reviewing.   Today's schools are dominated by the need to assess student performance. Test scores and grades measure the wrong things and thus cause the wrong things to be taught. What is important is achievement. Good software should allow its users to achieve goals that are worth achieving. Eliminate test scores and grades, and the endless repetitive reviewing and cramming for tests that go with it, and replace this with levels of achievement that are objective, relevant, and highly motivating. This can be done with good software, but it could also be done in today's classroom.

2. Possible Answers, not Right Answers.   Today's schools, and the culture in which those schools live, are obsessed with the accumulation of facts. We have so many lists of what everyone should know that we have succeeded in convincing people they are ignorant, but to what end? Real measures of knowledge are not fact based at all. Experts may not be able to recite facts, but they usually can do things that only experts do. Facts are useful only when they help one accomplish some goals; they should not be learned out of context. Knowledge should be taught when it is helpful for accomplishing some goal. There should be less emphasis on right answers and more discussion of open questions, for which no answers are known.

3. Fun, not Discipline.   Many parents and educators have confused instruction with discipline. Just because there is little discipline in today's schools, it does not follow that when there was discipline there was also a great deal of learning. The two have little to do with each other. Learning is best accomplished by children when what they are learning interests them, relates to their goals, and is fun.

There is no reason why we cannot make everything in school enjoyable. Discipline must be self-imposed to be of any real use, and it will be self-imposed by any child who cares about the goal he is trying to accomplish. Children are quite apt learners when they really want to know something. We must create environments in which children are curious.

4. Interest Groups, not Age Groups.   Today's schools are organized by age groups in grades. Why? Because they always have been. This causes us to lose the use of some available teachers, namely the other, more experienced, children. Children can learn from each other and will do better if they were organized by similar interests instead of similar ages. We must eliminate the concept of first grade, and so on and replace it with achievements within interest-based groupings. We must learn to ask what children have learned to do, not what grade they are in.

5. Visible Projects, not Invisible Rejects.   Today's schools emphasize the production of good scores. We must abandon entirely the whole notion of scores, grades, exams, and all other competitive measures. Children need to feel a sense of accomplishment, to show others what they have produced. We must enable them to produce. What they produce ought to be visible, real accomplishments, skills, or actual work products that can be shown off, not as objects in a competition but as a show of pride in what they can do.

6. Hearing and Needing, not Listening and Reading.   Today's schools are essentially passive experiences. Teachers teach and children listen. Learning is better when it is active not passive. Instruction should occur only when children express the desire to know. Every time teachers ask children to listen, they ought to ask themselves if they believe the children genuinely want to hear what they are saying. If the students don't want to hear it, they won't hear it, no matter how much we threaten them.

7. Motivation, not Resignation.   Children are discouraged from pursuing their own interests in school. The job of a teacher is to expand the horizons of the student, to cause the student to have more interests, not less. It is a good idea to allow teachers to advertise different possibilities and let teachers teach what they know best in response to the expressed interests of the children. Motivation is a terrible thing to waste. Everyone doesn't have to learn the same stuff. No more standard curricula!

8. Fun Fun Fun.   Learning is fun and school isn't. Making school fun doesn't mean having the teacher dress up in a clown suit, or making teaching into "Jeopardy." It does mean making learning fun in school in the same way that it is fun out of school.

This list does not detail everything that could be done to fix education. Nevertheless, it gives an idea of where to begin. High-quality software could help make these changes possible.

THE STUDENT'S BILL OF RIGHTS

School should not be a place where teachers and administrators make students jump through arbitrary hoops that could not possibly matter in real life. How does a student tell the real things to be worked on, the stuff that matters, from the junk, the stuff that is part of the curriculum because no one ever thought about it much, or the stuff that is part of the curriculum to help make teachers' lives simpler?

One way to improve matters is to allow students to have some say in their own education. I do not mean by this that students should be part of curriculum committees. Students are not prepared to determine what other kids should know any more than teachers, administrators, book publishers, or cultural literacy advocates. But students can determine what interests them, and they should have the right to complain when outmoded teaching methods are in use.

For the use of students and teachers everywhere, and by way of summing up the real issues in education, I present the Student's Bill of Rights:

1. Testing : No student should have to take a multiple-choice or fill-in-the-blank test.

2. Real-Life Skills: No student should be have to learn something that fails to relate to a skill that is likely to be required in life after school.

3. Memorization: No student should be required to memorize any information that is likely to be forgotten in 6 months.

4. Goal Clarity: No student should be required to take a course, the results of which are not directly related to a goal held by the student, nor to engage in an activity without knowing what he can expect to gain from that activity.

5. Passivity: No student should be required to spend time passively watching or listening to anything unless there is a longer period of time devoted to allowing the student to participate in a corresponding active activity.

6. Arbitrary Standards: No student should be required to prepare his work in ways that are arbitrary or to jump through arbitrary hoops defined only by a particular teacher and not by the society at large.

7. Mastery: No student should be required to continue to study something he has already mastered.
8. Discovery: No student should be asked to learn anything unless there
   is the possibility of his being able to experiment in school with what
   he has learned.
9. Defined Curriculum: No student should be barred from engaging in
   activities that interest him within the framework of school because of
   breadth requirements imposed by the curriculum.
10. Freedom Of Thought: No student should be placed in a position of
    having to air his views on a subject if the opposing point of view is not
    presented and equally represented.

References

Bell, B., Bareiss, R., & Beckwith, R. (1993/1994). Sickle Cell Counselor: A prototype Goal-Based Scenario for instruction in a museum environment. *The Journal of the Learning Sciences*, *3*(4), 347–386.

Chi, M. T. H., Bassok, M., Lewis M., Reimann, P., and Glaser, R. (1989). Learning problem solving skills from studying examples. *Cognitive Science, 13*(2), 145–182.

Cleave, J., Edelson, D. & Beckwith, R. (1993). A matter of style: An analysis of student interaction with a computer-based learning environment. Paper presented at the 1993 American Educational Research Association Annual Meeting, Atlanta, GA.

Collins, A., Brown, J.S., & Newman, S.E. (1983). Cognitive apprenticeship: Teaching the crafts of reading, writing, and mathematics. In L.B. Resnick (Ed), *Knowing, learning, and instruction: Essays in honor of Robert Glaser*. Hillsdale: Lawrence Erlbaum Associates.

Cremin, L. A. (1961). *The transformation of the school; Progressivism in American education*, 1876–1957. New York: Knopf.

Dillon, J.T. (1987). Question-answer practices in a dozen fields. *Questioning Exchange, 1*, 87–100.

Gardner, H. (1991). *The unschooled mind: How children think and how schools should teach*. New York: BasicBooks.

Gentner, D. (1989). Mechanisms of analogical learning. In S. Vosniadou & A. Ortony (Eds.), *Similarity and analogical reasoning.* New York: Cambridge Universlty Press, 199–241.

Greenberg, J. (1993). "Libyans cut short a visit to Israel." *The New York Times*, June 2, 1993.

Hirsch, E. D. (1987). *Cultural literacy: What every American needs to know*. Boston: Houghton Mifflin.

Hirsch, E. D. (Ed.). (1991). *What your first grader needs to know: Fundamentals of a good education*. New York: Doubleday.

Holt, J. (1964). *How children fail.* New York: Dell.

Holum, A. & Beckwith, R. (1993). The role of questioning strategies in story understanding. Paper presented at the 1993 American Educational Research Association Annual Meeting. Atlanta.

Holyoak, K. (1985). *The psychology of learning and motivation.* New York: Academic.

Palinscar, A. S. & Brown, A.L. (1984). Reciprocal teaching of comprehension-fostering monitoring activities. *Cognition and Instruction, 1,* 117–175.

Percy, W. (1982). The loss of the creature. In *The message in the bottle: How queer man is, how queer language is, and what one has to do with the other.* New York: Farrar, Straus, and Giroux.

Porter, M. E. (1990). The competitive advantage of nations. New York: Free Press.

Ross, B. H. (1987). This is like that: The use of earlier problems and the separation of similarity effects. *Journal Of Experimental Psychology: Learning, Memory, and Cognition, 13*(4), 629–639.

Royko, M. (1993). "Jay, David don't click with everyone." *The Chicago Tribune,* January 19, 1993.

Schank, R. C. (1982). *Dynamic memory: A theory of reminding and learning in computers and people.* New York: Cambridge University Press.

Schank, R. C. (1982). *Reading and understanding: Teaching from the perspective of artificial intelligence.* Hillsdale: Lawrence Erlbaum Associates.

Winslow, R. (1994). "Blood feud: Heart-surgery battle in Michigan is struggle over cost, care, profit." *The Wall Street Journal,* May 24, 1994.

"King of Saudi Arabia urges a formal peace with Israel." *The New York Times,* June 2, 1993.

Author Index

Subject Index